LGBTQ

LGBTQ

(Lesbian, Gay, Bisexual, Transgender and Queer)

Identities in
Select Modern Indian Literature

Kuhu Sharma Chanana

Suryodaya Books

Cataloging in Publication Data — DK

[Courtesy: D.K. Agencies (P) Ltd. <docinfo@dkagencies.com>]

Sharma Chanana, Kuhu, 1973- **author.**

LGBTQ (lesbian, gay, bisexual, transgender and queer) : identities in select modern Indian literature / Kuhu Sharma Chanana.

pages cm

Includes bibliographical references (pages).

ISBN 13: 9788192570242

1. Sexual minorities in literature. 2. Identity (Psychology) in literature. 3. Indic literature (English) — History and criticism. I. Title.

DDC 820.9954 23

ISBN 13: 978-81-925702-4-2

First published in India in 2015

Printed and published by:
Suryodaya Books
"*Suryodaya*", D-36A/1, Mohan Garden
Najafgarh Road, New Delhi – 110 059
Phone: (011) 2535 3435

and

Distributed by:
D.K. Printworld (P) Ltd.
Regd. Office: "Vedaśrī", F-395, Sudarshan Park
(Metro Station: Ramesh Nagar), New Delhi – 110 015
Phones: (011) 2545 3975, 2546 6019; *Fax*: (011) 2546 5926
e-mail: indology@dkprintworld.com
Website: www.dkprintworld.com

To

My PAPA

(A father who is also mother and teacher to me)

K.K. SHARMA

(Former Professor of English, University of Allahabad)

My father recited a story in a low voice.
I watched his lovely face and not the blade.
Before the story ended, he'd removed
the iron sliver I thought I'd die from.
I can't remember the tale,
but hear his voice still,
a well of dark water,
a prayer.

And I recall his hands,
two measures of tenderness
he laid against my face.

— Li-Young Lee, "The Gift"

To

[illegible]

(My father who is my mother and teacher for me)

[illegible] SHARMA

Former Professor of English, University of Allahabad

My father recited a story in a low voice
I watched his lovely face and not the blade
Before the story ended, he'd removed
the iron sliver I thought I'd die from
I can't remember the tale
but hear his voice still
a well of dark water
a prayer
And I recall his hands
two measures of tenderness
he laid against my face

Li-Young Lee, The Gift

Preface

The inappropriateness of the overturning of the High Court Judgement (2009) regarding Section 377 by the Supreme Court of India in 2013 has raised a furore among the writers and the critics alike. The absurdity of this outdated law is explicitly exposed in the writings such as *Inside Gayland* by Rajesh Talwar. This play depicts the turbulence faced by an Indian man who ends up being on a planet where heterosexuality is against the law. Thus the protests through writings, against the unfair treatment meted out to queers at every level, have been an integral part of LGBTQ activism.

This book is primarily concerned with the production and the counter production of the queer literary tools to lay bare the intricate web of silencing and visibilizing the alternative sexuality at the same time as presented in the Indian literary texts. Subsuming one of the most marginalized identities like *hijras* within the larger ambit of the queer writings that leaves very little space for the exploration of this unique identity has been a major handicap of the Indian homoerotic writings. No wonder the excavation of the Indian literary texts that primarily concern transgender and *hijra* identities has been an uphill task. The subversive potential of the third gender in creating radical ruptures in the sphere of familial sexual citizenship (because the alternative family disposition of the *hijras'* unmasks the oppressive structure of heteropatriarchal family that in turn problematizes the issue of sexual citizenship when claimed through the unit of family) is revealed through the texts such as Khushwant Singh's *Delhi*, Dattani's *Seven Steps around the Fire*, Satya's "I Hate Wet Tissues" and Abdul Khalid Rashid's "Incomplete Human". Also from the feminist perspective, their unusual gender blending adds another dimension to the whole issue of women's empowerment. Though there is mimetic appropriation of feminine behaviour by *hijra*s in terms of their feminine names, feminine attire, long hair, feminized language coupled with demands to be counted as females in census, there is a potent incongruity emerging out of their sexually suggestive behaviour. And this is due to the fact that though they ape feminine corporeality, they are dramatically different from sexually suppressed Indian women (who are perpetually on sexual dieting due to the middle-class issues of respectability). And this at one level creates voyeuristic titillating laughter in male audience and on the other works as a subversive tool to lay bare the repressed module of feminine sexuality. They, by appropriating female corporeality and behaving in an unabashed manner like dancing in public, sexually suggestive gesturing and smoking, surely produce a counter-culture against patriarchy. They present an effective foil to heterosexual patriarchal propriety. Indeed in a quite unique fashion within queer world, they are in one way able to bridge the much debated gap between feminism and lesbianism (specially in the Indian context) that has been meticulously discussed by authors like Maya Sharma in *Loving Women: Being Unprivileged in India*. Thus the marginalized groups within queer world not only redefine the basic premises of LGBTQ activism, but also reorient and reframe the heteropatriarchal hegemonies. Thus to counter the new emerging phenomenon of homonormativity (which creates an allowance for the specific sort of gays and lesbians who do not threaten the basic fabric of heteropatriarchy to a great extent and form a very specific kind of unholy alliance with heteronormativity), the marginalized identities within the LGBTQ world need to be visibilized and critiqued. In order to provide a holistic share to various kinds of sexual minorities, it is imperative to include bisexuals, queer diasporas, *hijras* and transgenders within the larger LGBTQ umbrella that has been to some extent partial to gay and lesbian identities. Thus this work aims at exposing the margins within margins, present in the form various types of sexual minorities, through modern Indian homoerotic writings and critiquing their positions as potent agents to radicalize and counter the hierarchal dispositions prevalent both in heteropatriarchal and homosexual world. Precisely for this reason the inclusion of Suniti Namjoshi who is a queer diaspora is extremely significant as her writings succinctly chart out the issue of sexual citizenship. The anxiety of subsuming the specific Indian lesbian experience and language within the ambit of the white queer world is exposed through her novel use of language, imagery and lesbian fabulation of seemingly straight myths. Also the issue of the consumption of the public, private and heterotopic spaces by the privileged homonormative queers at the expense of the stigmatized homosexuals like *hijras*, transgenders, bisexuals and sexual diasporas has been addressed through various literary representations across regional languages and genres.

For the above-mentioned purpose, I have amalgamated the Western and the Indian literary tools and have also borrowed the theoretical framework from the various other disciplines such as medical science, anthropology, sociology, journalism, film studies, geography and law. The texts under analysis include fiction, short story, poetry, drama and autobiographies and thus an effort has been made to represent major literary genres by critiquing works written originally in English and also literatures available in translations and Bhasha writings.

I am deeply grateful to Prof. Malashri Lal for incessantly guiding and encouraging me to write this book. I am indebted to the Sahitya Akademi Library, the British Council Library, the Shastri Indo-Canadian Library, the Nehru Memorial Museum & Library and the IIAS Library for permitting me to use their resources. My special thanks are due to my dear friend Balbir Krishan whose painting entitled "Rebirth" has adorned the cover page of this book.

Also, I acknowledge the precious support of my dear friends, Suman, Rachna, Ruchi, Saroj-ji and Alka.

Kuhu Sharma Chanana

Contents

Preface vii

Introduction 1

1. Dichotomic Representation of Lesbianism as an Act of Resistance in Contemporary Indian English Women Writers with Special Reference to Abha Dawesar and Anita Nair 26

2. Violence on Hijras through the Lens of Biphobia and the Contemporary Literary Representations: Mahesh Dattani, Khushwant Singh, Abdul Khalid Rashid and Satya 49

3. Lesbian Fabulation in Suniti Namjoshi's Poetry: A Tool to Familiarize or a Means to Escape? 100

4. The Polyvalent Power Structures in the Gay Writings of Contemporary Indian English Writers with Special Reference to R. Raj Rao and Hoshang Merchant 127

5. Plurality of the Significance of Lesbian Existence in Modern Indian Writers: Geetanjali Shree, Manju Kapur and Rajkamal Chaudhary 161

6. Lesbophobic Anxiety and the Contradictory Fissures in Modern Regional Women Short Story Writers: Shivani's "Manik" and Hiranmayee Mishra's "The Tale of a Rainy Night" 195

7. Queer Identity and Homosexualization of Spaces in Contemporary Indian Literary Texts 208

Bibliography 259

Index 270

Introduction

THE SUPREME COURT'S decision to uphold Section 377 and the refusal to even review the ban clearly indicate the dismal situation of subaltern sexual identities. Little wonder the queer writings even now inhabit just the margins of the Indian literary world, and the visibility of homoerotic literature at the Indian literary map is still a tantalizing dream. However, there are works ranging from gay, lesbian and *hijra* anthologies such as Hoshang Merchant's *Yaarana*, Sukthankar's *Facing the Mirror*, Maya Sharma's *Loving Women* and Revathi's *Our Lives, Our Words* to Revathi's autobiography entitled *The Truth About Me*, and Suniti Namjoshi and Merchant's fictionalized biographies named *Goja: An Autobiographical Myth* and *The Man Who Would Be Queen*. The fiction and poetry of Raj Rao and Namjoshi, the plays of Mahesh Dattani, Amruta Patil's *Kari* (the first graphic lesbian novel of India), the stories of Parvati Sharma, and the short story collections titled *Out* and queer-erotica called *Close Too Close* are also fine specimens of Indian queer literature. Despite the fact that recently there are also homoerotic writings in *Bhasha* literatures (*An Evening Rainbow: Queer Writings in Bhasha Literatures*), other than full length exhaustive queer literary critical writings by Ruth Vanita and Saleem Kidwai (*Same-sex Love in India*) and Merchant's (*Forbidden Sex, Forbidden Texts*), there is a severe dearth of books on Indian queer literary criticism. There can be two reasons for this: first, the Indian queer writing is still at a nascent stage as compared to the Western writings, and second, in India, unlike the West, there are no separate departments of alternative sexualities in most of the universities and inevitably, there is a serious paucity of specific queer literary tradition in Indian writings and as a result biographies and fictionalized accounts of biographies are the major forms of Indian queer literary production. Indeed there is not only a serious need for promotion of Indian homoerotic writings, but also for the development of queer literary tools to lay bare the depths of existing homosexual literary productions. This book of mine aims at developing an exclusive literary framework to analyse the Indian queer literary works. For this purpose I have amalgamated the Western and the Indian literary tools and also borrowed the theoretical framework from various other disciplines such as medical science, anthropology, sociology, journalism, film studies, geography and law. The texts under analysis include fiction, short story, poetry, drama and autobiographies and thus an effort has been made to represent the major literary genres by critiquing works written originally in English and also literatures available in translations and *Bhasha* writings.

In all there are seven chapters which deal with the themes of plurality of lesbian existence, overlapping of class and homosexuality, the doubly marginalized identity of lesbian diaspora and the specific rift between lesbianism, feminism and queer activism in Indian context as presented in literary studies. They also focus on ambivalent adaptation techniques adopted by the writers to grant visibility to subaltern sexualities and the development of exclusive queer aesthetics by the inversion of the accepted mode of literary language, imagery and techniques. The last two chapters deal with the issues of biphobia, violence on *hijra* identity (perhaps one of the most marginalized identity in LGBTQ movement), the homosexualization of spaces and the depiction of symbiotic relationship between space and sexual identity in Indian literary texts.

The three chapters which primarily focus on lesbian fiction, include apparently disparate texts like Manju Kapur's *A Married Woman* in English, Rajkamal Chaudhary's *Machali Mari Hui* in Hindi (written by a male writer), Geetanjali Shree's *Tirohit*, Abha Dawesar's *Babyji*, Anita Nair's *Ladies Coupé*, Hiranmayee Mishra's "The Tale of a Rainy Night" (an Oriya story in English translation), and Shivani's Hindi story "Manik". These works have been woven into a single thread due to the common themes of malleability and contradictory plurality of lesbian experiences of Indian upper middle-class married women. In these chapters the Western tools that have been employed are Terry Castle's notion of "ghosting of lesbians" and Patricia Juliana Smith's concept of "lesbian panic", which are indicative of the authors' own anxieties regarding the portrayal of the lesbian longings in their writings. Terry Castle in her work, *The Apparitional Lesbian: Female Homosexuality and Modern Culture* has given the concept of "self-ghosting". According to her, since lesbianism is a potential threat to the patriarchal structure, there is a tendency to juxtapose lesbian characters with apparition like creatures to invisibilize them. Similarly Patricia Juliana Smith has argued that whenever there is a chance of culmination of lesbian relationship, the panic strikes the writer and there is a sudden abortion of the relationship due to the abrupt decision of one of the partners. Manju Kapur's *A Married Woman*, Geetanjali Shree's *Tirohit*, Rajkamal's *Machali Mari Hui*, Shivani's "Manik" and Hiranmayee Mishra's "The Tale of a Rainy Night" have been analysed from this perspective which provides potent techniques to lay bare the writers' lesbophobic anxieties and their latent ambivalent intentions pertaining to the lesbian representations. On the one hand the revered identity of the motherhood has been wrapped around lesbianism to provide it respectability, and on the other it endorses the notion that the alternative family structure which is possible within queer family and homosexuality is not deficient in anything. For this purpose the old Indian myths of King Dilipa's queens (who without any male partner gave birth to Bhagirathi) and the birth of *agni* by multiple mothers as depicted by Ruth and Kidwai in their book, *Same-Sex Love in India*, have been cited as classic Indian examples to build linkages between Indian lesbian motherhood and the depiction of it in contemporary Indian queer writings. Significantly this notion of alternative family structure is not bereft of sinister back hand agenda and for exposing this malicious design, the tool from popular Western visual culture has been borrowed. Sara Warn in her insightful essay, "T.V.'s Lesbian Baby Boom" exhibits that so many American T.V. serials start with the theme of homosexual women coming to terms with their sexuality but later on the stories invariably veer around the issues of gay parenthood. And the reason for this is that motherhood is a mainstream identity and lesbianism is a marginalized existence and hence in order to make it palatable to the straight audience, the writer has to present it under the garb of the mainstream accepted identity of motherhood. Thus apart from the exclusive Indian tools borrowed from the ancient religious texts, the Western framework of popular visual culture has also been used to critique the Indian literary texts vis-à-vis lesbian motherhood.

For depicting the voyeuristic male pleasures emanating from lesbian double bonanza, specially demonstrated by the male writers like Rajkamal Chaudhary, there are frequent references to Rangeen's *Chaptinama* (A form of *Rekhti* poetry written in Urdu in nineteenth century) which catalogues the sinister agenda of many male writers to present lesbianism as a precursor to heterosexual mating to titillate male readers. In this sort of representation, towards the end, the lesbians are shown as being cured of homosexuality due to the exhaustive joys of heterosexual mating even if it is imposed upon them. Rajkamal Chaudhary's *Machali Mari Hui* clearly evinces this horrific idea and stresses that many a time lesbian visibility is fraught with serious lesbophobic anxieties on the part of the author. Interestingly contrary to this at times the apparently lesbophobic tales have potent potential to challenge heteronormativity as in Hiranmayee's "The Tale of a Rainy Night" and Shivani's "Manik". Both the stories are important lesbian signatures, for first, they are written in Hindi and Oriya respectively, and not in English, and this bursts the myth that homoeroticism is a Western import popularized in India by the English-speaking middle class for the benefit of the exclusive English-reading public, and second, these tales, despite homophobia, constantly reveal the opprobrium suffered by many married women in the so-called conjugal bliss. Also, the Sapphic relationships in these stories are not shown purged of sexual intimacies. These writers have boldly located the lesbian longings outside the desexualized *sakhi* space where homosexuality of a woman is limited to only romantic friendship. Thus the inclusion of lesbian tales from *Bhasha* literature has a specific agenda of creating a history of Indian lesbian literature which has been systematically erased and even the feminists have shown indifference towards lesbian movement for various reasons as has been demonstrated by Maya Sharma in *Loving Women*. Thus even the Indian feminist writings do not exhibit overt lesbian longings by and large.

Another aspect of the Indian literary lesbian writings is the depiction of specific problems faced by the diasporic lesbian writers. And this issue has been explored in the chapter entitled "Lesbian Fabulation in Suniti Namjoshi's Poetry: A Tool to Familiarize or a Means to Escape?". The doubly marginalized identity of sexual and racial minority poses specific problems of linguistic articulation in an alien space because the threat of submerging the lesbian experience of South Asian identity under the white lesbian articulation looms large. In order to counter this problem Suniti Namjoshi devises a unique literary tool of lesbian fabulation, through which she twists both the Indian classical stories and the popular European tales to fit in the exclusive South Asian homoerotic experiences. For instance in "Beauty and the Beast" she has changed the beast into a homosexual woman. Similarly in "Snapshots of Caliban" she has depicted Caliban as a lesbian woman who is in love with Miranda. No doubt her own particular problem of being a racial and sexual minority finds the fullest expression in twisting the tale of Shakespeare's *The Tempest* in this fashion. In fact in *Sycorax: New Fables and Poems,* she has gone to the extent of showing Sycorax coming back to her native land after the departure of Prospero to claim her land and she has a lesbian daughter named Caliban and naturally after the death of Sycorax the land will be appropriated by lesbian Caliban, and it is in this fashion that the issues pertaining to sexual citizenship emerge. The issue of sexual citizenship is raised vociferously by geographers like Bell and Binnie in their seminal work, *The Sexual Citizen: Queer Politics and Beyond* in which they try to view sexuality through the lens of citizenship, and this is still a neglected area in Indian queer studies. They try to broaden the area of sexual citizenship by including pink economy or consumer citizenship (the role of the market in providing sexual minority a citizenship right), the nation and city as sites for citizenship and familial citizenship (by accepting alternative gay family structure, as family is the smallest unit of nation) within the purview of the discourse on sexual minorities.

In addition to it, Michael Brown in *RePlacing Citizenship: AIDS Activism and Radical Democracy* talks about the dubious AIDS citizenship. According to him,

> AIDS citizenship considers the AIDS quilt as public enunciation (or memorialization) of grief and rage — a kind of subaltern counterpublic — which is simultaneously a site for both consciousness-raising (and fund-raising) and

> for the public affirmation of kinship and collectivity: a time–space event of citizenship in civil society, that is many layered, polysemic, both personal and public. — 1997: 18

In India, unlike the West, there is no strong tradition of emergence of AIDS novels and hence in the present scenario, this cannot be used as a tool to negotiate queer identity in Indian literature. But the citizenship claim through alternative family structure is present in Geetanjali Shree's *Tirohit* and *Across the Mystic Shore* by Suroopa Mukherjee. In both these texts, there is a depiction of a lesbian family consisting of the two lesbians and a son, and in this way they form the smallest unit of nation and hence assert a right on nation to consider them as legible citizens. Similarly Suniti, through the claiming of the land by Sycorax and her having a lesbian daughter, lays bare a complex web of signification. Sycorax reveals her understanding of female-colonial subject through her relationship with Caliban and the land occupied by Prospero. At the very outset the blue-eyed Syocrax proclaims:

> . . . as I'm still here/I'm able to say clearly that when Prospero/said he took over an uninhabited island/save for Caliban and the enslaved/Ariel, he lied./I LIVED ON THAT ISLAND/it was my property (at least as much as it was anybody else's)./He drove me away, made himself king, set up/his props and bided his time/Now that they've gone/I may return, and ask myself, not who/they were, but who I was and what I mourn.
>
> — *Sycorax: New Fables and Poems,* Namjoshi 2006: 1

After Prospero's departure, she tries to reclaim her lost land which is to be ultimately inherited by lesbian, Caliban. Significantly it catalogues the appropriation of land by a lesbian. Thus the issue of sexual citizenship finds manifestation in the writings of Suniti, though in a slightly oblique fashion. Likewise in Abha Dawesar's *Babyji,* the very name of a lesbian lover is rechristened as India by the protagonist. She has gone to the extent of saying that India (her lover Tripta) is the "essence of being Indian" (2005: 166). Similarly in Khushwant Singh's *Delhi*, the very capital of India has been anthropomorphized as *hijra* Bhagmati to evince horrid vandalizing that Bhagmati suffers and thus reveals the relentless ravaging, loot and plunder thrust upon the city for centuries:

> I return to Delhi as I return to my mistress Bhagmati when I have had my fill of whoring in foreign lands. Delhi and Bhagmati have a lot in common. Having been long misused by rough people they have learnt to conceal their seductive charms under a mask of repulsive ugliness. — 1990: 1

Thus sexual citizenship, though primarily a tool borrowed from geography, can be effectively used by the literary researchers to excavate the depths of the queer texts.

While discussing Suniti's poetry and *Babyji* in the same breath during the discussion on sexual citizenship, a sharp contrast between these two diasporic writers emerges in their use of language to articulate queer concerns. Queer aesthetics is a term used by Raj Rao frequently. In an interview with me he states that

> . . . you take something as you know it, as it actually exists, and turn it on its head. This is achieved through the use of literary technique. It's what one may call a queer or transgressive aesthetics, which is radical, and only has legitimate place in the world of representation, be it literature, cinema, theatre, painting or sculpture.
>
> — Chanana 2011: 134

In 1995 William Leap in *Beyond the Lavender Lexicon* talks about the need for interrogating the specific use of language by the gays and the lesbians. Further Rusty Barrett postulates the idea of "speech community", (http://en.wikipedia.org/wiki/Speech_community) according to which the queer community can forge a bonding through sharing specific linguistic traits. However, on account of different hierarchal dispositions within queer community due to the class, gender, race, active, passive, butch, femme, the need for resisting and reinventing the popular linguistic codes also arises. The members might try to oppose the cultural hierarchy by inventing their own distinctive variety. The concept of "swardspeak" is a classic example of it. Swardspeak is a specific gay lingo of homosexuals in the Philippines. It is a unique amalgam of Taglog, English, Spanish and Japanese along with the novel juxtaposing of trademark brands and celebrities' names and this variety of gay lingo helps them to assert their unique individual identity within larger queer umbrella. This language community formation can also be seen in Indian context in the specific *hijra* terminology used by *hijra*s. Another patent aspect of the lavender linguistics is "code switching" which is used to critique the dominant oppressive culture. Rusty Barrett gives an example of code switching by citing the example of Black drag performers who deliberately use "female white English" as a tool of inversion and create ruptures in the stereotypical biases regarding ethnicity and gender. Similarly "the bikes on dykes" phenomenon reverses the historically pejorative connotations of the word "dyke", as it completely reorients the meaning of the term. "The dykes on bikes" is a motorcycle group that frequents the gay pride march and tries to displace the dominant lesbian culture by exhibiting that

> the terms 'diesel-dyke', 'bull-dyke', 'bull-dagger' and dyke all have historically negative connotations but have been re-appropriated as self-referential terms of endearment and empowerment distinct from *lesbian* and indeed awards and events utilizing those names are now used by the LGBT community.
> — Ilyasova 2006: 21

Another re-appropriation of the word "dyke" is visible in the way it has been linked with the glorified identity of motherhood by coining the term "dykes with tykes" which means lesbian motherhood. In this light it is specially significant to mention the idea of "dyke diction". In fact Leonard R.N. Ashley catalogues a list of slang words used exclusively by lesbians. Thus the marginalized identities within the sexual minorities group tend to reinvent and reclaim certain terms, linguistic patterns and coin their own language to cement their place in dominant queer culture.

It is in this tradition that we can notice the purpose of the deliberate break from the conventional aesthetically appealing language as has been used by Rao and Dawesar. In Abha Dawesar's *Babyji* and Raj Rao's *The Boyfriend*, there is a raw realism and deliberate sensationalization coupled with the inversion of aesthetically appealing literary language to protest against the traditionally accepted literary mode of writing, for the traditional literary language is coded as heterosexual and the global gay language is still "white" in essence and hence there is a need for reinventing a specific queer language, imagery and technique by the Indian writers. Apropos of this Rani Kawale highlights the fact that the South Asian lesbians deliberately use to speak in broken English to reinvest the white spaces with their unique Asian identity so that they are not submerged under the overwhelming whiteness of the space. Thus the language and imagery become important markers to assert the unique queer individuality of the Indian writers who have linkages with the global gay but have their unique significance as well. And this reinventing of queer language is visible even in the nineteenth-century *rekhti* poetry. Since homoeroticism cuts across respectable *grihastha* (domesticated) woman and courtesan — both speak quite a different language from each other — there is a curious amalgam of the language of both these types of women which helps in forming a unique queer language. Ruth Vanita, by quoting Rangin, catalogues this aspect of *rekhti*:

> I do not restrict this to prostitutes (*kasbi*) *or to domestic* (*gharelu*) women/I am interested here only in women's speech (*zanani boli*).
> — Ruth Vanita 2012: 28

In fact, the blurring of this binary opposition finds an interesting articulation in the language of *khangis*. *Khangis* were married women who were also involved in sex-work with both men and women, and therefore their lesbian experience and its expression had a distinct hybrid flavour. Ruth writes how Rangin pays special attention to the speech of *khangis* to learn language for penning down women's specific sexual experiences:

> . . . he used to pay attention to the speech of every member of the group. Having spent some time thus, I acquire knowledge (*ilm*) of many of their idioms and sayings. . . . This fourth (*rekhti*) collection of poetry is in their language (*zuban*).
>
> —Ibid.

In this light the imperfect and broken language of Caliban's journal in Suniti Namjoshi not only represents the lack of lesbian vocabulary, but is also indicative of the emergence of a new queer language created by mixing the lesbian native language and the language learnt through the white, heterosexual colonizers. Suniti as an Indian lesbian living in the West confronts this problem and finds a unique solution through her specific writing techniques. Her hyper-elegance, unique lesbian fabulation, juxtaposing of various interspecies identities, creation of imaginary spaces, broken narration coupled with ambivalent symbols present the diametrically opposite side of the "lavender lexicon".

The use of animal imagery (specially the symbol of cow) is another specific feature of Indian queer writings successfully used by many writers like Suniti, Indu Menon in "A Lesbian Cow" and Nazir Mansuri in "The Sea Hawk" for blurring the gender boundaries. The reason is, as Suniti states, that when one sees an animal then one cannot determine its gender because the sartorial and cultural markers of masculinity and femininity are not inscribed on its body and thus in a way the animal symbol works as a potent tool to deconstruct stringent gender and sexual boundaries. Contrary to this belief Ruth in her essay, "The Many Colours of Love: Homoerotic Tropes in Modern Indian Fiction" states that the use of animal imagery in Keval Sood's Hindi novel, *Murgikhana* (*Hen Coup*), Shobha De's *Strange Obsession* in which Minx is constantly compared with animals like black cat, dead rats and ferocious wild beasts, Bani Ray's Bengali story, "Sappho" which has a lesbian protagonist who has been compared to reptile, and the short story "Pratiksha" in which the homosexual woman is imagined to be a spider swallowing flies document the authors' intentions of showing queer characters as debased as animals. To quote her words:

> Many of these stories employ the language of beastility and demonization, comparing lesbians to lizards, snakes, rats, cockroaches or spider swallowing flies.
>
> — Ruth Vanita 2005: 194

In fact Harshad Mehta in his Gujarati story, "Leech" also depicts the lesbian lover as a leech who ultimately kills her supposedly bisexual partner. However, Ruth later changes her stance and in her brilliant essay in the same book entitled "I'm an Excellent Animal" reveals how animal imagery is being used to forge possibilities of alternative sexualities through texts like *Manu-Smriti*, the poems of Bahinabai and Rukun Advani's *Beethoven Among the Cows*. These symbolic riddles on the one hand open up loads of fluid spaces through which pan-sexuality can be prescribed, but on the other they seem to camouflage the lesbian identity through suggestive ways of narration and unusual symbols. Ruth argues:

> Non-human animals are less containable in categories of gender and nationality than are humans. Hence they often function, in mythologies and literatures, to subvert or undo these categories, revealing the surprising commonalty of apparently distinct traditions and groupings . . . non-human animals are a strong device than a child is, as a site for

> ungendering, because the imposed nature of gender roles and sexual roles can be defamiliarized more easily when a non-human animal is the locus for such roles. —2005: 290

Similarly Suniti Namjoshi in "A Quiet Life" clearly tells us as why symbolizing woman as an animal is an effective device for dissolving gender boundaries because when one looks at a rabbit or a squirrel the sex is not evident, whereas in human beings such freedom is not there because of sartorial and other gender discriminatory markers. Therefore the use of animal imagery for queer existence is not always a means to degrade the homosexual identity but is also effectively employed by many writers to deconstruct essentialist categories. Little wonder Suniti constantly uses animal fables to dismantle these fixities and definities.

In fact in Suniti's *The Conversations of Cow*, the cow not only turns lesbian but also constantly changes gender and race by being white man Baddy intermittently and dismantles all binary dispositions effectively. In "Her Form in Clear Water" Namjoshi reverses the tale of the fall of Eve who finds a mate in a snake rather than in Adam, which is counterproductive of heterosexual matrix. In the similar vein, "A Lesbian Cow" by Indu Menon is a story about the stalking of a married pregnant woman by a lesbian cow. Throughout the story, there appears to be an implicit sympathy towards the cow, but in the end the killing of the cow by stones puts question marks on the intention of the writer. Thus if there are texts in which the animal symbol is used explicitly for degrading queer existence, there are also literary works which make use of animal trope to mitigate the sex and gender boundaries. Moreover there are also texts like *Machali Mari Hui* and "The Sea Hawk" by Nazir Mansuri in which the employment of the animal symbol is debatable. As in *Machali Mari Hui*, the fishes have no hands and no feet and can only come close by leaping towards and upon each other. Naturally it reflects the obvious lack of means of making love in the conventional fashion, and also reveals the new forms of making love in the absence of the coded sexual behaviour. In addition, the use of the death trope in this novel is also ambivalent because time and again death symbol has been juxtaposed with sexual orgasm as Ruth Vanita postulates in her essay, "The Many Colours of Love: Homoerotic Tropes in Modern Indian Fiction". Referring to this novel, she contends:

> Death, a symbol of orgasm in many European discourses of sexuality, is depicted as unattainable, yet the fish, trope for female fertility and genitalia, are figured as dead.
>
> — Ruth Vanita 2005: 205

Likewise in the short story, "The Sea Hawk", an interesting parallel has been drawn between the bisexual heroine, Janu and the sea hawks. Apparently the destruction of the nests of the sea hawks bears a close semblance with Janu's negation of motherhood. Surely it is a progressive move when viewed from the lesbian perspective but the ultimate triumph of heterosexual love at the cost of lesbian affair clearly makes the intentions of the author opaque. Also, the story throughout demonstrates sea hawk as a forceful but destructive force. Another dimension has been added to this discourse on animal symbol in queer texts by Shohini Ghosh. She argues that at times the animal trope for homosexual intimacies is used to catalogue the social gap even in homosexual individuals who are conditioned not to consider their intimacies as primary, and thus the above discussion leads one to assume that animal imagery has been employed in polyvalent ways in Indian queer texts.

Another not much discussed aspect of Indian queer literary texts is the viewing of homosexuality from the lens of class dynamics. Invariably the gay movement has been described as a Western import that primarily caters to privileged upper middle class. Therefore there is an entire chapter, "The

Polyvalent Power Structures in the Gay Writings of Contemporary Indian English Writers with Special Reference to R. Raj Rao and Hoshang Merchant" dedicated to the issues of class and caste vis-à-vis homosexuality. Regarding the complex matrix of class and homosexuality and the effects of market forces on altering the sexual orientation of an individual, John D'Emilio contends in his classic essay, "Capitalism and Gay Identity" that the emergence of queer identity is in a way directly proportional to the rise of the capitalism. According to him, with the gradual rise of family as an institution that offers "emotional satisfaction and happiness" rather than an institution that provides goods, there is an undermining of the significance of family's "economic rationale". Obliquely this gives an individual ample opportunity to work outside the restricted domain of family. It automatically paves way for the new ways of loving and living, especially in urban areas. Clearly the changing climate allows deviant sexualities to emerge, but it also consolidates the pressure on the family to reproduce itself. So at one level it gives rise to queer opportunities, but at another it gives impetus to internalized homophobia due to which the availability of partners is reduced and gay individuals are compelled to transcend the barriers of class and caste. Their being outcast make them collude with other marginalized entities. Thus the sexual minorities, in a quite potent way, invert the existing hegemony of class and caste and create fractures in the essentialist hierarchal structure of the heterosexual world with regard to class and caste.

Little wonder the liaison between *dalit* Miland and Yudi has been described by Raj Rao in *The Boyfriend* as a panacea for dismantling the caste and class discrimination. Citing another reason for this casteless and classless assimilation in the queer world, Raj Rao, quoting Dollimore, points out the need for the "other" in a romantic relationship. He contends that for any romantic relationship to flourish there is constant need of the presence of that elusive "other" between the partners. In heterosexual intimacies the need for the "other" is satiated through the difference in gender whereas in the same-sex relationship the gender is the same and thus the need for the "other" is being fulfilled by the tremendous gap between social class, caste or age. Unmistakably we notice that in "The Slaves", "Moonlight Tandoori", "Manik", *Tirohit* and *The Boyfriend* there is a huge difference in the age and class of the partners. In fact, Yudi, the hero in *The Boyfriend*, is so obsessed with the romantic notion of the working-class "other" that he goes to the extent of writing a sexually surcharged poem on Chinchpokali, a slum in Mumbai.

Yet one more unexplored arena of the impact of class on homosexuality is the effect of social class on active/passive dichotomy. There is a deep-rooted cultural bias according to which, being "passive" is linked with being effeminate and hence is a despicable identity. This notion has emanated from the slave tradition where slaves by and large were passive sex objects to their masters. As Paul Veyne argues in his essay entitled "Homosexuality in Ancient Rome" that in a slave-owing society the master had a sexual dominance and so the moral stands varied with social status. Thus in *The Boyfriend* an egalitarian structure is formed through the role reversal when Yudi, the provider, becomes passive and this helps Miland to counter his homophobic anxiety. In fact, Yudi has made it a habit to offer an active role to his one night partners who belong to lower social strata, as his long experience has taught him that if men are allowed to penetrate there is hardly any fear of their returning afterwards to demand money or beat him up out of homophobic guilt and rage. Thus this chapter excavates the eclectic functioning of class on homosexuality through a close analysis of gay writings like "The Slave" by Hoshang Merchant, "Moonlight Tandoori", "Six Inches" and

The Boyfriend by Raj Rao and helps in providing another tool to unearth the rich layers of Indian gay literature.

Apart from chapters on lesbian and gay writings, there is a full-fledged chapter devoted to the *hijra* identity which is the most neglected and marginalized entity within queer literature. The chapter, "Violence on Hijras through the Lens of Biphobia and the Contemporary Literary Representations: Mahesh Dattani, Khushwant Singh, Abdul Khalid Rashid and Satya", unearths the specific case of mental, social and physical violence on the third sex on account of biphobia, the effects of which are much more hazardous than homophobia. The major reasons ascribed to the social, cultural and legal opprobrium are the long and persisting effects of The Criminal Tribes Act of 1871 and biphobia. The supposedly androgynous identity of *hijras* tears the veil formed to segregate homo/hetero existence. The so-called male and female twin identity, encapsulated within *hijra* existence, naturally tends to challenge the dichotomous paradigm of sexual orientation and poses a threat to the dominant heteropatriarchal society, for the in-between identity of eunuchs negates the assumption that gays as a category are very different from straight people. We live in a culture where we are trained to have bipolar thinking and we assume that each category has its mutually exclusive opposite. Homosexuals are

> "that category, way over there", very different from heterosexuals. If they are so different then heterosexuals do not have to confront the possibility of acknowledging same-sex attractions within themselves and the attendant anxiety of possibly, "becoming like them".
>
> — Robyn Ochs 1996: 225

The amalgam of male and female existence in *hijras* poses the possibility of their having relationships with both men and women, and therefore in an oblique fashion puts them in the category of bisexuals and this becomes the reason of the emergence of biphobia. Illustrating it further, Robyn Ochs argues that there is indeed not only an overlap between homophobia and biphobia but also a distinct gap. Thus bisexuals face discrimination at the hands of homosexuals on account of their attendant privileges of being able to have heterosexual partners. She states:

> . . . Bisexuals, who fit neither the prioritized category nor its perceived antithesis, create discomfort and anxiety in others simply by the fact of their existence. There is pressure for those of us who do not fit to remain silent about our deviation, because there is a great deal at stake. Perpetuating the silence of bisexuals allows the dominant culture to exaggerate the differences between heterosexual and homosexual and to ignore the fact that human sexuality exists on a continuum. —Ibid.

Also there is an effort to showcase that despite its abolition in 1962, the debilitating effects of the Criminal Tribes Act of 1871 (that had described even *hijra*s as a de-notified tribes and hence catalogued them as criminal caste) has a deep-rooted impact on the collective consciousness of Indian citizens and due to that *hijra*s undergo immense emotional, physical and mental torture. The literary texts that have been discussed to explore these cultural biases are Mahesh Dattani's "Seven Steps Around the Fire", Khushwant Singh's *Delhi* and Rashid's "Incomplete Human". In addition to this Satya's "I Hate Wet Tissues" reveals the crippling effects of sex-reassignment surgery (which is performed in order to transform transsexual individual into a so-called full man or woman) on transgender body and mind. This chapter aims, through contemporary literary productions, at unveiling the complex network of oppression of *hijra*s on account of biphobia coupled with other factors, and the ingenious ways through which this neither man nor woman identity can actually work in favour of *hijra*s. It also focuses on how their twofold gender existence encapsulates a more holistic identity because it demonstrates the assimilation and concurrence of contradictory threads in multiple ways. Also as Gayatri Reddy contends in her book entitled *With Respect to Sex*, their twin existence imposes a unique corporeal asexuality that symbolically puts them in the category of *sannyasi*s. The detailed discussion regarding this forms a part of the chapter.

True, the negation of the internalized biphobia and the acceptance of their unique corporeality, which in an interesting fashion suggests their symbolic non-sexual existence and presents them in a peculiar way as ascetics, are the keys to the real uplift of *hijra*s. In addition, they are also able to create fissures and radical ruptures in the domain of familial sexual citizenship because *hijra*s' alternative family disposition unmasks the oppressive structure of heteropatriarchal family by presenting a contrast. This in turn problematizes the issue of sexual citizenship when claimed through the unit of family. Thus from the feminist perspective also their unusual gender-blending takes the whole issue of women's empowerment to another trajectory.

The overlapping of space and sexual identity, or in other words the erotic geography, is a fast emerging area in the field of sexuality studies, and therefore any discussion pertaining to sexual identities without negotiating the role of space in shaping them is incomplete. The last chapter entitled "Queer Identity and Homosexualization of Spaces in Contemporary Indian Literary Texts" aims at excavating the overlapping of sexual identity and space and the consequent spatial anxiety arising from it in relation to exclusively gay, bisexual, lesbian or transgender identities in the Indian context. It also focuses on the techniques of erasure for silencing sexual minorities with a special emphasis on the specific mode of surveillance of transgenders and lesbians in terms of re(appropriation) of spaces. For this purpose Foucault's concept of heterotopias (in which he talks about the liminal spaces that work as fertile ground for the flourishing of non-normative sexuality because these spaces belong to nowhere specifically and thus the identities that are not accepted anywhere find their exploration there) has been applied to the texts like Suroopa Mukherjee's *Across the Mystic Shore,* Mayur Patel's *Vivek and I,* Abha Dawesar's *Babyji,* Mridula Koshy's "A Large Girl", Anita Nair's *Ladies Coupé,* short stories like "Conference Sex", Sarojini Sahoo's "Behind the Scene" and Michael Malik's "Dreams and Desires in Srinagar". According to Foucault,

> There are also, probably in every culture, in every civilization, real places — places that do not exist and that are formed in every founding society — which are something like counter-sites, a kind of effectively enacted utopia in which the real sites, all the other real sites that can be found within the culture, are simultaneously represented, contested and inverted. Places of this kind are outside of all places, even though it may be possible to indicate their location in reality, because these places are absolutely different from all the sites that they reflect and speak about, I shall call them, by way of contrast to utopias, heterotopias. I believe that between utopias and these quiet other sites, these heterotopias, there might be a sort of mixed, joint experience.
>
> — http://foucault.info/documents/heteroTopia.en.html

He further divides them into "heterotopias of crisis" and "heterotopias of deviation". "Heterotopias of crisis" are spaces that are outside the dominant spatial domain both structurally and ideologically and hence ideal for forbidden activities. Motel rooms, train, etc. are fine examples of it. In this chapter, through the use of roof (*chat*) (a very specific Indian space), train and boat, the negotiation between fluid spaces and sexual identities has been demonstrated. For instance, the story, "A Large Girl" and the novels, *Tirohit* and *Across the Mystic Shore,* postulate the immense possibilities that *chat* (roof) offers because of the curious juxtaposing of private and public spheres at such places. Sarojini Sahoo's "Behind the Scene" and Michael Malik's "Dreams and Desires in Srinagar" expose the radicalizing effects of fluid spaces like boat and train (that are constantly in motion and without geographical markers) on sexuality.

An interesting dimension has been added to the discussion through the use of "festival site". According to Michel Foucault, there are heterotopias of indefinitely accumulating time, for examples museums and libraries that will encompass in one place "all times, all epochs, all forms, all tastes, the idea of constituting a place of all times that is itself outside of time and inaccessible to its ravages, the project of organizing in this way a sort of perpetual and indefinite accumulation of time in an immobile place" (http://www.foucaullt.info/doc/documents/heterotopia/foucault.heterotopia.en.html). It is opposed to those heterotopias that in contrast represent time in its most transient, ephemeral and flowing nature. According to him, one example of such heterotopias is "festival". He further elaborates it by giving the example of fairgrounds. To quote his words:

> These heterotopias are not oriented towards the eternal, they are rather absolutely temporal [chroniques]. Such, for example, are the fairgrounds, these marvelous empty sites on the outskirts of the cities that teem once or twice a year with stands, displays heteroclite objects, wrestlers, snakewomen, fortune-tellers such as those Polynesian villages that offer a compact three weeks of primitive and eternal nudity to the inhabitants of the cities.
>
> — http://foucault.info/documents/hetero Topia.en.html

The examples of *Dahihandi* festival in Raj Rao's "Six Inches" and new year festivities in Mayur Patel's *Vivek and I* illustrate the brilliant use of "carnivalesque spaces" for the purpose of reinvesting these places with dissident sexualities in a unique fashion. Propounding the concept of "carnivalesque", Mikhail Bakhtin argues that these festival sites recreate a symbolic "second life" where hegemonic structures are dismantled because the spirit of festivities provides an entry into the symbolic space of utopian freedom. Little wonder when Siddharth in *Vivek and I* has been chided by his partner for an open indulgence in sexual gesturing and groping during a public celebration of New Year, he replies back that it is a wanton night and everything is forgiven at such places at these times. All these are perfect examples of heterochronies or temporarily excluded spaces that transform sexual norms.

Moreover apart from the temporal openings in public spheres during carnival times, there is also a need for radicalizing the largely heterosexual public spaces through homosexual interventions. Most of the public spaces are largely straight and the so-called gay bars, public loo and parks are also queer only at a particular time of night. The depiction of such places and the subsequent queer encounters figure in Raj Rao's *The Boyfriend* and Dattani's "Night Queen". Significantly such ephemeral experiences at transient sites are by and large absent in Indian lesbian narratives. The mutability of these fleeting experiences at equally ephemeral sites has a very important advantage as has been charted out by Larry Knopp in "From Lesbian and Gay to Queer Geographies: Pasts, Prospects and Possibilities". According to him,

> Cruising is not so much tied to a fixed site but is all about the flows of movement and passings. Clubbing, meanwhile, is an ephemeral experience — both the ephemerality of erotic encounters with others on and off a dance floor, but also the ephemerality of the club night itself, coming together to use a space for one night a week or one night a month, congregating and then dispersing. Such queer experiences and practices might be understood in terms of Thrift's idea of an "ecology of place" as a "spectral gathering", in which various practices, meanings and "actants" are examined

> for their myriad and ephemeral interconnections. Similarly, "placelessness" might be productively reconceptualized as an embodied and material practice, one that offers certain pleasures and other benefits (such as security) through its various perceived qualities (heterogeneity, temporariness, anonymity, cosmopolitanism), rather than just a lack.
> — 2007: 23

Importantly in the story "Conference Sex" there is an emergence of lesbian site in the form of transient space of conference. The temporality and anonymity regarding both space and identities (as people are there for a very short period of time) are the distinguished features of a conference site. This story revolves around the two lesbians who have a fleeting sexual encounter at a conference, and they part without even greeting each other. Indubitably the "placelessness" of the conference site provides a fertile ground for the flourishing of deviant desires as the protagonist cogitates:

> It was a conference, I reassured myself; no one expects anything like this, and there are no set rules for behaviour.
> — L.R. Ellen 2012: 183

Thus the ephemerality of such places is indubitably not a "lack" in any sense of the word but contributes to the rewriting and bending of the rules of desire. The chapter also documents the fact that through the techniques of inversion, various specific religious Indian spaces (like *ashram* and temples) are radicalized. For instance in *Across the Mystic Shore* the *ashram* space not only exhibits the lesbian liaison but also the formation of alternative family structure with the two lesbians and a son. *Ashrams*, like university spheres, are autonomous spaces to a great extent, where the rules of inclusion and exclusion operate at an entirely different paradigm as compared to the normative society. Thus on the one hand there is a more disciplined order, but on the other since the usual societal rules do not operate here, there are more slippages and fissures at such sites which can be effective in producing counter-culture. Likewise by deliberately placing homosexual relationships right inside the religious temples and *math*, both Suroopa and Dibyajyoti Sarma in "Let Me Sin Then" reverse the stringent heteropatriarchal order of spatial sexuality. In fact the first flush of lesbian longing flowers between the two lesbian lovers in *Across the Mystic Shore* inside a Shiva temple before a *shivaling* which is a significant marker of heterosexual mating. In the similar vein the school and university spaces, on account of their specific autonomy, help in breaking the sexual stereotypes and therefore have been effectively used by the authors like Ismat (*The Crooked Line*), Mayur Patel (*Vivek and I*), Raj Rao (*Hostel Room 131*) and Ellen ("Conference Sex"). Yet one more effective strategy to radicalize education spheres is the clever use of manipulating the strict boundaries of curriculum in sex-education counselling sessions. Thus the curriculum, whether in the form of biology class or sex-education sessions, plays a pivotal role in reinvesting school and college environment with a certain openness that is a fertile ground for any sort of discussion on dissident sexualities as well. Even if the formal curriculum is only about heterosexuality, the informal curriculum which is called "hidden curriculum" by Nairan is a significant key for breaking the stereotypes and Dawesar's *Babyji* fully illustrates it. In this text, the formal sexual education is imbued with heteronormative assumptions but the informal counselling session creates ruptures and non-normativity becomes the focal point of the discussion. Indeed, the correspondence between the formal and informal curriculum plays a key role in reorienting the taken for granted heteronormativity of the university space and this aspect has been effectively showcased in *Babyji*. Thus the mutually reciprocal and radicalizing impact of space over subaltern sexuality and the vice versa have been effectively demonstrated in these Indian texts. Besides, the use of very specific Indian spaces like *chat*, *ashram*, *math* and temples add all together a different tangent to the whole discussion. Obviously the tools are drawn, apart from reworking of specific Indian spaces, from Western philosophy and geography to open up new areas in Indian queer academia vis-à-vis space.

Hence the major concerns of this book, negotiated through the exclusive Indian literary texts, are the demonstration of the lesbian issues and the potent lesbian activism in seemingly lesbophobic regional tales, the depiction of the phenomenon of formation of a gay group that consists of queers from all social and cultural groups (on account of their outcast queer identity) and consequently creates ruptures in conventional heterosexual hierarchies of class and caste, the tense negotiation between sexual dissidents and space and the specific problem of biphobia and its consequent impact on *hijra* identity. In addition, as a part of broader framework, the present study is meant to reveal the fact that the perennial mutability of queer existence due to the non-acceptance by patriarchal society is able to create fractures, though in a quite inverted fashion, in the revered but highly oppressive idea of middle-class stability and permanence generated out of the false sense of security. Through the reversal of paradigm, the same transitoriness of queer relationships which is constantly sneered at can actually work as a catalyst to burst the myth of middle class stability and non-anarchic heteropatriarchal society and hence the lack of marriage sanction, the dubious AIDS citizenship (which forms a counter-culture by forming a shadow state as has been mentioned earlier) and the assimilation of both lower and higher castes and classes under the ambit of outcast queer identity are not markers of subjugation only, but in an oblique manner annihilate the larger hegemonic structures of heteropatriarchal society by producing counter-culture in every sense of the word.

1

Dichotomic Representation of Lesbianism
As an Act of Resistance in Contemporary Indian English Women Writers With Special Reference to Abha Dawesar and Anita Nair

> May Eros, the formless one, be gracious/and give to each one of us a double life.
>
> — Vijaydan Detha, "A Double Life", *Same-Sex Love in India*, p. 318

THE NON-EGALITARIAN structure of heteronormativity, which aims at the regulation of feminine sexuality at different measures, has long been debated in lesbian circles in the form of academic papers such as Cheryl Clarke's "Lesbianism: An Act of Resistance" where she vociferously argues that hetero-normativity is a male supermasist chauvinistic measure to oppress women. In India works by Giti Thadani, Ashwini Sukthankar and Ruth Vanita endorse these views through critical apparatus, and the creative rendering of it finds their manifestations in the writings of Geetanjali Shree (*Tirohit*), Suroopa Mukherjee (*Across the Mystic Shore*), Manju Kapur (*A Married Woman*), Vijaydan Detha ("A Double Life"), R. Raj Rao ("The Gang Rape") and Indu Menon ("Oru Lesbian Pashu") . In fact what Cheryl Clarke argues in her sophisticated academic paper, Vijaydan Detha's "A Double Life" explores it through an age-old Rajasthani folk tale. In this story when the lesbian lover turns into a man, the horror faced by her wife knows no bounds and ultimately sanity and love return to marriage when the husband once again transforms into a woman. This overtly expresses that coercive subjugation is inherent in a heterosexual marriage, irrespective of man's internal complexion, and proclaims that feminism can only be fully realized outside heteronormativity. In this brilliantly crafted story Detha, without using any sophisticated obscure Western theoretical apparatus, bursts the myth of glorified motherhood (a very specific Indian identity of woman) and recommends all women homosocial space:

> Thanks to the ghost chieftain's magic, not only the filthy seed of man but Teeja's womb too burned up forever. This creature named man dare not venture within a distance of twenty-four and twenty-four, a total of forty-eight miles around that place. — Vanita and Kidwai 2000: 324

Despite the post-colonial agenda and the fact that there is a distinct Indian tradition — viz. a very specific way of locating desire in the context of nationalism, citizen subject, public culture, linguistic and cultural identity, gender and civilization-myth — due to globalization in the last decade (both the writings belong to the last decade), the inclusion of the diasporic writer Abha Dawesar in this paper and the inherent "intranational cultural differences" (as Spivak calls it), somewhat justify the use of the certain Western theoretical tools along with the specific Indian critical positions while analysing the position of lesbianism in the feminist context. Apropos of this complex problem of transcultural/ transnational similarities and differences, Jyoti Puri argues:

> Lesbian and gay scholarship in India cannot help but be influenced by the search for a universal gay identity that is, at best, offset by the culturally specific gay. This only reproduces the effect of differences between the gay West and non-West, between the global and culturally different gay.

Hence while analysing Abha Dawesar's *Babyji* and Anita Nair's

Ladies Coupé as significant additions to the radical feminist debate, which argues that no holistic realization of feminism is possible without the displacement of heterosexuality, it is important to locate the negotiation between the specific national and cultural construction of female desire and the global universal politics of shared lesbian identity, and this renegotiation creates a unique third space. This space needs to be carefully understood in terms of specific lesbian resistance. However, locating lesbianism in the domain of "resistance" poses certain problematic questions, for it reaffirms somewhat that the homoerotic passion is an aside to heterosexuality rather than an instinctive choice and becomes a dominant form of identity only as a revolt to heteronormativity and obliquely re-establishes heteronorm as a primary signifier. Also the issue of the egalitarian structure of same-sex love is somewhat plagued in these texts because they exhibit the overlapping of the class and caste dynamics and evince that at times class and caste trump over sexuality. By doing so they do not fix their narratives into inflexible categories of experience that follow the stringently dichotomic model of assimilation/resistance. This sort of ambivalence, contradiction and slippage on the one hand makes the texts in question somewhat regressive, and on the other gives impetus to the alternative readings that challenge the essentialist identity categories.

The story of Abha Dawesar's *Babyji* is of a young girl named Anamika who has lesbian relationships simultaneously with her maid Rani, her classmate Sheela and the working mother Tripta, whereas Anita Nair's *Ladies Coupé* revolves around the lives of six women travelling in a ladies coupé and narrating their life stories. The last story of this novel centres around Marikolanthu, a working-class maid who has homoerotic passion for her upper-class mistress Sujata Akka. The common concern of both the texts is the relentless exposition of the oppressive coercive heterosexuality. They tend to deconstruct the patriotic nationalistic construction of the middle-class heterosexual monogamous "mother" image that fixes woman into the over glorified image of mother and caretaker of the future generation and hence divorcing sexual mating from pleasure and casting it into a mould of procreation only, and all this further gives impetus to the heterosexual capitalist ideology by fulfilling its incessant need for free labour. These texts share the common ground also on the basis of their exploration of plurality and multiplicity of lesbian experience within the heterosexual space and using it as a tool to familiarize and normalize the homoerotic passion. However, the lesbian anxiety is also apparent in these works in the depiction of the dismantling of the so-called non-exploitative nature of the same-sex love by showcasing power operations based on class and caste dynamics within the lesbian framework. Thus these authors problematize the whole issue by seeking answers to the question whether the assimilation and coalition politics of becoming a single category on the basis of being sexual minority (lesbians), irrespective of their class and caste status, provides a non-exploitative space to these women or the caste and class categories trump over this assumption and become a greater tool of oppression. Sukthankar talks about the utopian notion of all women-space thus:

> When we name ourselves we can see ourselves for who we are: a group of women utterly diverse in terms of religion, class, community, age, marital status, but with this one thing in common. Our love for women — that which marks us as different from the rest of the world, which brings us together.
>
> — 1999: xx

This kind of blunting of hegemonic structures and over-simplification of a complex problem under the overarching phenomenon of lesbianism is somewhat fallacious and both the texts under consideration quite systematically argue the contradiction and the partial falsity of this kind of position.

The first text *Ladies Coupé* focuses on the life-stories of six women travelling in a train who choose to narrate their tales of coercive heterosexuality in an all-female (ladies coupé) homosocial space. To quote from the text:

> There was silence in the coupe. For a moment, Akhila had thought they had established a connection. Fetuses jostling within the walls of a womb, drawing sustenance from each other's lives, aided by the darkness outside and the fact that what was shared within the walls wouldn't go beyond this night or the contained space. — Anita Nair: 22

Thus the space plays a vital role in reincarnating the sexual identities of these women when they tell their stories through memory and recreate it in a heterotopic site of train. Both in *Babyji* and *Ladies Coupé* the relocating of same-sex desire within a middle-class heterosexual household and that too on the conjugal bed of a married woman is indeed a progressive move by Abha Dawesar and Anita Nair. No wonder all the encounters of Anamika and Marikolanthu take place in their bedroom right inside the patriarchal format. To quote from *Babyji*:

> At home the servant was stooped over the kitchen sink doing the dishes. When she did the dishes in my presence she always squatted with her sari hitched half way up, and I could see her legs. Her legs were covered now.
>
> — Dawesar 2005: 258

Similarly she takes Rani to her room and asks her to lie down on her bed so that they both may cuddle up each other to which Rani instantly says "no" due to her inferior caste and class. Thus the bed becomes the site of deconstructing hegemonic structures of class, caste and sexuality. In fact, the mutually reciprocal relationship between space and self has been effectively portrayed in the thought-provoking scene in which cajoling Rani to come to bed, Anamika says:

> From now on I want you to treat me like an eqûal when we are alone. In front of other people you can behave as usual. "I can't do that, Baby ji. It wouldn't be right", she said, lowering her eyes. I walked up to where she was standing at the threshold of my bedroom and ran my fingers along her lips. She reached out. A thrill shot up my spine. I pulled her into my room and flung us both on the bed. Instead of the disturbing *Kamasutra* dream where I had failed to make an entrance on the scene, I saw Rani and myself in an erotic position.
>
> — Ibid.: 32

Another oppressive category is demolished by these texts and that is the annihilation of juxtaposing of the mother image with the Indian land and cultural identity. There is a systematically politicized nationalist construction of Indian woman as a symbol of Indianness and associating her with Mother India (Indian land), and thus giving impetus to the cultural construction of Indian woman as a heterosexual, monogamous nurturing mother of the future citizens and this clearly ascertains deferral of the non-procreative identity of lesbian women. Apropos of this Sridevi K. Nair comments:

> In many nationalist contexts "woman" signifies the nurturing wife and mother, monogamous and heterosexual who gives material form to abstract ideas like culture and nation. Scholars have theorized that the woman chosen to represent "India" and "Indianness" is the upper-caste, middle-class educated woman who is seen essentially nurturing and raising future generations.
>
> — http://deepblue.lib.umich.edu/bitstream/202742/64620/1/nair-1.pdf

This can be further substantiated by quoting the exact words of Mahila Aghadi's (the women wing of Shiv Sena) petition against the screening of Deepa Mehta's *Fire.* They argued in the petition to ban the film stating that

> If women's physical needs get fulfilled through lesbian acts, the institution of marriage will collapse and the "reproduction" of human beings will stop.
>
> — Praveen Sami in www.hinduonnet.com/fl1526/

Patently this sort of position where women's sexuality is deployed in the service of nation only and this kind of connection between India (the motherland) and feminine sexuality have been vociferously rejected by many lesbian feminists. Little wonder, Qamar Roshanabadi through her poem, "Vande Mataram!", annihilates this overlapping. In this connection Sridevi K. Nair also suggests that Roshanabadi tries to challenge masculine cultural patriotism. She rewrites the "whole notion" of Mother India by using the same tool of oppression and that is reversing the nationalist patriotic cult song, "Vande Mataram" and placing women's desire for another woman (irrespective of heterosexual mother image) at the centre of it. Thus she puts lesbianism at the very heart of the nation rather than displacing it. In this poem she valorizes "the motherland" as she celebrates women's love for women and makes an obvious connection that motherland is not only a place for heterosexual citizens and recasts the masculine desire for nation and woman. To quote from the poem:

> On the solemn occasion/of the fiftieth year/of Indian Independence/I salute our motherland/Home of the most beautiful women. — Sukthankar 1999: 408

The exclusion of homosexuality from nationalist culture is not exclusively for lesbians only but extends its vicious boundaries with equal potency to the male homosexuality as well, as Ruth Vanita points out in *Chocolate and Other Writings on Male Homoeroticism.* She situates Pandey Bechan Sharma's writings in relation to Indian nationalist struggle. In the pre-Independence era, many critics fallaciously believed that the representation of Indian man as gay portrayed an effeminate picture of Indian man before the imperial British powers and hence gave a backlash to freedom struggle. This creates ambivalent homophobic anxiety in the stories of "Ugra". Hence there is a desperate need for counter-strategies to combat against the othering of sexual minorities and their displacement as authentic citizen subjects. Brinda Bose aptly remarks in this connection:

> The alternatively sexualized citizens — just like the "second-sex", perhaps — is instrumental, through the very performance of his/her sexuality, in rendering unstable all universalized notions of citizenship (modelled on the male heterosexual). The nation-state then becomes a site of anxiety as well as of negotiation, where the dissident sexual subject threatens the social, cultural and economic boundaries of the national imagination and challenges the ideological apparatus employed by the state for vigilance and containment. — Bose and Bhattacharyya 2007: xvii

Thus in *Babyji* the renaming of Tripta (Anamika's lesbian partner and divorced single mother) as India can be seen as a deliberate act of radical resistance against the nationalist construction of woman as a heterosexual mother. While rechristening Tripta, Anamika thinks:

> I felt the urge to call her something. Something that no one else was called. A word that was not a name and that was still proportional to the immensity of the revelation unfolding within me. "India" was the first thing that slipped silently from my lips. — Dawesar 2005: 3

She has gone to the extent of saying that India (her lover Tripta) is the "essence of being Indian" (p. 166). According to Lisa Duggan, this "queering of the state" is absolutely imperative. This tactic enables to expose the complex and overlapping dynamics of citizenship, identity and sexuality. The debates surrounding the concept of sexual citizenship (specially in connection with homosexual identity) create a better understanding of the role of state in systematic red-lining of sexual subcultures into marginal spaces. Therefore the relentless description of Tripta's sensuousness by Anamika in a geography class is specially significant. She once even anthropomorphizes the map of India with Tripta's curly hair and breasts. At another moment she juxtaposes the images of her lovers Rani and Tripta and then compares them with the sun rising over the Ganges in Benares:

> I drew maps of India and wrote India in the centre. I anthropomorphized the map by adding curls on the states of Gujarat and West Bengal. I imagined India's body and the map of country liquefying the boundaries between various states so that they could overlap. —Ibid.: 46

Patriotism and lesbianism have been shown greatly linked when Anamika states that when she sees India she feels the same love as she feels for the whole country:

> Because when I first saw you I felt the kind of love I feel for the whole country, not just one part. For all her contradictions, her fierceness, her beauty, her rivers and her mountains. —Ibid.: 130-31

David Bell and Jon Binnie in *The Sexual Citizen* affirm that citizenship is another way of expressing compromise because every entitlement is freighted with a duty (2000: 3).

Thus every citizen has to perform a specific duty and for Indian woman her right to a legitimate citizenship is fraught with the burden of reproduction. No wonder in *Ladies Coupé* though the obvious connections have not been made between nationalism and lesbian desire, there is a powerful and sustained effort to challenge the glorified notion of motherhood (a byproduct of heterosexual invasion and a major tool of deferral of female transgressive longings) which is considered the essence of womanhood in the nationalist construction of ideal Indian woman. At another level these six stories unfold the oppression faced by a woman because of this essentialist identity where her entire being seems to stem out of being a mother. This regulation of feminine sexuality by procreation is poignantly described through a powerful scene in *Ladies Coupé* where Janaki's husband tells everyone how she has been instrumental in taking a pregnant woman to hospital and making her deliver the child. Her husband tells this story time and again as if it is her highest and the only achievement. This sort of linking of her identity to only being either a mother or helping the other woman becoming a mother irks her beyond measures and in a larger context is an obvious backlash at the non-procreative homoerotic passion. Janaki in a fit of rage yells:

> She wanted to fling down the spatula, upturn the bowl that held the dosa batter and slap his face till the pride crumbled in his eyes and scattered in the air. She wanted to scream, 'Don't call me mummy. I'm not your mummy. I am your wife. Remember you used to call me janu once. Wife. Darling. Sweetheart. And if you find it hard saying those call me woman, but don't call me Mummy".
>
> — Anita Nair 2001: 34

The mass apathy to the horrible violation of feminine desire under the garb of procreative identity is also reflected in one of the scenes where the doctor makes a generalized sweeping statement that it is natural to feel horrible during pregnancy. Likewise Akhila, a spinster, is shown constantly bothered by the annoying and disturbing sounds of her sister's daughters. Similarly another aspect of subjugation due to coercive procreative sex, viz. the forced abortion, finds its expression in the story of Margaret Shanthi, who suffers from severe anxiety, guilt and pain at being forced into aborting her first born. An unborn child that evokes so much of passion and compassion in her heart has been seen by her husband as a tiny cell only:

> Right now that cell in you is just that: a cell with no soul or feelings. If you had a boil that turned septic wouldn't you

> have it lanced? Just think it as a tumour that has to be removed. — Ibid.: 106

The reason behind this gory act is that he does not want her body to change. The gross appropriation of her body is the sole reason for this forced abortion. She will cease to be a little girl and turn into a full-fledged woman is what irks her husband. Thus the control over a woman's body whether she should be a mother or not ought to be of a man. Hence the procreative sex, the biggest argument in favour of heterosexual marriage, works actually in turn to regulate feminine body and sexuality in all possible forms. Ebbe states:

> So untainted and clean. My little darling. My lovely girl. With no big bouncy breasts and horrible woman's bush. I never want you to change. I want you to remain like this all your life. — Anita Nair 2001: 111

This control over productivity through the forced abortion is the way to appropriate Margaret's body, whereas in Marikolanthu's story in the same text, the forced pregnancy as a result of rape becomes the sole reason of her oppression at every level. She has been thrown out of job and home. She completely rejects the child born out of rape and deconstructs the so-called notion that pleasure of motherhood is the ultimate panacea for heterosexual onslaught. To quote from the texts:

> The sight of one's own baby; the feeling of holding your own baby in your arms — Periamma thought all this would make me want the child. But she didn't know me well enough, nor the power of hate. — Ibid.: 248

In fact, dismantling the fallacious concept of all consuming motherly love, she goes to the extent of selling her own child to his rapist father as a labourer and accepts him wholeheartedly only after the death of that rapist when the patriarchal structure is completely annihilated in her mind and the child ceases to be a living symbol of it. However, another contradictory dimension can be added to the whole issue. By exhibiting the same-sex desire of both the respectable middle-class mothers, Sujata and Tripta, the fictionists are trying to assert that being a mother as well as a lesbian clearly proves that procreative sex aims at the perverted satisfaction of penis alone and leaves woman wounded and dissatisfied both emotionally and physically. Naturally the whole idea of the nationalistic cataloguing of woman as a tool to nurture future generations gets demolished here and the sinister politics of transference from clitoral to procreative vaginal sex is exposed blatantly. Furthermore to reveal the fact that even alternative family structure and motherhood are also possible within the same-sex framework, the writers exhibit two women nurturing a child without the pernicious presence of father as in *Tirohit* and *Across the Mystic Shore*. Likewise Anamika taking up the role of a guardian, even gets admitted Tripta's son to a school despite all stumbling blocks and envisages a home where she sees herself with Tripta and her son. Thus this kind of positioning on the one hand appears to be writing back to heteronormative family structure, but on the other confirms that lesbian love is holistic in every possible way and to counter the patriarchal privileges there is an answer in alternative family structure and hence transgressive desire is not deficient in any form. Similarly tracing back the complex identity of lesbian motherhood through religious, mythological and historical texts, both Ruth Vanita and Giti Thadani in *Sakhiyani* talk about the birth of Bhagirathi by the two wives of King Dilipa after his death and the birth of Agni who is not only born of two mothers but also nourished by a group of mothers. True both these positions, despite their contradictions, make a strong case for lesbian love as a potent solution to counter horrible appropriation of female body and at the same time expose the politics of deliberate deferral of lesbians as authentic citizens.

Similarly in yet another attempt to showcase lesbianism as an act of resistance against heterosexual invasion, all married women — Rani, Sujata Akka, Tripta and Marikolanthu who have been victims of marital rape and domestic violence — get comfort and sexually rejuvenate themselves through the tender body mating with other women. In fact the very title of the chapter of the story of Marikolanthu is "Sister to the Real Thing" clearly exhibits that it is not lesbianism but heterosexuality that is an aside to homosexuality. Bombarded with media images and heterosexual romances, a woman's mind is conditioned to think it to be the only way of sexual resuscitation. But soon she discovers the power manifestations of this structure and questions whether it is the "real" thing:

> In all the films that we see they make such a fuss about love. All those dialogues they speak, the songs they sing, if only those heroines knew what came after. . . . What comes after is revulsion. When he comes near me, I feel as though a lizard is crawling up my skin. But I close my eyes and let him do whatever he wants to. I know he goes to other women, but if I don't let him do it once in a while, he'll find a mistress like his father did, and flaunt her beneath my nose. Every night when I go to bed, I wait for his touch. Only when he turns on his side and goes to sleep do I fall asleep. Marikolanthu, I worry, that something is wrong with me. What if I go mad like his mother did? Was it this revulsion for the physical part of marriage that turned her into a mad woman.
>
> — Anita Nair 2001: 259

This horrible conditioning of mind engenders so much anxiety in women that they not only suffer physically but are also mutilated and crippled psychologically by this schizophrenic split identity. Again Rani's marital rape leaves horrible permanent scars on her soul and body on which Anamika very tenderly puts medicine and later on further soothes her by becoming intimate with her. This clearly exhibits the author's intention of evincing homoerotic liaison as the only space available for the complete and unexploitative exploration of feminine sexuality. Anamika asks Rani:

> "Have you ever enjoyed yourself with your husband? I asked, struggling to be precise." He is an animal. Don't pollute yourself mentioning him. Women are not meant to enjoy. — Dawesar 2005: 49

Not only the barriers of class but also of caste are also shattered when Rani (a shudra) is shown copulating with Anamika and Marikolanthu with Sujata Akka. Another bias against homoerotic passion in India is that it is a middle class, English-speaking, non-Indian (an import from the West) phenomenon. Divorcing lesbianism from Indianness has been somewhat mitigated in these two texts and another fallacious construct that it is only a middle-class phenomenon is also challenged when the maidservants Rani and Marikolanthu have been shown having an all-consuming passion for their upper-class employers, Anamika and Sujata Akka respectively. However, there is a regressive move by the author when she depicts that Marikolanthu has been initiated into homoerotic passion by aping the model of her foreigner white employees, two nurses called Missy V and Missy K. But overall, the spontaneous sensuous absorption of Sapphic desire by both the working-class women, Rani and Marikolanthu, clearly breaks the assumption that same-sex desire is exclusive to middle class only. One of the obvious reasons is that lack of availability of lesbian partners gives impetus to classless and casteless assimilation. Citing another reason for the blunting of hierarchal privileges in the same-sex union, R. Raj Rao, for example, asserts: "What is same/similar in non-transgressive sexuality is same here" (Rao and Sarma 2009: xvi). Thus the need for the "other" is satisfied in these relationships on the basis of the differences in class, caste and age (as in the case of Tripta and Rani in *Babyji* and Marikolanthu in *Ladies Coupé*), for unlike the heterosexual structure, here the constant "other" on the basis of gender is altered and becomes the "same". Neither Rani nor Marikolanthu (unlike the maidservants Rabbu in "Lihaf", Miland in *The Boyfriend* and Lalana in Geetanjali Shree's *Tirohit*) exploits her socially superior partner for money. This lesbian passion is a spontaneous instinctive overflow of emotions, bereft of any motive of extracting economic benefits from their upper-class mates. But there appears a problem in the paradise when viewed from the perspectives of the socially superior mates, Anamika and Sujata Akka. Anamika almost rapes both Rani and Sheela (a lower-caste classmate). Nevertheless, this horrible scene occurs when she and Sheela have been savagely molested and humilitated in full public view in bus and Anamika avenges herself by brutally ravaging Rani:

> I threw her on the bed and started ripping open her blouse. She closed her eyes as if she didn't want to see me . . . . I had an image of the two men from bus again, but this time it did not leave me cold. It made me angry and I started pushing Rani more vigorously. The German guy from the porn magazines, but with Chakkar Deva's face, the brahmin from the movies with his servant, positions from the *Kamasutra* all mixed up in my head till I could no longer think.
>
> — Dawesar 2005: 95

Also the opaque intentions of Dawesar and Anita Nair are visible because despite representing homosexuality in the working class, the partners of these maids always belong to the upper class (there are never two exclusively working class mates) and the reason could be that being doubly marginalized both by class and sexuality, there is a sense of power that these women gain through appropriating "upward social mobility" by associating themselves with upper-class women. But when viewed from the perspective of the upper class mate, the reason could be that women are culturally trained to love women only through masculine appropriation of power and this dynamics cannot be realized between the same class partners. This power operation is possible only with the lower class or lower caste (the finger rape of Sheela, a *dalit* schoolmate, by Anamika is another example of it) women even if the direct transaction of money is not involved. In *Babyji* Anamika brutally forces herself on Rani by constantly remembering the physical humiliation suffered by her in a bus by *chepad* men. In the very next chapter she affirms that this sort of forcible act is not possible with Tripta, who is also from upper class. This, according to Sridevi K. Nair, is an attempt of masculine appropriation and transference of physical atrocities committed on Anamika's body, and so in turn avenges herself by savagely appropriating Rani's body. On the one hand the class dynamics comes in the picture, and on the other the realization by Anamika that appropriation of masculinity and money are the only ways to get empowered, and that being a woman means constantly regulated and policed. Anamika herself acknowledges it in a poignantly portrayed scene:

> But standing like this that while having a man polish my shoes made me feel like a grown-up man. My society allowed the molestation of young girl in public, but if you had money then people always bowed down to you. Sheela stood near me looking at the guys bending over my right foot and then my left, applying shoe cream and buffing the leather with a cloth. — Dawesar 2005: 98

This episode and certain other incidents clearly establish Anamika's overt "butch" identity which evinces a "gendered structure" relationship rather than an egalitarian one. According to many lesbian feminists, this sort of aping of heteronormative masculine/feminine category is quite regressive. But the various episodes in the text evince that the terrible appropriation of masculinity is a strategic tool deliberately adopted by the fictionist to highlight the fact that without masculine identity empowerment is not possible in a viciously subversive patriarchal system, and so at the back hand it is an oblique way of the exposition of power paradigm. Thus whether the "butch" identity of Anamika is a backlash at lesbian feminism or a carefully crafted tool to showcase the power mechanisms of heterosexual world is debatable. In fact, these "butch" and "femme" identities are completely negated in the relationship between Marikolanthu and Sujata Akka, but the class dynamics ultimately trumps over sexuality and the exploitive nature of even same-sex relationship is also vehemently exposed. Marikolanthu loves Sujata Akka unconditionally and in order to save her from her husband's brutal sexual needs she offers herself to him:

> All my capacity for loving and giving had found a vent in Sujata Akka. So it was to preserve her happiness, her position in the household, her hold over Sridhar Anna that I welcomed Sridhar Anna into my body. As long as I fed his appetites, he would never seek another woman. As long as I was available, he would never trouble Sujata Akka on the days he was at home. — Anita Nair 2001: 261

This provides useful points of entry for considering slippage between exclusive lesbian love and playing out the ultimate male fantasy of double bonanza whereby the female bonding between a wife and her lover ultimately works for resuscitating husband's sexual desires. And unlike Gayatri Gopinath's argument in favour of this kind of triangulated desire which can open a third space where both hetero- and homoerotic relationships coexist, this reversal of heterosexual triangle in *Ladies Coupé* ultimately subjugates the working class Marikolanthu. She has been exploited both emotionally and physically by her upper-caste and upper-class employers (both the husband and wife). Despite this act of utter selfless love and horrible mutilation of her body, Marikolanthu has been labelled as a home-snatcher and gold digger. Sujata accuses her of being a whore and in fact their unexploitative free flowing love is seen by her as unnatural. She even blames Marikolanthu for initiating her into this and throws her out of home, and the latter leaves her home without salary. So she has been completely devastated physically, mentally and economically. This is how the classless and casteless paradig of same-sex love is shown annihilated completely an lesbianism appears not an answer to patriarchal subjugation but rather an extension of it. Here once again class supersedes gender and sexuality. It puts various question marks on the intention of the author. To quote from the text:

> You are unnatural. Do you know that? Turn away from your own child. You prefer a mad woman's company to your mother's. In the day-time you pretend to be my friend, at night you feed on my husband's lust. What kind of friend are you? . . . You are a wicked creature. I know you used black magic to make me your slave . . . make me do things no woman would . . . but not any more . . . get out of this house before I have you thrown out. — Anita Nair: 263-64

Significantly enough, the debatable positions of both these writers are visible in the way their characters are stricken by "lesbian panic" and fail to show the culmination of their homoerotic passion into something permanently fruitful. Apart from Sujata Akka's act of suddenly throwing away Marikolanthu, the two foreign lovers, Miss K and Miss V, have been shown abruptly breaking their relationship when Miss V suddenly decides to go back to England, and in a very disruptive fashion the sudden end of their relationship is depicted symbolically through the destruction of roses (planted by Miss V) by Miss K. To quote from the text:

> She rose from her chair and went into the garden with a pair of garden scissors. And quietly she set about snipping the rose plants till they stood just about six inches high. Then she took a hoe and dug up the bed till all the rose

> plants lay with their roots exposed and shivering . . . "Kate, what's wrong with you?" Miss V screamed from the window.
>
> "You", she said. "These were for you. I don't want them here reminding me of you."
>
> Miss V turned away from the window. When the rose bed was wrecked beyond redemption, Miss K went back in.
>
> — Anita Nair 2001: 252

Then, Anamika in *Babyji* leaves for America for higher studies suddenly (like Piplika Khan in *A Married Woman*) and other than Rani she does not feel the need to tell anyone, and this clearly aborts her relationships with all the three women in her life, Rani, Tripta and Sheela.

Despite this sort of disruption of lesbian desire, both Dawesar and Anita Nair take a very progressive stand when they portray the resexualization of lesbian longing instead of showcasing it only as a romantic leaning devoid of any underbelt activity. Desexualization of lesbianism is vehemently opposed by A. Koedt, E. Levine and Diane Richardson. The emphasis on the eroticization of lesbian intimacies as a political agenda also finds manifestation in the writings of Giti Thadani and Ashwini Sukthankar who point out the problem with the term *saheli* or *sakhi* that tends to divorce physical passion from lesbian experience and consequently works as a systematic tool of coercion. In this regard both the texts are surcharged with the description of overt sexual indulgence among major women characters. Anamika goes to the extent of asserting:

> I didn't think any one of them as pure minds. I saw them as women. I liked their flesh. Did it detract from my love for them that I loved their bodies, not just their souls.
>
> — Dawesar 2005: 130

In addition to this, the plurality and multiplicity of Anamika's relationships (she is involved with three women of different ages and classes at the same time) definitely reveal the overwhelming enormity, possibility and freedom that same-sex love offers to women because it does not include the propertization of their bodies. Also the main characters, Anamika, Marikolanthu, and even the minor characters like Miss V and Miss K are shown exclusively lesbian rather than bisexual. Similarly, Rani and Sujata are bisexuals on account of forced marriage against their own choice and volition. Bisexuality as a safer label as opposed to exclusive homosexuality has been long debated in feminist circles. Obviously both these authors adopt a very clear-cut strong position.

A close study of the form of these novels gives rise to certain disturbing arguments. For instance the lesbophobic anxieties on the part of the authors are also visible not only due to the thematic representation, but also on account of form. As one can notice that the lesbian life story of Marikolanthu is narrated only in the end after the stories of five upper class heterosexual women and the novel closes with Akhila's heterosexual encounter as if to reaffirm the heterosexual superiority. In the similar fashion in *Babyji* there is a deliberate sensationalization and forced realism that lack Ismat's spontaneous, instinctive charm. She writes in a crass sexual language of commercial pornography while describing the finger rape of Sheela by Anamika (she points out in an overtly insensitive manner about the blood in her finger after the forceful breaking of Sheela's hymen) and the brutal sexual assault on Rani. According to Raj Rao, this strategic inversion of literary language is at times intentional to emphasize the exclusively "queer or transgressive aesthetics", which operates in conformity with the principle of resistance against the accepted norm of literary language. The question is whether it is only a political agenda or there is something more sinister behind this sort of blunt language. Apropos of this Ashwini Sukthankar writes:

> When we write erotica and make it public in this manner, are we merely replicating the ways in which society objectifies us, turning our lives into sexual commodities for the entertainment of men. Are we unable to think of being sexual with each other without a male voyeur validating us.
>
> — 1999: xxviii

Giti Thadani traces back this sort of male voyeurism of lesbian act to "Radha–Krishna" tradition and locates it in various scenes where Radha's *sakhi*s erotically play in the water and Krishna adopts the role of a male voyeur. The detailed analysis of it can be found in the chapter entitled "Plurality of the Significance of Lesbian Existence in Modern Indian Writers: Manju Kapur, Rajkamal Chaudhary and Geetanjali Shree". This sort of titillating depiction in a particular kind of sensational (in the name of realism) and insensitive language at times is a means to provide lesbian double-bonanza to a male reader and mars the political position of resexualization of Sapphic desire. Laura Mulvey in "Visual Pleasure and Narrative Cinema" famously calls it "masculinization" of female gaze and terms it as "to-be-looked-at-ness". Another significant aspect is the difference of language and symbols between the writer's entry into the psyche of a straight character and that of a homosexual. Anamika's internalization of the fluidity and non-fixities of her homoerotic passion has been articulated in a very poetic and symbolic mode through physics theories on wave particle and "uncertainity principle". Thus the fictionist's affinity with a homosexual character is explicitly visible. However, in *Ladies Coupé* while describing Akhila and Margaret, the two straight women, the various stages of their mental states are depicted through persistent water-imagery and different kind of chemicals respectively, but this kind of suggestive inquiry into the psyche of lesbian Marikolanthu is not visible despite the extremely dramatic and painful events in her life. Hence this sort of partial treatment raises questions in the mind of the reader.

To conclude, both the writers do take a radical lesbian feminist approach by evincing homoerotic passion as the elixir for dismantling the subversive heterosexual pattern by repeatedly referring to the atrocities and violence of men's love as opposed to the fluidity, spontaneity, polyvalence and tenderness of female to female desire. Further the depiction of the horrors of the procreative sex and the forced motherhood, as in the case of Rani and Marikolanthu, endorses the writers' belief in the supremacy of the lesbian love as opposed to the heterosexual intimacies. The fictionists demonstrate queer affirmative stand through depicting explicit resexualization of homoerotic passion, by negating the exclusion of lesbianism from the purview of "Indian identity" and locating it within the very centre of nationalistic patriotism and thus exceeding the boundaries drawn for citizen subject and through reframing Sapphic desire within the very heterosexual domestic spaces such as in bedroom, bathroom, kitchen, conjugal bed and familiarizing and normalizing it. But, at the same time, the regressive approach in their writings is also visible on account of description of heterosexual hierarchal privileges of caste, culture and religion within transgressive relationships, and this indubitably bursts the myth about the utopian non-oppressive nature of same-sex love. Also the close scrutiny of form and language as presented above reveals some sort of insincerity (despite raising the issues of "queer aesthetics") in portraying lesbianism as a political tool of emancipation and exhibits the writers' lesbophobic anxieties. Though Indian writers have surely come a long way from the days of Pandey Bechan Sharma "Ugra", Rajkamal Chaudhary and Shobha De, the authors' anxieties are explicitly visible at many places and put various question marks on the catholicity of their genuine intentions to highlight lesbianism as an ultimate solution to patriarchal subjugation. These fissures and slippage are not pertinent to specific texts, but raise a bigger question: since power operates at multiple contradictory levels and lesbianism is forged into the very matrix of heterosexual structure propelling it as an ultimate panacea against patriarchal subversion, is a monolithic approach and requires a scrutiny. The complete annihilation of eclectic hegemonic hierarchies through the same-sex love, which definitely somewhat negates the atrocities committed on account gender differences and challenges the ideological heteronormative apparatus by creating a site of anxiety and space for renegotiation, is an utopian ideal because the privileges of class, caste, age and education still operate, though not quite conspicuously because the divide between the oppressor and the oppressed is somewhat blunted in the same-sex union, and thus it is certainly a partial answer to patriarchal subjugation but not the ultimate elixir.

2

Violence on Hijras through the Lens of Biphobia and the Contemporary Literary Representations

Mahesh Dattani, Khushwant Singh, Abdul Khalid Rashid and Satya

As the third sex (*tritiya prakriti*) as it has been called in Sanskrit or *kothey* in Thailand, and *xanith* in Omani — as it bears a close semblance with *fa'afafine* of Polynesia, sworn-virgins of Balkans, berdaches of North America, *waria* of Indonesia, *ashtime* of Southern Ethiopia's Maale culture, *muxe* of Southern Mexico, *mashoga* of Kenya and *shamans* described in Inuit culture — *hijra* identity has been largely ignored in queer academia. Despite the sea changes in law and social visibility through artistic representations — viz. Election Commission's instruction that *hijras* (eunuchs) should be on electoral rolls and be allowed to choose their gender in 1994, the repeal of Section 377 (though it has been again upheld in 2014) and the resultant decriminalization of homosexuality followed by the spurt in filing of the nominations by *hijra* community for parliamentary positions and the publication of PUCL report on "Human Rights Violations against the Transgender Community" in 2003 — the social and cultural acceptance has eluded them. Apart from this there are other so-called major reforms in the form of Municipal Corporation of Delhi's (MCD) declaration of providing security net to eunuchs by making them eligible for monthly pension of Rs. 1,000 (*Asian Age*, 10 November 2003, p. 13); passport authorities decision to include "E" as a separate category for transgender, transvestites and *hijras*; Law School's decision to have "others" categories for transgenders in application forms (*Times of India*, 6 February 2011, p. 4); Tamil Naidu state's decision to carry on "others" option in ration cards, passports and admission forms for government schools and colleges in 2007 (*Times of India*, 14 May 2008, p. 19) and in 2014 Supreme Court's decision to provide reservation to transgenders in educational institutes under OBC quota after which for the first time University of Delhi gave admission to nine transgenders in P.G. course in 2014 (*The Telegraph*, 13 August 2014, p. 1). Further the academic and legal discussions surrounding the Criminal Tribes Act (1871), the decision of Planning Commission on 17 January 2010 to hear out transgenders before the next five-year plan (*Deccan Herald*, 8 January 2010, p. 5), Delhi Legal Services Authorities (DLSA) decision to amend its charter to include transgenders and making them eligible for legal aid in February 2011 (*Times of India*, 6 February 2011, p. 4) contribute to the cataloguing of *hijras* as an accepted separate category. Not only the legal and social activism has given impetus to their mainstreaming, but also the media and popular culture have played their part — and one such example is the positive media publicity of projects such as Sahodari in 2010 that focuses on getting transgender women equipped with skill training for jewellery designing. Besides there are also widely circulated success stories of second elected eunuch mayor Kamla Bua, the first MLA Shabnum Mausi, *hijra* celebrities like Kalki Subramaniyam (who is a media professional and founder of the first matrimonial website for transgenders, Thirunangai.net), Rose the first transgender television host of the programme, "Ippadikku Rose" or "Yours Rose" and Laxmi Tripathy, the owner of event management company, and a known TV personality who organizes transgender beauty contests. All this indubitably has given impetus to break the gender and sexual stereotypes surrounding *hijra* identity.[1]

However, despite these socio-cultural changes and spurt in academic researches focusing on the depiction of ancient and contemporary visibility of *hijras* at religious spaces and stories — such as Shikandi/Amba story, the tale of Sukumarika[2] as delineated in Sanskrit play of the same name, the myth surrounding Krishna's son Samba[3] known for his female attire and homosexual activities, the rituals surrounding the goddess of Bahucharji in north Gujarat, specifically worshipped by eunuchs as this goddess is associated with sex-change, and the Aravani festival celebrated at Villupuram, exclusively by *hijra* community — the miseries of these outcast identities are still unnoticed and they remain both in terms of

---

1 In the same vein the making of exclusive transgender documentary movies such as *Gulabi Aaina* by Rangayan, *Ek Tha Lal Pari* by Rajdeep Randhawa, and prominent sculptors made exclusively of *hijras* by George Kurivilla, depict systematic subjugation of *hijras* within queer community.

2 Sukumarika is the heroine of an ancient Sanskrit play of the same name and she is denounced for being sexually insatiable. According to O'Flaherty, "A character in a Sanskrit play is a prostitute named Sukumarika 'Good Little Girl' who is referred to as 'third sex' and is an inauspicious thing to see. She is accused of having a heart insatiable by any amount of sex, but she has certain advantages in her profession: she has no breasts to get in the way of a tight embrace, no monthly period to interrupt in the enjoyment of passion, and no pregnancy to mar her beauty" (Wendy Doniger O'Flaherty, 1980, *Women, Androgynes and Other Mythical Beasts*, Chicago: The University of Chicago Press, p. 299).

3 Krishna's son Samba was infamous for being dressed as a pregnant woman and for indulging in homosexuality. A detailed reference of it can be found in Bullough's work. (V. Lern Bullough, 1976, *Sexual Variance in Society and History*, Chicago: University of Chicago Press, p. 267).

even literary production and consumption largely invisible. No wonder A. Revathi's *The Truth About Me* (2010) is the first autobiography in India by a *hijra* and despite a number of gay and lesbian anthologies published in the last decade, the first *hijra* anthology *Our Lives, Our Words* by Revathi came in 2011. The major reasons for this sort of neglect and the consequent violence lie in biphobia (which is significantly different from homophobia because it is both an overlap and gap, and this will be discussed in the later part of the chapter) and the colonial hangover of the Criminal Tribes Act of 1871 which target *hijra*s in a very specific fashion. This chapter aims (through contemporary literary productions) at unveiling the complex network of oppression of *hijra*s on account of biphobia coupled with other factors, and the ingenious ways through which this neither man nor woman identity can actually work in their favour. This chapter focuses on how their twofold gender existence encapsulates a more holistic identity because it demonstrates the assimilation and concurrence of contradictory threads in multiple ways. Hence, the negation of the internalized biphobia and acceptance of their unique corporeality, which in an interesting fashion suggests their symbolic non-sexual existence and presents them in a peculiar way as an ascetic, are the keys to the real uplift of *hijra*s. Also they are able to create fissures and radical ruptures in the domain of familial sexual citizenship because *hijra*s' alternative family disposition unmasks the oppressive structure of heteropatriarchal family that in turn problematizes the issue of sexual citizenship when claimed through the unit of family. Thus from the feminist perspective also their unusual gender-blending adds another dimension to the whole issue of women's empowerment.

It is a daunting task to find a literary representation of exclusive *hijra* identity even within queer literature and after much deliberation one can discover only few literary texts that have *hijra* protagonists. The texts discussed in this regard are Khushwant Singh's *Delhi,* Dattani's *Seven Steps around the Fire,* Satya's "I Hate Wet Tissues" and Abdul Khalid Rashid's "Incomplete Human". They are of diverse nature in terms of both genre and language as *Seven Steps around the Fire* is a play whereas *Delhi* is a novel and the rest of the two texts are short stories and out of them "Incomplete Human" is a Pashto story which has been recently translated into English. But the common ground among these contemporary literary works is that they all deal with the structural violence inflicted upon *hijra*s and the diverse means to counter that subjugation. The primary two reasons assigned to transphobia (namely "Criminal Tribes Act" and biphobia) at the start of the chapter might not be overtly described under these labels but systematic violence emanating from these factors has been fully explored by these writers.

Seven Steps around the Fire is a play that revolves around the murder of the *hijra* Kamla by a minister (whose son has been secretly married to Kamla) and another *hijra* Anarkali is falsely implicated and put behind the bars. Khushwant Singh's *Delhi* cleverly juxtaposes Delhi, the city with *hijra* Bhagmati, and lays bare many questions pertaining to violence, space vis-à-vis sexual identity and the sexual citizenship. The third text under discussion is "Incomplete Human" which poignantly highlights the issue of invisibility of *hijra*s through a nameless *hijra* and the gory death rituals of *hijras* which symbolically represent the internalized transphobia of eunuchs. The last story, "I Hate Wet Tissues" examines the hazardous psychological and physical effects of sex-reassignment surgeries. Though in "I Hate Wet Tissues" the main characters do not have culturally inscribed *hijra* identity and are rather more close to being transsexual men and the ostracization faced by *hijra*s are of different order as compared to transsexuals, yet there is a lot of overlapping, specially regarding sex-reassignment surgeries. Thus the reason for including this story is primarily for this purpose. It stresses the point that the bipolar method of fixing individuals into man/woman category creates such tremendous self-hatred for transgender body that it results in a horrible defacement and self-inflicted violence. Thus the acceptance of unique transgender body is the ultimate empowerment and mainstreaming should not be done at the cost of jamming them into the binary sexual model only.

Let us first examine the Criminal Tribes Act of 1871 which is a product of biases against *hijra*s along with certain other communities and tribes, and how the biases on account of this act are still prevalent in the cultural memory of our contemporary society and get reflected in the literary texts under discussion. According to the statutes, certain communities are "Addicted to the systematic commission of non-bailable offences" (Section 2 of the Criminal Tribes Act). Those communities and tribes were considered criminals genetically and believed to pass criminality from generation to generation as Leela Gandhi rightly states in *Affective Communities*. In this work, she tries to draw an analogy with a carpenter to argue that there has been a fallacious understanding that just like a carpenter would pass on his trade to the next generation, similarly criminal castes can transfer their criminality genetically to their successive generations. However, this connection between sexual dissidence and criminality was made more conspicuous in the amendment of the Criminal Tribes Act of 1871 in 1897 which was subtitled, "An Act for the Registration of Criminal Tribes and Eunuchs". According to the Section 24A of the Criminal Tribes Act,

> The local government was required to keep a register of the names and residences of all the eunuchs who are reasonably suspected of kidnapping or castrating children or of

committing offences under section 377 of the Indian Penal Code.

Further the Sections 26 and 27 of the Criminal Tribes Act forbade eunuchs to dress like a woman, drawing up a will or adopting a son. Though the act has been repealed, but the social prejudices regarding the attachment of criminality to *hijra* community still continue as has been recognized by the Naz judgement in which the judge notes that "while this act has been repealed, the attachment of the criminality to *hijra* community still continues" (Naz Foundation vs. Government of New Capital Territory of Delhi and Others (2009), para 50). Thus *hijra*s are further redlined by the state in the larger structure of exclusion of sexual minorities. The all-consuming social impact of this act even in contemporary India can be seen in Dattani's *Seven Steps around the Fire* in which a eunuch is wrongly implicated and put behind the bars on account of the false murder charge of fellow *hijra* who has actually been killed by a minister owing to her/his love affair and secret marriage to the minister's son. But everyone seems to be more than willing to believe that *hijra* Anarkali is the actual culprit, for it is embedded in cultural memory that *hijra*s are bound to delve in criminal acts by dint of their *hijra* identity. Apropos of this Uma's husband who is a police officer states that "they all are castrated degenerate men. They fought like dogs everyday" (Dattani 2000a: 238). She has been conveniently called liar by Uma's husband who is a police officer. The sweeping generalization and the mass apathy of the state are reflected conspicuously when Suresh asks Uma not to have any compassion for them and cogitates: "Don't believe a word of anything it says. They are all liars" (ibid.: 237). Similarly in *Seven Steps around the Fire* Anarkali has been constantly mentioned as "it" in order to emphasize that they are no better than the animals and so no human status should be accorded to them. When Uma says that whether she (Anarkali) will talk to her, Manuswami immediately reacts: "She! Of course it will talk to you. We will beat it up if it doesn't" (ibid.: 233). Later on, he bullies Anarkali and yells at her: "I will come inside and beat you up, you worthless pig" (ibid.: 235). There is a preconceived notion that lying and stealing come naturally to *hijra* community and it is clearly demonstrated in Uma's statement when she jokingly states that if she tells her husband that Anarkali (the *hijra*) has stolen his cigarettes, he will readily believe this lie. Likewise Munuswami, the investigating officer, evinces the prejudice of the state when he remarks about the jewellery worn by the dead *hijra* Kamla:

> So much jewellery she was wearing when she died! Even a bride will not wear so much. That too gold. All stolen, I am sure. How will *hijras* get so much gold if they can only beg for a few rupees. —Ibid.: 247

Thus the ready acceptance of *hijras* as a tribe indulging in stealing, crimes and lying (which this play effectively showcases) can be traced back to the pernicious effects of the Criminal Tribes Act that persists in the cultural memory for centuries even when legally it is repealed.

Another remarkable feature of this text is that throughout in it Anarkali has been addressed as "that thing" or "that creature". Similarly in Khushwant Singh's *Delhi*, when *hijra* Bhagmati narrates her story, she unwittingly mentions that not only *hijras* but even her own father calls her "it". First, she narrates an incident when *hijras* come to her home to take her away: "Show us your last born. If it is one of us, let us take it away" (Singh 1990: 29). Finally when his father begets more children he gives *hijras* twenty-one rupees and says: "Now I have three sons and two daughters, you can take this one. It is one of you" (ibid.). There is a constant mention of "it" whenever *hijras* are addressed. Thus naming is a conspicuous marker of denouncing their presence which is beautifully highlighted in yet another story, "Incomplete Human". This story categorically talks about the prejudiced behaviour of the society that invisibilizes *hijras* through a nameless *hijra* protagonist. In this story the *hijra* in the disguise of a woman is a co-traveller with two other men in a train, and during the conversation when she is constantly asked to disclose her name, she evades the issue and after constant persuasion ejaculates that she is a *hijra*. Thus the namelessness of *hijra* is suggestively employed to showcase the erasure and non-acceptance of eunuchs. And second, since naming is a process of cataloguing gender demarcation and there are no specific *hijra* names unlike the clear-cut male and female names, therefore the eunuch in the story remains a nameless person and once again it brings forth our stringent conceptualization of male/female binary. To quote from the text:

> And then I asked the same question again, "what is your name?"
>
> This time she laughed and answered unhesitatingly.
>
> "Why do you need to know my name? I am just a human being and your co-passenger." But I am not going to surrender and I reasoned.
>
> . . . "I am just asking your name. Is it a sin? I don't have even a slightest doubt that you are a human being but after all every being has a name.". . .
>
> "What if I tell you that I don't have a name? Would you accept it?"
>
> "I don't think that there is any man who does not have a name."
>
> "But after all I am not a man."
>
> "I know that you are not a man, you are a woman. But even a woman has some name."
>
> "I am not even a woman." . . .
>
> "What else are you if you are neither a man nor a woman?"
>
> She replied in a very humble and dejected tone when she

> realized that my patience had crossed its boundaries. Else . . . I am a eunuch. — Singh 1990: 204-05

In this context it is significant to note the observation of A. Mangai, who is the translator of the first *hijra* anthology, *Our Lives, Our Words*. According to her, in the afterword to Revathi's book in Tamil, the novelist, Perumal Murugam, pointed out that *Tolkappiyam*, the earliest Tamil grammatical and aesthetic treatise, accorded the status of *uyar tivani* (living beings with a gender marker as masculine or feminine grammatically) to transgenders, while in a later work *Nannud* they have been called *ahrinai* (non-living objects with no gender markers and therefore called *adhu*). To quote his words:

> An acknowledgement of the coexistence of different permutations and combinations in gender identity had given way to a normative polarization into masculine and feminine. The in-between was lost or demanded in the process. — Mangai 2011: xi

Thus their banishment from the lesbian and gay subcultures and consequent subjugation can be attributed to biphobia which is significantly different from homophobia and the specific biases faced by the inherent twin identity of male/female are generally subsumed under the ambit of queer studies. Little wonder in all the three texts, discussed above, the *hijra* protagonist is either addressed as "it" or has been denied a name as in "Incomplete Human". This invisibilizing, though presented symbolically through naming practices, clearly posits the problem pertaining to the acceptance of specific third gender. This is specially ironical in the Indian context because it is a well-known fact that in Vedic astrology, the nine planets are classified in one of the three types of genders and in the cataloguing, the third gender or *tritiya prakriti* is associated with Mercury, Saturn and Ketu in particular. In the Puranas, there are also references to three kinds of *deva*s of music and dance: *apsarase*s (female), *gandharva*s (male) and *kinnars* (neuter). Similarly in Buddhist *Vinaya* there are four main sex/gender categories: male, female, *ubhatobhyanjanaka* (person of a dual sexual nature) and *pandaka* (person of various non-normative sexual natures, perhaps originally denoting a deficiency in male sexual capacity). With the development of the *Vinaya* tradition, the term *pandaka* came to refer to a broad third sex category which encompassed intersex, male and female bodied people with physical and/ or behavioural attributes that were considered inconsistent with the natural characteristics of man and woman.[4] Thus it is a matter of great surprise that despite religious, astrological and spiritual presence of the third gender, the transphobia is so rampant in modern India. And because of the apparent bisexuality, inherent in the bodies of *hijras*, they not only become victims of the homophobia of the heterosexuals but are also considered traitors by the homosexuals.

According to Robyn Ochs, the writer of "Biphobia: It Goes More Than Two Ways", there is indeed not only an overlap between homophobia and biphobia but also distinct gap as well. Thus bisexuals suffer discrimination from homosexuals on account of their attendant privileges of being able to have heterosexual partners. She states:

> . . . bisexuals, who fit neither the prioritized category nor its perceived antithesis, create discomfort and anxiety in others simply by the fact of their existence. There is pressure for those of us who do not fit to remain silent about our deviation, because there is a great deal at stake. Perpetuating

[4] The reference of it can be found in Peter A. Jackson, 1996, "Non-normative Sex/Gender Categories in the Theravada Buddhist Scriptures", in *Australian Humanities Review* (australianhumanitiesreview.org/archive/issue-April 1996/ Jacksonrefhtml) and in J. Gyatso, 2003, "One Plus One Makes Three: Buddhist Gender, Monasticism, and the Law of the Non-Excluded Middle", *History of Religions* **43**(2): 89-115. doi:10.1086/423006. JSTOR 3176712.

> the silence of bisexuals allows the dominant culture to exaggerate the differences between heterosexual and homosexual and to ignore the fact that human sexuality exists on a continuum. — Robyn Ochs 1996: 225

It unmasks the veil formed to segregate homo/hetero identity. The so-called male and female twin identity, encapsulated within *hijra* existence, naturally tends to challenge the dichotomous paradigm of sexual orientation and poses a threat to the dominant heteropatriarchal society, for the in-between identity of eunuchs negates the assumption that gays as a category are very different from straight people. We live in a culture where we are trained to have bipolar thinking and we assume that each category has its mutually exclusive opposite. Homosexuals are

> "that category, way over there", very different from heterosexuals. If they are so different then heterosexuals do not have to confront the possibility of acknowledging same-sex attractions within themselves and the attendant anxiety of possibly, "becoming like them". — Ibid.

Preserving this clear-cut distinction becomes an obsessive need for dominant cultures in order to maintain their hierarchy. When we cannot place something in clear-cut dichotomy, then the anxiety arises. This anxiety is on account of being compelled to acknowledge that the "other" is not as different and there is no exclusively explicit binary opposition between homo/hetero. This creates what Udis Kessler describes as "crisis of meaning" for straight people.

Also since there is a fallacious assumption that twin desire is inherent in bi-sexuality, they have been falsely stereotyped as infidel and promiscuous by both the groups. Although the fact is that the "fluid continuum" of their desire cannot be fixed on the assumption that at a particular juncture of time they compulsively desire both the straight and the same-sex partners at the same time. Their twin-identity can be a fluid phase of their pansexuality, where in one phase and at a specific space and time their desire can be exclusively located in one category only. But there is an illusion of considering bisexuals as having a perennial desire for both homo and hetero partners, irrespective of phases, space, time and subjectivity factors. In fact, bisexuality has been divided by Klein into four categories namely transitional, historical, sequential and concurrent. And out of these only concurrent bisexuality points towards non-monogamous sexual orientation. Thus this sweeping and generalized belief in the inherent infidelity of eunuchs (who unwittingly fall into this category on account of their corporeal androgynous self) is grounded on an incomplete understanding of the term and is quite fallacious. In India the so-called, hyper-libidinousness of the third sex (*napumsakaveda*) can be traced back to the religious texts such as *Devendrasuri* and *Catvarah Karmagranthah* in which it is argued that

> just as a burning city burns for a great period of time and spreads to a great degree, in the same way when the third-sex sexuality (*napumsakaveda*) comes to fruition there is an intense desire to have sex with women and men which does not disappear for a great period of time, nor is there satiation in sexual relations. — *Catvarah Karmagranthah*: 44

This insatiable libidinal desire is supposed to be directly proportional to third sex and clearly creates strong cultural biases that perpetuate inadvertently the notion that they are bound to be non-monogamous. Thus due to this false assumption of their unbridled sexual prowess, they are not only forced into prostitution (*dhandha*) as it is known in *hijra* terminology, but also at times have to entertain five to six customers in a day as has been mentioned in Revathi's autobiography.

Similarly in *Seven Steps around the Fire* Anarkali, who is falsely charged of the murder of another *hijra* Kamla, is forced to perform oral sex incessantly in jail, and on account of falsified notion of their hyperlibidinousness the physical fatigue faced by those ceaseless sexual acts is completely neglected. When Uma wants to interview her she states nonchalantly: "After servicing all those sons of whores, my mouth is too tired to talk" (Dattani 2000: 236). We know that within the oppressed group there are hierarchies. Thus how homophobia affects *hijras*, gays and lesbians differently is an important issue to address. According to Allport, there are numerous ways in which individuals react negatively to stigmatization. He calls them "traits of victimization". Robyn Ochs argues that the discussion on biphobia needs to be centred on two characteristics: (i) aggression and blame directed at one's own group, and (ii) prejudice and predilections directed against other minorities. Apparently there is a significant internal homophobia and also the hostility towards bisexuals and transgendered people by others who are also members of the stigmatized group. Apropos of this Ochs states:

> Feelings of victimization may get acted out through anger and rejection of those within or outside of one's group who are perceived as even less acceptable than oneself. One reason for this is the fear that these "marginal people" will give all gays and lesbians an even worse image than that they already hold in the eyes of those within the dominant culture, further impeding gays' and lesbians' struggle for acceptance.
>
> — 1996: 222

Obviously there is a tendency in them to identify themselves with either a man or preferably a woman, and many times the third gender relationships with men have been oversimplified and are considered gay relationships in order to fix them into the Western heteropatriarchal division of homo/hetero. Whereas the truth is that the complexity of the third gender sexual encounters cannot be simply categorized as gay mating and this further endorses the assumption that we are paranoid about the liminal spaces and feel comfortable only in the strict bipolar model. However, the reason for the female representation can also be adduced to the fact that they have to feed male fantasy (which is largely heterosexual) in order to extract money. The identification of *hijra*s primarily as a woman can be traced back to the tradition of harems where their ambiguous sexuality ought to be like a female in order to negate even an iota of desire in women kept in harems. In *Sabdangal* by Basheer, the transgender person is dressed like a woman.

Similarly in *Seven Steps around the Fire*, Kamla has been transformed from a man into a beautiful woman, and in "Incomplete Human" the *hijra* is such a beautiful woman with long hair that she has been asked to sit in women's compartment. Dattani, commenting on this issue, states that even among *hijra*s those who can pass for women are considered superior, and as Bhaswati Chakravorty notes that long hair is a matter of great pride among *hijra*s and this fetish for long hair can be traced back to Patanjali's *Mahabhashya* in which while describing feminine gender he mentions that one who has breasts and long hair is feminine. According to Zwilling and Sweet,

> This position is then criticized by pointing out the discrepancies between natural and grammatical gender which would proceed from such a view, as in the case of the masculine noun *bhrukumsa* ("a man who dresses as a woman", specifically a male-actor *en travestie*) which should logically be feminine as the actor appears as one possessed of both breast and long hair. — 2000: 108

Breaking all the stereotypes of sartorial gender identity the narrator of *Delhi* views Bhagmati in shirt and pants, and in a way finds her a classic symbol of pansexuality:

> Now it is a different Bhagmati . . . . Very chic! No one can tell whether she is a *hijda* or a boy who looks like a girl.
> — Singh 1990: 47

But ironically enough, bereft of sartorial identity marker the very sight of *hijra*'s naked body can bring forth the transphobic anxiety in its most concentrated manner as has been depicted in this novel when the narrator is perplexed and anxious at the very thought of viewing a nude *hijra*. To quote from the text:

> But what did a *hijda* look like with nothing on? . . . I tried to put it out of my mind. A sick scruffy *hijda* — how could I? I picked up a journal. Her naked figure kept coming over the print. What kind of breast did a *hijda* have? What shape were her genitals? Did she shave her pubis? I put away the journal and switched off the lamp. — Ibid.: 39

In fact, when she came in the bathroom the protagonist could not muster the courage to look at her naked body. Thus the clothing becomes an extremely important aspect of their gender cataloguing and is certainly not an issue exclusively related to an individual choice. It participates in developing a counter-strategy to negate the ambiguity of their twin gender identity. Revathi in her autobiography, *The Truth about Me,* mentions that the long hair is considered as the primary symbol of womanhood among *hijra*s and nothing is considered more disastrous than chopping their hair.

However, Khushwant Singh gives a very interesting and an entirely different argument when he states:

> The reason why they prefer to wear women's clothes is because it being a man's world every deviation from accepted standards of masculinity are regarded as unmanly. Women are more generous. — Singh 1990: 29

This non-acceptance of their twin identity and arranging them into the categories of either a man or preferably a woman find a very interesting manifestation in the Kamla Jaan case. Kamla Jaan was elected mayor of Katni in Madhya Pradesh in 1999. A member of the opposition party filed a petition that she lied about her gender because Kamla had contested and won a seat reserved for women, while the electoral rolls declared her a "male". According to her, she had "not bothered to check" her gender on the rolls before contesting (*The Telegraph*, 4 February 2003 and *Asian Age*, 7 January 2010, p. 3). She lost the case on this basis. Likewise the illustrious athlete Soundarajan was stripped of her Asian games medal in Qatar in 2007 on account of her intersexed identity and forced to attempt suicide and yet the media shamelessly tried to capture the sensational element of her intersexed identity rather than focusing on the ostracization she suffered in sport world due to her fluid identity. In yet another less reported but equally poignant case Sanju Behra who was sacked from her job of constable from Central Industrial Security Forces (CISF) in November 2007 after the medical reports revealed that she had underdeveloped uterus ("Caught between the Sexes" by Jaya Shroff, in *Hindustan Times*, 28 November 2007, p. 10).[5]

Now nothing could be more tragic and glaring examples of our obsession with neat clear-cut division of genders and negation of the acceptance and recognition of two-gender mould identity. Likewise there is also an infamous case of Chandni, a *hijra* from Bangalore who was burnt to death on 1 December 2002 and whose so-called husband Gnanaprakash claimed that she did it after he rejected her on discovering that she was genetically male. Although the local activists

---

[5] The case was referred to the All India Institute of Medical Sciences (AIIMS), where Swati's (name changed as real name Sanju Behra was revealed in the later article published in *Hindustan Times*, 29 August 2008, p. 9) genetic sex was defined as 46XY (constituent with male as opposed to the XX of female. "The CISF unfairly sacked her saying she had applied as a female while her sex was male but it was not her fault as she was not aware about her condition, says the doctor treating Swati in the department of endocrinology, AIIMS" (*Hindustan Times*, 28 November 2007, p. 10).

believed that she was killed by her husband. The local police of Banaswadi Police Station had in fact initially refused to even register the complaint of Prema (Chandni's *guru*):

> They said that they do not recognize the *hijra* community or its relationships. They said they would act only if Chandni's biological parents issued a complaint.
>
> — http// ai.eecs.umich.edu/people/Conway/TS/PUCL/PUCL5 20 Report.html

Despite the documentary proofs of the marriage (given by Sangama, an NGO that works for the rights of LGBTQ community) of domestic violence, and the fact that her husband knew that she was a *hijra* prior to her marriage there was general sympathy for the victimizers in such cases who use "transpanic" as an excuse.

Thus "transpanic" is an easily recognizable notion across all sections and works against *hijra* community at every level. The transphobia of the state is also visible in the gory atrocities committed on Kokila, a 21-year old *hijra* from Bangalore who was brutally assaulted at police station as reported in Sangama's report.[6] She was constantly taunted for not having vagina and *lathi* was pushed inside her genitals and she was incessantly asked lewd questions regarding the absence of an actual vagina. Thus not having a vagina and lack of being identified as a complete biological woman become the key causes of severe hatred and transphobia and the justification

6 "The police also burned her nipples and *chapdi* (vaginal portion of *hijras*) with a burning coir rope. One policeman of the rank of SI (Sub-inspector of Police) positioned his rifle on her *chapdi* and threatened to shoot her. He also tried pushing the rifle butt and *lathi* into the *chapdi* and saying. 'Do you have a vagina, can this go inside' while other policemen were laughing. This is to humiliate a transsexual woman by insisting that she is not a woman, as she was not born with a vagina" (http// ai.eecs.umich.edu/people/Conway/TS/PUCL/PUCL5 20 Report.html, pp. 11-12).

in their minds for inflicting terrible violence. Further the prejudice of state against a transbody is much more as compared to a homosexual body which is visible from the fact that the first reported case of implementation of Section 377 is quite obviously against a *hijra* known as Khairati in 1884. Justice Straight was called to abjugate whether a person who wears a woman's cloth and has syphilis and shows signs of sodomite can be punished. This case is known as *Queen* vs. *Khairati.*[7] Thus the state recognizes transbody as a more easily recognizable and visible site of transgression as compared to homosexual individual is crystal clear from the fact that the very first recorded case against so-called unnatural desire is against a *hijra* and not against a lesbian or a gay man.

One can easily trace the state operated structural violence against *hijras* in *Seven Steps around the Fire* in which there is a complete immunity regarding the bashing of a *hijra* Anarkali as if it is the logical consequence of her being a *hijra*. To quote from the text:

> Munuswami (*hitting the bars*). Back! Beat it! Kick the *hijra*!
> *The other inmates begin to beat Anarkali up.*
>
> Anarkali (*hitting back at first*). *Ai*! Don't touch me!
>
> *The other inmates scream with pleasure as they beat up Anarkali*
>
> *Aaagh*! *Aaaagh*! . . .

---

[7] The session court judge noted that he "was found singing dressed as a woman among the women of certain family. Having been subjected to examination by the Civil Surgeon . . . he is shown to have the characteristic mark of a habitual catamite — the distortion of the orifice of the anus into the shape of a trumpet and also to be affected with syphilis in the same region in a manner which distinctly points to unnatural intercourse within the last few months" (*Queen Empress* vs. *Khairati* I. L.R. 6 All 205). Justice Straight though could not convict him because "neither the individual with whom the offense was committed, nor the time of the committal nor the place is ascertainable" (ibid.), yet he admired the efforts of authorities of Moradabad to restrain this kind of "disgusting practices".

Uma. Why did they put her in a male prison? . . . Suresh, why is she in a cell with men?

Suresh. They are as strong as horses. . . .

Uma. She is being beaten up by all the male prisoners.

— Dattani 2000: 236

Another classic example of transphobia is the unique case involving a love affair between Shi Pei Pu, a Chinese transgender opera singer and spy whose sexually convoluted love affair with a French Embassy worker created one of the strangest cases in 1983 in international espionage and was inspiration for the Broadway show, *M. Butterfly*.[8]

Likewise the dilemma of Punjab and Haryana government regarding this issue was evident when they categorize eunuchs as male for government jobs and ask the central government to clarify its stand on this issue because a separate identity irrespective of male and female has still not been assigned to them (*Deccan Herald,* 2 April 2010, p. 9). This gender confusion and their desire to catalogue themselves into fixed categories create deep-rooted internalized biphobia that results in the horrible maiming of their bodies and gives impetus to self-destructive masochistic behaviour, which is evident from *nirvanam* (emasculation ceremonies). Within the *hijra* community

[8] Bernard Boursicot had an affair with a transgender Shi Pei Pu who could befool him for about more than a decade that he was a woman and could get more than 500 confidential papers out of him. Boursicot always had affairs with men but when Boursicot got to know about it more than the cheating the fact that he was not with a woman or with a man (as Boursicot was a known gay) but with a transgender irked him so much that he attempted suicide by slitting his own throat. Thus his own homosexual/heterosexual leanings were acceptable to him but not the desire for the transgender and it ones again proves that biphobia is much more difficult to counter as compared to homophobia. A detailed description of it can be found in Joyce Walder's *Liaison: The Gripping Real Story of the Diplomat Spy and the Chinese Opera Star* whose affair inspired *M. Butterfly.*

there are hierarchies such as the *badai hijras* (who has the power to confer fertility on account of their emasculation) are considered superior to *kandra hijras*, who are involved in *dhandha* (sexual work). However, even within the emasculated *hijras* the medically operated ones are considered inferior to those who have gone through *thayamma nirvanam*, which is done by a *hijra* through crude methods and involves excruciating physical pain. It is believed by the *hijras* that *thayamma nirvanam* makes one look more like a woman as compared to the emasculations done at the hospitals. Thus serious discomfort with twin identity becomes once again a reason enough for going through such mangling of body.

John Irving's novel, *A Son of Circus* and Revathi's autobiography along with *hijra* anthology, *Our Lives, Our Words*, are replete with gory descriptions of crude emasculation. These texts point to a brutal ritual in which the wound is deliberately kept open by relentless and repeated poking so that the puckered scar may resemble vagina. Similarly hot oil is being poured in vagina in order to make it bleed profusely, for it is believed that through this the so-called bad blood, the entire maleness of the *hijra* body will be washed out. Radha's description of her *thayamma nirvanam* as catalogued in the recent *hijra* anthology is heart wrenching. To quote from the text:

> I stood naked in front of a photograph of Goddess Mata. They put strands of my hair into my mouth and asked me to keep uttering the name of *Mata*. . . . As I was doing it, Thayamma pulled my penis and cut it in one blow with knife. It was not painful when she cut it. After cutting she made me sit. It was burning like hell. It was like sitting on burning fire. I could not do anything. I fainted. They took the oozing blood and rubbed it all over my body. It is believed that if we rub this blood all over the body, all the body hair will drop off. I did not look down. They sat me up with spread legs onto a wall. My eyes were dizzy. Thayamma slapped me hard on my cheeks and woke me up. We should

> not sleep at that time. . . . I could not bear the burning sensation. After a while, hot sesame oil was applied on the operated spot. It felt good when they applied it. But after a while there was a prickly pain. . . . They made sure that we did not sleep till 7 a.m. by beating us every now and then. Even when we begged for water they gave me dried ginger.
>
> — Revathi 2010: 65-66

Another major tool of physical abuse among *hijra*s is popping hormone pills in alarming measures in order to develop breast. The most common of these hormonal products are oral contraceptives for women, commonly called as Sunday, Monday *goli*s which are sold across the counter in all pharmacies. *Hijra*s would take as many as nine to twelve pills a day in order to scalp a female body. Despite knowing the hazardous effects of these drugs, they keep on consuming it in huge amount in order to fulfil the elusive dire need for that symbol of femininity. Lactating potential is another marker of femininity which is highly valorized. Gayatri Reddy narrates how Lekha, one of the *hijra*s, proudly states:

> "See Gayatri, I am more like a woman than any of these *hijra*s here. Only I can produce milk from my breasts. None of these people can. See I'll show you. Do you know what this means? Of all the *hijra*s here, I am more like a woman," Lekha told me proudly while demonstrating her femininity for my benefit. — Reddy 2006: 132

Indeed they are unable to perceive themselves outside the binary frame of gendered reference. This internalized biphobia is so conspicuous as Vinay Sitapati mentions in the article entitled "Sex Change for Free" while referring to a news (published in *Indian Express*, 9 March 2009) that Chennai corporation's decision in 2009 to build separate toilets for eunuchs face opposition from them because they consider that it will further segregate them. This distinct desire to emulate feminine attributes and their discomfort with fluid identity are major setbacks to transgender activism because merging in mainstream of culture should not be at the cost of annihilating their unique identity and pansexuality. Acceptance at the cost of transforming them into either a complete male or a female is a mutilation of their fluid distinct self and this sort of merging into the mainstream of culture after a certain sort of correction in their liminal sexuality is indeed a farce and a sort of mockery of the acceptance of transgender identity. They should be made comfortable as a third sex without having any need to go through horribly hazardous and painful sex-change surgeries. Specially when the law and the medical practitioners both mirror the fact that even after the sex reassignment surgery the transbody cannot be recognized as a complete male or female. In this respect it is significant to cite the oft-quoted and much debated case of *Corbett* vs. *Corbett* ([1970] 2 ALL ER 33) of England in 1971.[9]

We do not recognize neatly the difference between social sex and the genetic sex. Hence these anomalies further complicate matters for transgenders and *hijra*s and the ideal proposition for them is to transgress the boundaries and division of male/female and have a distinct identity. And in this way they will be able to have a separate unique space without going through the demoralizing rigidities of law and the horrors of post-operative surgeries. Colette Chiland in his book, *Transsexualism* insightfully states that at best these sex reassignment surgeries provide just apparent physical

[9] It concerns the marriage of April Ashley (a male to female transsexual). Her husband wants to nullify the marriage on the ground that since she was a trans woman the marriage has never been consummated and April remained a male. The judge Ormrod decided the case on the basis of a test in which the sex has to be determined on the basis of chromosomal, gonadal and genital features at the time of the birth. And on this basis April remained a man and hence the marriage was nullified. But it raises serious concerns regarding our lack of capacity to distinguish between the notion of man and woman, and the ideas of femaleness and maleness.

tokens of social sex and ultimately create all the more intersex bodies because the chromosomal complexion of an individual cannot be changed, and motherhood or semen ejaculation still remains distant dreams for these transbodies. Hence the acceptability and valorization of their unique liminal position are more healthy and progressive steps.[10] Indubitably the need to counter internalized biphobia is all the more urgent. In a recently published book, *Close, Too Close* by Meenu and Shruti, there is a wonderful story, "I Hate Wet Tissues" by Satya which primarily deals with the issues pertaining to transbody, sex reassignment surgery and non-acceptance of body even after surgery which result in internalized transphobia and extermination of sexual urge. This is a story of two supposedly transmen who meet at a drink joint and the Indian man has already gone for the surgery whereas his Pakistani counterpart is in the process of searching for the right clinic and enquires about the procedures. His inquires and probing questions regarding sex-change surgeries transport the Indian narrator into flashback and make him

---

[10] Apropos of this in her essay, Khartini Slamah offers an inspiring vision of what a self-critical transgender movement could look like: "Over the years, our politics as transgenders has shifted considerably. We are no longer asking the law to recognize us simply as men and women — which is what earlier generations of transsexuals fought for — rather, we want a status that goes beyond the dichotomous structures of sex and gender roles recognized within and by the law. We define ourselves using a mobile logic based on self-identification rather than corporeality. . . . There is no one version of being a *mak nyah.* Some of us feel that it is important to have breasts, others do not. Most of us want a woman's shape but some of us do not see this as important. And only half of us feel that a sex-change would improve our lives." (Khartini Slamah, 2005, "The Struggle to Be Ourselves, neither Men nor Women: *Mak Nyahs* in Malaysia", in *Sexuality, Gender, and Rights: Exploring Theory and Practice in South and Southeast Asia,* ed. G. Mishra, and R. Chandiramani, New Delhi: Sage Publications, p. 107.)

reveal his dreadful internalized transphobia which he has encountered at sex-reassignment surgery centre. S/he recounts how the discomfort with the unwanted sexual organs and the consequent hiding of them curb and restrict sexual desire in both the partners. To quote from the text:

> . . . But he wants to witness with his own eyes. The chest hair sprouting from the scars of my mastectomy. The meatiness of the constructed penis. The bloodiness and spread of the glance. But unzipping my trousers is not as easy as unbuttoning my shirt. There is another coming out that I know will seal this connect forever. . . . Rules of engagement: I am not allowed to open his shirt or take his pants down. Yes I can kiss him. On his face but not his lips. Between desire and the risk of his self, we agree that I can rub him on his packer without touching him directly. The rest can flow and we can call stop when we want to.
>
> — Satya 2012: 185-86

The narrator further remembers that the discomfort with the transbody creates such terrible anxiety that the hatred for one's own body gets translated into mutilating sexual urge for the partner as well, and the very thought of exposing once nude body before the partner creates jitters in the heart of the person concerned. Thus the non-acceptance of one's own transbody makes one indulge in horrible violence in the form of physical, emotional and sexual assault. The narrator ruminates that while he embraces his partner he could not understand that from where he should hold him so that the unwanted sexual organs of his partners are not touched, for it will result in extreme internalized transphobia in the heart of his partner. He states:

> Where should I hold him? I remember what it was for me. When you are not in your body. When your nude body is not your desire. And when the impossibility of this desire, to inhabit and act through this body, can lead you to a bottle of sleeping pills. — Satya 2012: 186

The narrator has gone through the sex-reassignment surgery and the story symbolically presents the hazardous psychological effects of the sex-reassignment surgery. It is suggestively told in the form of an incident when the story-teller performs oral sex on the ward boy in the same clinic facing dead bodies which creates a terrible havoc in the mind of the narrator. There is constant overlapping and personification of the ward boy and the sex-assignment clinic. To quote from the text:

> His crotch brushes against the trolley frame, pushing it further towards OT. As the largeness between his legs comes near my face, recedes and moves closer again, I meet his gaze; we know we are family and I am not alone anymore. The dread of what they call Sex Reassignment Surgery lessens in the assurances of his presence. — Ibid.: 188

Thus a close parallel has been drawn between the ward boy and the sex-change clinic and when the reassurance generated due to the presence of the ward boy turns into a nightmare with dead bodies all around, the entire episode is surcharged with internalized homophobia and significantly the backdrop is a sex-change clinic. In the words of the author:

> Suddenly the smell of dead embalmed bodies hits me, over and above the smell of my saliva on his organ, and over and above the smell of his piss in his underwear. The movement in my stomach begins to rise and I can taste the *dal* and *palak paneer* and my night medicines in my mouth. Vomit from fellatio in a morgue, vomit dripping from phallus, vomit held in the bottom of the very tight underwear of an almost naked, standing man. But so many dead dicks, of men lying behind me, that don't witness my vomit. — Satya 2012: 191

This whole vomit symbol as a trope for homophobic anxiety is specially significant (Raj Rao has also used it in *The Boyfriend*) in the light of the Reparative therapies introduced by Sandor Rado (Freud's disciple) to cure homosexuality. The Reparative therapies include administration of nausea inducing drugs and thus the vomiting trope is a significant symbol of homophobic anxiety. True the whole experience at sex-change clinic is loaded with internalized transanxiety which finds manifestation in various forms such as the granting of the permission of mastectomy to him when he ingeniously hides his transbody and is able to befool doctor who has diagnosed him as having gynecomastia (a condition in medical science described as the abnormal development of the mammary glands in males resulting in breast enlargement). He says that this "diagnosis gives Dr. K a place to hide" (ibid.: 189). However, at the very beginning of the story the protagonist talks about the meatiness of his constructed penis. Thus the traspanic is all-pervasive flowing from the doctor's mind to the patient and his partner. It is precisely for this reason that the protagonist, after the hazardous mental and physical effects of sex-reassignment surgery, wants his partner to accept his body in all its ambivalence because only that can bring permanent assurance and can mitigate self-hatred and internalized biphobia.

> . . . I lay naked, exhausted, nestled near the bound chest of a fully-clothed man. He made a very satisfying lover and it's true that the hold of the large hands can be very substantial. Was that a look of love? The look of being somewhere else . . . was he seeing with the naked eyes the possibility of becoming a man . . . could there have been a more honest way to tell him how *this* man had become a man. . . .
>
> — Satya 2012: 187

This self-inflicted internalized transphobia due to the non-acceptance of their body can also be seen in the death rituals of some *hijra* communities as has been described in detail in "Incomplete Human". Here the protagonist (a *hijra*) talks about the dilapidated condition in which the dead body needs to be sent to God so that it should not come again in this world in the *hijra* form. In fact, the basic dignity accorded to a dead human body is not granted to a eunuch body and it is their own internal ritual and thus clearly unmasks the self-hatred and deep-rooted transphobia. The protagonist observes:

> We give a severe beating to the dead body and bid farewell to it in such a miserable condition so that God should not send it amidst those human beings in the next birth.
>
> — Chanana 2012: 226

Likewise in the process of describing the death rituals of Hyderabadi *hijras*, Gayatri Reddy highlights that these practices encapsulate fear of their own anatomy and the sense of incompleteness that they feel. After the death a man known as *ghasl*, who does the washing of a *hijra* after death, is given jewellery from one side of the body that is one bangle, ear ring, toe ring, etc. Naturally the sense of inadequacy and incompleteness persists even after death (Reddy 2006: 107). In fact, Dayanita Singh, the Indian photographer in her conversation with a *hijra* known as Mona Ahmed, candidly talks about the acceptance of the two-spirited third gender identity in some *hijras*. She writes that when Dayanita Singh once asked her if she would like to go to Singapore for a sex-change operation, she said:

> You really do not understand. I am the third sex, not a man trying to be a woman. It's your societies problem that you only recognize two sexes.
>
> — http://en.wikipedia.org/wiki/third-gender

Thus the traditional wisdom might consider Tamil Naidu's decision to pay for the sex-change surgeries as a progressive move but it ultimately perpetuates the agenda of jamming them into male/female dichotomy and considers them as aberrations that need to be corrected, and this is certainly not an affirmative action. The matter gets further complicated as for the legalized sex-reassignment surgery one ought to have a self-identification as a transgender person, as Padma Govindan and Aniruuddhan Vasudevan argue, "is a condition that some will be able and want to meet, and others will not" (2011: 103). But the argument in favour of the assertion of the individual choice further complicates this issue as has been mentioned by Ashwini Sukthankar, who, by quoting from the International Bill of Gender Rights, states:

> . . . It would be worth remembering that the right, when stated in the abstract, is as over-inclusive and under-inclusive as its critique: to state, as the International Bill of Gender Rights does, that "All human beings have the right to control their bodies, which includes the right to change their bodies, cosmetically, chemically, or surgically so as to express a self-defined gender identity" (International Conference on Transgender Law and Employment Policy 1995), is to deny that public policy might have any role to play in the shaping or limiting of such an absolute right.
>
> — Sukthankar 2011: 170

Although the picture further gets murkier due to the participation of doctors, psychiatrists and the state (in the sex-reassignment saga) with their own agenda of control over body. Thus by and large the comfort with the unique and exclusive trans-body seems to be a better solution.

It is all the more significant in the wake of a number of recent scientific studies which catalogue that transsexualism is not simply a lifestyle choice but has a genetic basis. According to the recent findings of Vincent Harley (Head of Molecular Genetics at Prince Henry Institute, Melbourne), these genetic differences might reduce testosterone action and under-masculinize the brain during foetal developments and hence transsexualism "is something that people are born with and its certainly not a lifestyle choice as some have suggested" (*Asian Age*, 28 October 2008, p. 10). Likewise various studies focusing on homoerotic behaviour or bisexuality in animal world clearly indicate that pansexuality is a part of natural order. In the entire animal kingdom more than 500 species are found to have behavioural and even bisexual traits. According to chimpanzee and gorilla expert, Jane Goodall, chimpanzees form small bisexual social groups. He contends that bisexuality is being observed in orca whales, bottlenose dolphins and humboldt penguins and even among some fish, flatworms and crustaceans. Similarly Bruce Bagemihl in his book *Biological Exuberance: Animal Homosexuality and Natural Diversity*, says that animals like gazelles, bison and antelope form bisexual bonds that extend much deeper than sexual activity.[11]

Thus when there are so many examples of bisexuality and homosexuality in natural world, it is indeed quite improbable to ostracize human species for alternative sexual choices. In this regard it is significant to note that the door attendant in Khushwant Singh's *Delhi* lies to the story-teller in order to prevent *hijra* from meeting his owner. He says:

> Excuse me, Sir, your *hijda* came to see you. I told her you have not come back from *phoren.* I hope you are not angry with me. Take a woman, take a boy, but a *hijda.* . . .
>
> — Singh 1990: 12

[11] He saw long-term coupling behaviour in some animals. A male bottlenose dolphin, for instance, will engage in heterosexual sex early in life, but as it ages, it will partner with a male dolphin for many years, forming a sometimes sexual, and often a protective and an intimate relationship. (Sabrina Buckwalter, 2 July 2006, "Chimps too Star fish Even", *Sunday Times of India*, New Delhi, p. 15). In the similar fashion evolutionary biologist Joan Rough Garden argues in *Evolution's Rainbow: Diversity, Gender and Sexuality in Nature and People* (especially in chapter six, "Multiple Gender Families") that more than two genders exist in hundreds of animal spices such as red deer, Plainfin midshipman fish, Coho Salmon and Bluegill sunfish. Likewise Petter Beckman, academic advisor for the "Against Nature?" has done an exhibition on homosexuality in The Natural History Museum, University of Oslo to showcase that it is not unnatural. (*Times of India*, 29 June 2008, p. 20).

There is a constant repetition of this line in the text which clearly evinces that even gay copulation is acceptable but the liminal space of neither man nor woman creates an irrepressible biphobia which is much more difficult to counter as compared to homophobia. In fact, physical and emotional defacement is such an integral part of a *hijra*'s existence that when Bhagmati first meets the narrator, she is obviously shown as battered, dishevelled and in a state of semi-consciousness.

On the one hand they are being feared on account of having a power to confer fertility or curse, but on the other the public opprobrium is a daily reality of their life. The basic right to live with dignity has been denied to them by man and nature. Significantly in Dattani's *Seven Steps around the Fire* Uma states that "not for them the seven rounds witnessed by the Fire God, eternally binding man and woman in matrimony, or the blessings of 'May you be the mother of a hundred sons'" (pp. 239-40). Coming back to Khushwant Singh's *Delhi* in which he employs a very clever tact to evince horrid vandalizing that Bhagmati suffers by juxtaposing Delhi and Bhagmati, and this exposes the centuries of relentless ravaging, loot and plunder thrust upon the city:

> I return to Delhi as I return to my mistress Bhagmati when I have had my fill of whoring in foreign lands. Delhi and Bhagmati have a lot in common. Having been long misused by rough people they have learnt to conceal their seductive charms under a mask of repulsive ugliness. — 1990: 1

Likewise this overlapping also opens up an interesting site of citizenship rights as well. It has not been long that the category "T" (implying transgenders) or "O" (meaning others) has been included in the passports and the reason of this can be adduced to their exclusion from the purview of the authentic citizen subject. The entire text is saturated with historical and fictional documentation of the ravaging of Delhi followed by violence inflicted on Bhagmati. It is a very interesting technique because it not only exhibits a gross appropriation of transgender identity, but also addresses a larger question of the authentic citizenship claim. He elaborates that in order to make the city and *hijra* palatable one has to

> cultivate a sense of belonging to Delhi and an attachment to someone like Bhagmati. Then the skies over Delhi's marbled palaces turn an aquamarine blue; . . . the earth exudes the earthy aroma of *khas*, of jasmine and *maulsri*. Then the dusky Bhagmati glides towards you swaying her ample hips like a temple dancer; her mouth smells of fresh cloves and she speaks like her Imperial Majesty the empress of Hindustan.
>
> — Singh 1990: 1-2

In a quite progressive move he tries to queer the entire nation by anthropomorphizing Delhi, the very capital of the nation, as Bhagmati, the *hijra*. The constant overlapping of the city and the eunuch Bhagmati is all-pervasive as the writer himself explains at the very outset of the novel:

> I make Delhi and Bhagmati sound very mysterious. The truth is that I am somewhat confused in my thoughts. What I am trying to say is that although I detest living in Delhi and am ashamed of my liaison with Bhagmati, I cannot keep away from either for too long. . . . I will explain the strange paradox of my lifelong, love–hate affair with the city and the woman. — Ibid.: 2

In fact, at one place Bhagmati even calls herself the Purana Kila of Delhi. Similarly in a quite ingenious fashion the Republic Day parade is used to affirm the juxtaposing of Bhagmati and India. The narrator does not feel like going to the Republic Day parade and feels superior in this sort of isolation as he can read about it in newspapers and hear commentary on radio and thinks that his celebration of the Republic Day can have a fitting ending, "if that Bhagmati has any sense, sing the national anthem and hoist the tri-colour flag atop her quivering torso" (Singh 1990: 104). It is not surprising that when Budh Singh, disgusted with the loot and corruption of the so-called free Indian state, loses his sanity and wants to traverse back to the British rule, he forms a society called British Retention League, and Bhagmati becomes its first and the only signatory. This is a semi-comic and satirical presentation of the sorry state of India and the resurrection of it, even if in a jocular fashion, has been guaranteed by Bhagmati's participation in it and her sex and profession have been categorically mentioned without any sense of shame. The scroll that she signs for the regeneration of the country bears her name "Bhagmati — Sex: neutral *hijda*; Profession: prostitute" (ibid.: 375). Hence throughout the novel, the reshaping of land by the *hijra* and the vice versa are all-pervasive themes and the chapter scheme is also in accordance with it because each chapter that traces the history of Delhi is followed by the chapter named Bhagmati. The *hijra* is thus shown travelling through time, space and history to evince the symbiotic relationship between the land and the *hijra*s.

However, the entire issue of appropriation of land by transsexual identity takes a twist in the chapter, "Alice Aldwell" that describes 1857 mutiny and the plight of a half-white and half-Muslim woman who becomes a living symbol of British atrocities in the minds of the Indians. She has been brutally ravaged by a *hijra*, Basant Ali Khan. The rape of a white woman by the natives has been continuously used in post-colonial literature as a trope of revenge on the white colonizers. It is translated in this fashion that if the colonizers have usurped their land then the natives want to appropriate the white woman's body as a revenge. Though from feminist angle it is an appalling tale of female subjugation and puts *hijra*, Basant Lal, as a perpetrator of extreme violence but in a very dark and twisted fashion it obliquely presents him/her as an authentic native subject who is fit to take revenge on behalf of her/his plundered and ravaged land. Thus the rights of *hijras* on the land have been asserted through various tropes.

Moreover this citizenship claim becomes absolutely imperative as Steven Seidman writes:

> Citizenship rights make it possible for individuals to protect themselves against social threat, to participate in public decision-making, to make claims about national policy and culture, and so on. At stake is how the lesbian and gay movement approach questions of citizenship. Contestation should be over the basis of citizenship and the meaning of sexual and intimate citizenship. In short we need queer articulation of democratic theory. — 1998: 189

Significantly in the context of *hijras*' citizenship rights (due to the lack of the separate identity), the gender confusion leads to lack of property rights and adoption rights as has been mentioned in Revathi's autobiography. Revathi has been denied share in property for being born as a man and living like a woman, and in order to get her share she has to assume masculine name and sartorial identity. So it is indeed of singular importance to identify eunuchs and *hijras* as authentic citizen subject from that angle. Thus turning the national capital into Bhagmati the *hijra* is indeed a radical attempt at queering the entire nation and asserting citizenship rights in a nation.

However, interestingly enough, within *hijra* community whereas death rituals and other forms of public opprobrium indicate a sense of incompleteness, there are other practices that create gender trouble through specific *hijra* claps, feminist ritual songs loaded with sarcasm at patriarchy and *sari* lifting (to expose their ambiguous genital organs) practice. These practices clearly draw attention to their gender liminality rather than resignifying normative gender ideals. They employ these practices to not only decode their *hijra* identity but also to gain advantage in a paradoxical fashion because by showing the mutilated genital organs they want to create a phobia mixed with awe in the minds of the onlookers that *hijras* can curse them to have similar fate (see Reddy 2006: 138). Also it is an act of mocking at the male genital prowess that has been overrated. Thus they try to reclaim a phobic respect in this inverted fashion and use their in-between sexuality to empower themselves, though in a slightly twisted manner. To quote Gayatri Reddy's words:

> Both these practices serve as unambiguous markers of muddied gender (as well as critical symbols of abjection and asceticism). . . . These gender performances explicitly counter a reading of *hijras* as merely reinscribers of normative femininity. At the very least, by focusing attention on themselves as liminal figures both in terms of embodiment and gender ascription, *hijras* appear as potentially subversive agents, serving self-consciously to cause "gender trouble". — 2006: 140-41

Likewise the *badhai* songs sung at marriages have potent undercurrents of casting aspersions on the groom's family (though in a jocular way) by taunting the groom for imagined poverty and bad looks. These verbal shots aim at undermining the so-called higher status of groom's family. According to Serena Nanda,

> . . . the *hijra*'s verbal play functions as a kind of "ritual of reversal", a phenomenon in many cultures in which those who are in high and mighty positions are brought lower and humbled. — 1999: 5

Though there is an overwhelming burlesque feminine behaviour among *hijras* in terms of their feminine names, feminine attire, long hair, feminized language and their insistence on occupying "ladies only" seat coupled with demands to be counted as females in census, there is a significant incongruity emerging out of their sexually suggestive behaviour. And this is due to the fact that though they ape feminine corporeality, they are dramatically different from sexually repressed Indian women (who are perpetually on sexual dieting due to middle-class issues of respectability). And this at one level arouses voyeuristic titillating laughter in male audience, and on the other works as a subversive tool to lay bare the repressed module of feminine sexuality. *Hijras* surely produce a counter-culture against patriarchy by appropriating female corporeality and behaving in an unabashed manner like dancing in public, sexually suggestive gesturing and smoking. Indubitably they are an effective foil to heterosexual patriarchal propriety. In *Seven Steps around the Fire*, *hijra* Anarkali is childless and penniless, and Uma who meets her for her research thesis (Uma comes from an upper middle-class family and is a wife of a senior police officer) tells Anarkali that she has no money of her own and has to give an account of every penny she spends. Likewise Anarkali is childless and due to her *hijra* identity she is naturally sterile but even Uma's barrenness, in an inadvertent fashion, is adduced to her anatomical fault. When she tells her husband that the doctor finds no fault with her and her husband has to go for the checking of sperm counts, he immediately retracts back and states that he will not go for it. Little wonder while addressing Uma, Anarkali spontaneously utters: "Maybe you are more unhappy than I am" (Dattani 2000a: 243). In a very suggestive manner the myth about the heterosexual conjugal bliss is busted when Suresh tries to make love to her while she wants to talk about Anarkali and the conditions of *hijras* in general. To quote from the text:

> *Uma starts to say something but Suresh is kissing her. He immediately jumps up.*
>
> SURESH. Ow! You bit me! You bit me!
>
> *Uma apologizes while he checks his tongue.*
>
> Hmmmmm. It's okay, sweetheart. I know you didn't mean to.
>
> UMA (quietly). No, Suresh. It's just that you put your tongue

in my mouth while I was trying to talk to you.

Suresh looks at her trying to figure out if she means more than what she said. Uma gives him an innocent smile.

SURESH. (*checking his tongue*). Excuse me.

Suresh exits. — Dattani 2000: 238-39

Importantly enough this scene is immediately followed by Uma's loud thinking about *hijras*:

> . . . A brief note on the popular myths on the origin of the *hijras* will be in order, before looking at the class–gender-based power implications. The term *hijra*, of course, is of Urdu origin, a combination of Hindi, Persian and Arabic, literally meaning "neither male nor female." — Ibid.: 239

And then quiet dramatically, even when the voice-over continues, Uma and Anarkali are shown together on the stage. Obviously the overlapping of Uma and *hijra* Anarkali is a constant feature of the play. And many times Anarkali serves as a projected identity of Uma and in a unique fashion the *hijra* identity and her unabashed exposition of it create the much needed gender bender, that defies the stringent codes for accepted female behaviour. *Hijras* due to their corporeality and through performative practices question the existing gender patterns. Thus the *hijra* identity projects an existence that is already outside the binary framework of gender and hence works as potential subversive agents to question the patriarchal order of thinking. And in this light, their overwhelming mimetic appropriation of feminine gender is indeed a backlash at their unique position as potent subversive tools to question gender inequalities. Apropos of this, quoting Roland Barthes, Gayatri Reddy talks about the "intentional" and "innocent signification". While she allocates a certain kind of spontaneity to the latter, the intentional signification is a deliberate construction according to her. She states:

> As such, the "visual ensembles of spectacular subcultures" by being "obviously fabricated", go against the grain of a mainstream culture whose principle defining feature according to Barthes, is "a tendency to masquerade as nature . . . to translate the reality of the world into an image of the world which in turn presents itself as if composed according to the evident laws of the natural order."
>
> — Reddy 2006: 132

She observes that in that sense *hijra*s seem to merge the difference between innocent and intentional signification and thereby become all the more powerful agents of reversing the paradigm from feminist perspectives. Significantly their obsession with the feminine accoutrements needs to be debated in the context of their position outside the bipolar gender framework because it is from this position that the heteropatriarchal subjugation can be critiqued in a very distinct fashion and *hijra*s can work as a catalyst for feminist concerns. Thus their specific neither man nor woman identity needs to be accepted holistically not only for their individual self-assurance but also for a larger cause of diffusing stringent gender categorization.

True the androgynous identity is not always a source of transphobia but at times encapsulates a uniquely holistic existence which generates a very different order of respectability. Apropos of this Gayatri Reddy in *With Respect to Sex* gives us a very interesting thesis by identifying different sort of *sannyasi*s (a very revered Indian identity) and demonstrating that *hijra*s are also in one way renouncers or *sannyasi*s. Starting with an analysis of the tool of "dissident androgyny" (to quote Leela Gandhi's term) employed by Gandhi to counter hyper-masculinity of colonial rulers, she contends how androgynous existence gained unique meaning in terms of various interpretations of *sannyas*. Quoting Ashish Nandy and Kakkar, Gayatri states that Gandhi by drawing upon the several ascetic traditions of India, "posited the ability to transcend the man–woman dichotomy through a self-conscious aspiration for androgyny. The desire to become 'God's eunuch', as he puts it was superior to both the essence of masculinity and femininity" (ibid.: 29). She further asserts that by doing so Gandhi is able to negate the stringent idea of cowardice or *kapurusatva* (failure of masculinity) and in this manner he re-conceptualizes the definition of "man" who admits his drive to become both sexes. In this fashion Gandhi dismantles the colonial logic of sexual binaries and deconstructs British hyper-masculinity to justify the imperial oppression. Thus by elevating the status of androgynous-self as opposed to stringent hyper-masculinity Gandhi paves the way for a reverence for twin-mould identity which no longer should be understood only in terms of deficient existence. This redefinition of masculinity and femininity in terms of androgyny further helps in reinventing the idea of authentic spiritual self or *sannyas*. There are clear-cut three instances of refurbishing the concept of true *sannyasi*. By and large *sannyasi* is understood as the renouncer of the world and the currency that is primarily used is sexual abstinence apart from denouncing the materialistic creed. Retention of semen ("semen anxiety" is commonly used to indicate that loss of semen is equated with loss of force whereas it is believed that the retention of it strengthens both the body and the spiritual self) is the key marker in this context. Thus bodily discipline and sexual renunciation become the primary requisites in this structure. J. Alter in *The Wrestler's Body: Identity and Ideology in North India* argues that in this manner the definition of an ascetic can include the north Indian wrestlers as well because

> [I]t is by virtue of the fact that the practice of *sannyas* has such profound spiritual, other-worldly significance that the practice of wrestling is meaningful as an ethical ideology with worldly implications. The agency through which one

> point of reference is translated into another is body discipline. — 1992: 223

However, this whole argument is quite androcentric and this semen anxiety, as it is popularly known, puts women *sannyasin*s out of its purview. Highlighting the specific position of women *sannyasini*s in this regard Mira Khandelwal redefines the idea of *sannyas* and puts more stress on emotional discipline to attain higher spiritual self as compared to bodily discipline. Quoting Meena Khandelwal (from *Sexual Fluids, Emotions, Morality: Notes on the Gendering of Brahmacharya* in *Celibacy, Culture, and Society: The Anthropology of Sexual Abstinence*) Gayatri Reddy argues in favour of more egalitarian model practised by *sannyasin*s. To quote her words:

> Rather than restricting its meaning to semen retention — an anxiety over which pervades Banaras wrestlers' articulations of *brahmacarya* — the *sannyasin*s' accounts highlight a more egalitarian model that emphasizes "moral purity, a lifestyle of self-control or self-restraint, and emotional detachment rather than the androcentric focus on "semen obsession". — 2006: 39

Furthermore taking an altogether different tangent to re-inscribe the meaning of *sannyas* in terms of non-Brahmanic caste ideology, Ravinder Khare cites the examples of a certain section of Lucknow *dalit*s and talks about making the other-worldly boundaries of *sannyas* porous and relocating it within worldly egalitarian moral values as opposed to other-worldly preoccupations of *sannyasi*s, and gives a more elaborate understanding of the term. In the process, they (the low caste *dalit*s of Lucknow) negate the brahmanic notion of *sannyas* and situate it within the discourse of non-hierarchal caste system. Thus the disengagement of *sannyas* from caste holism is quite explicit in this unique interpretation of *sannyas*. Thus the subjective and plural interpretations of *sannyas* reformulate the definition of a renouncer and take it out of the stringent confines of caste holism, semen retention, "other-worldly ethics" and include values of emotional detachment, bodily discipline and egalitarian "worldly ethics" in its purview. In this light the emasculated corporeal self (that symbolizes sexual abstinence), the consequent lack of progeny and worldly concerns make *hijras* potent contenders for a unique individualized form of renouncers. According to Gayatri Reddy, *hijras* seem to employ this highly subjective model of *sannyas* according to which they not only rely on the corporeal reality of their asexual identity due to the emasculation, but also heavily depend on emotional detachment and egalitarian ethics of self-control to project a higher spiritual self. She states:

> After all, as Irfan and Amir Nayak told me repeatedly, not only is the "male body [penis] . . . useless" for *hijras*, its excision merely underscored their (ontologically prior) asexuality rather than delineating the centrality of semen retention and power stemming from such control. Instead as many *hijras* emphasized, it is the emotional detachment and possession of *himmat*, or courage/strength — emotional, psychological, and physical — to undergo this commitment to permanent sexual abstinence that reveals *hijras*' greater authenticity and ultimately their greater *izzat*.
>
> — Reddy 2006: 40

No wonder *hijras* filing for nominations for electoral polls assert their emotional and materialistic detachment (because they have no progeny or a concept of future in worldly terms) as keys to establish themselves as honest and non-corrupt contenders and people accept this version which is evident from the wonderful track record of their victories. Again this is an affirmation of their being a worldly renouncer in a specific way. Hence emasculation, dual identity and lack of reproductive tools are not always sources of biphobia, but at times elevate their status due to the symbolic manifestation of the lack of worldly concerns which are forged into their existence.

Similarly duality at times becomes metaphor for more holistic and elevated self rather than a symbol of disabled entity. In fact, the hierarchies of class, culture and religion are completely dismantled in this assimilation of binary opposition within *hijra* identity as Gayatri Reddy argues (while tracing the ethnography of Hyderabadi *hijras*). Eunuchs in death rituals though get buried like Muslims but in all other ceremonies of widowhood and mourning practices follow Hindu rituals. For instances after the *guru*'s death, *chelas* wear white *saris*, break bangles and wear coloured dresses only when they find a new *guru* (all these rituals bears a close semblance with those of the Hindu widows). Significantly both the Muslim and the Hindu *hijras* worship Bedharaj Mata (a Hindu goddess) before emasculation. Interestingly enough *hijras* become the metonymic signifier of assimilation of two contradictory impulses. That is why Uma in Dattani's *Seven Steps around the Fire* contemplates:

> Nobody seems to know anything about them. Neither do they. Did they come to this country with Islam, or are they a part of our glorious Hindu tradition? — Dattani 2000: 246

Their neither here nor there liminal position is not a marker of a "lack" but a unique amalgam of divergent impulses, and one such example is their Hindu/Muslim secular disposition. Thus it is not a matter of great surprise that in Khushwant Singh's *Delhi* one of the characters proudly proclaims that Delhi is *hijda* by which he means that it is the combination of all divergent impulses and not a deficient and dysfunctional city. In fact, in the fourth chapter a character called Musaddi Lal who is shown being born in 633 Hijri corresponding to the year 1265 of Christian calendar is rumoured to have adopted the ways of the Muslims and consequently jeered at. And this confused identity creates an extreme anxiety and even his wife refuses to accept him but later a beautiful reconciliation emerges. To quote his words:

> I was disowned by the Hindus and shunned by my own wife. I was exploited by the Muslims who disdained my company. Indeed I was like a *hijda* who was neither one thing nor another but could be misused by everyone.
>
> — Singh 1990: 55

However, amidst the extreme hostility, this dual identity becomes their shield and the term *hijda* acquires a beautiful meaning signifying synchronization, harmony and assimilation of contradictory ideology. As Musaddi Lal affirms:

> If any one asked me whether we were Hindus or Mussalmans, we would reply we were both. Nizamuddin was our umbrella against the burning sun of Muslim bigotry and the downpour of Hindu contempt. — Ibid.: 62

He further elaborates that when his wife gave birth to a son he "chose the name Kamal for him — it could be either Hindu or Muslim. In Hindi it meant the lotus flower. In Arabic, pronounced with a longer accent on the second *a*, it meant excellence. We took the child to Jogmaya Temple and had the priest daub sandalpaste on his forehead. Then we took him to Ghiaspur and had the Khwaja Sahib bless him (Singh 1990: 62).

In the same vein Bhagmati also becomes a symbol of assimilation of all contrasting binary oppositions including various fanatic religious beliefs. The narrator opines:

> Even after the years I have known her I am not sure whether she is a Muslim or Hindu. She says she is both — and more because now she is also Sikh. — Ibid.: 105

Further at another place he affirms:

> She no longer talks of her *hijda* husband (perhaps he is dead) or of sex but of Ramji and of Hindu temples and Muslim *dargahs* she visits. — Ibid.: 380

She talks about her going to *haj* and spending her old age at the banks of holy river of Ganga at Haridwar with equal ease.

And like Musaddi Lal when there is a possibility of religious riots her ambiguous identity becomes her saving grace. When Budh Singh asks her if she is with Muslims or Sikhs, with the purpose of labelling her as a particular kind of religious believer, she answers:

> I am on no side — neither Emperor Aurangzeb's nor your *Guru*'s. You know what he says to me? So you are neutral, *hain*? If you were a man or a woman you would have been on one side or the other. . . I said, "*Arre,* son of Budhoo Singh"! The great *Bhagwan* who lives up in the heavens can perform many miracles. He can make a *bhangi* (sweeper) into a brahmin. He can turn a timid *bania* (shopkeeper) into a kshatriya (warrior). He can make a poor *hijda* into a man or a woman. But even *Bhagwan* cannot put sense into the skull of a *budhoo* like you. — Ibid.: 121-22

Significantly in the chapter entitled "The Untouchables", the writer explains that only two people could pass the gate of Shahjahanabad without being questioned and they were either the emperor or the untouchables. Thus the outcast identity assigns an extreme sort of isolation that in turn and in an inverted fashion can provide blanket safety guard against certain kinds of oppressions. In the same vein *hijra*s are extreme outcasts who are not willingly accepted by any religion and thus can have a mix of various religious beliefs that safeguard them against religious subjugation at one level because they cannot be labelled as practitioner of any specific religion exclusively. Gayatri Reddy gives a very significant example in this respect. She quotes a scene from the movie *Bombay* in which during a Hindu/Muslim religious riots the children of the protagonist could only be saved by a *hijra* because s/he belongs to no specific religion. Similarly in a recently released movie, *Agnipath,* the hero's sister could not be saved by anyone, and only *hijra*s along with hero could invade the space of extreme subjugation, because their twin identity and lack of being fixated into the confines of specific categories provide them a fluid power which makes them invade any religious, social and gendered space that otherwise can only be accessible to a particular group. In another movie *Majnu ki Bijli ka Mandola* the communication between the ultra left hero and the common villagers is made possible only by a *hijra*. Naturally amidst the 1984 Sikh riots that have been depicted in *Delhi*, the Sikh narrator is throughout comforted and supported by *hijra* Bhagmati and when the issue of safe place arises she immediately asks him to come with her to *hijra* locality known as Lal Kuan:

> "I am going to take you to Lal Kuan. Nobody will bend a hair on a *hijda*'s head. *Chalo*," she orders.
>
> — Singh 1990: 387

Thus their androgynous state does not always generate transphobia but at times makes them penetrate into impervious oppressive spheres.

Quite obviously other than non-materialistic *sannyasi* corporeality (even if it is only symbolic at times) and incorporation of divergent ideologies (an assimilation of Hindu/Muslim secular identity), *hijra*'s unique twin male/female identity creates an interesting rupture by also providing an alternative family structure. Their family pattern is significantly different from the traditional family structure and it is a well-established stance that "familial citizenship" is another currency through which citizenship is proclaimed, as family is the smallest unit of national formation. Gay marriage and alternative family structure endorse the view that the "so-called normalcy" is possible within homoerotic structure as well and it is not deficient in anything, but Gayatri Spivak, Carl Wittman, Judith Rauhofer, D'Emilio and Eva Pendleton negate the assimilationist strategy because they feel it is an aping of the heterosexual framework. This debate is not new because as early as in 1970, American activist Carl Wittman affirmed that gay marriages would have the same pressures as that on heterosexual marriages and the usual societal impositions of kids, older parents and neighbours would not be there to keep it intact and hence it can be more disastrous and would do no good to the real issue of the eradication of "self-hatred". In the similar vein John D'Emilio argues in favour of forming an "affectional community" which will broaden the possibilities of new ways of loving and living outside the confines of a family. This "affectional community" propagates an idea of utopian social project and thus questions the very structure of the restrictive nature of familial space. Michael Warner's assumption also challenges equal rights/citizenship framework because he affirms that this familial structure will reprivatize homoerotic desire by pushing it back to monogamous couple system. In fact, citing Dennis Allen's public discussion on the same-sex marriage in Hawaii (in the light of a suit filed by two lesbian couples and one gay couple (Baer vs. Lewin), Bell and Binnie argue that such cases problematize the very definition and idea of marriage and serve as destabilizing tools which further question the hierarchal exploitation inherent in heterosexual marriages. To quote from *Sexual Citizen:*

> . . . same-sex marriage is held as capable of undermining the most solid of social structures ('the family') by infiltrating it and exposing its contradictory logics from within.
>
> — Bell and Binnie 2000: 57

But this view is countered by assimilationist thinkers like Franklin Kameny, Morris Kaplan and Evan Wolfson. Franklin Kameny opines that homosexuals are indeed no different from heterosexuals and are simply another minority group like the religious or ethnic minority which makes up a nation. Evan Wolfson also supports gay marriage in the light of enactment of "basic human right" and constitutional freedom "because literally hundreds of important legal, economic, practical and social benefits and protections flow directly from marriage

. . . exclusion from this central social institution wreaks real harm on real-life same-sex couple every day" (1996: 79-89). Linking the right to marry and familial structure with broader citizenship claim, Morris Kaplan affirms:

> Lesbian and gay marriages, domestic partnerships and the re-conceiving of family institutions as modes of intimate association among free and equal citizens all efforts to appropriate, extend, and transform the available possibilities.
> — 1997: 222

In India the leading gay writer and activist Raj Rao in his interview, while sketching the current climate of sexual citizenship, supports Spivak's view by arguing that property and adoption laws are part of heteropatriarchal paradigm and thus the benefits incurred out of gay wedlock blunt the radical edge of queer activism. He supports gay marriage only as an individual choice and a means to destabilize normalcy but certainly not as a tool to claim familial citizenship of a nation (which has a heterosexual character). But on the other hand Ruth Vanita in her essay, "Democratising Marriage: Consent, Custom and the Law", takes a pro-marriage stand though only to justify the argument that the right should be available to people irrespective of their sexual orientation. Another important marker in this discussion is the inclusion of space variable by which one understands the place from where the people exercise their sexual citizenship rights. And this further brings forth the concept of the policing of the sexual activities of sexual minorities at public places. Familial citizenship in this line of argument places family as a private site of citizenship, and as Bell and Binnie affirm that this privatization perpetuates the notion that a particular family space is allocated so that the private act may remain invisible. To quote their words:

> From our perspective, such a programme is intensely problematic, not least because it sides with phobic

> arguments that grant sexual rights only on the understanding that they will be kept private; that is, invisible (Cooper, p. 993). While there is a need to protect some notion of privacy — if that means defining a space where law cannot intervene, for example — there is a bigger risk to be taken in stressing the private as a proper home of sexual citizenship.
>
> — Bell and Binnie 2000: 5

Now in this light the *hijra* identity brings about a tense negotiation between this public/private and pro-gay marriage/ radical anti-gay marriage stand. As these thinkers consider that the issue of individual right is perfectly justified but the so-called radical mutation through these measures of same-sex marriage can only happen at boundary and will not affect centre in alarming measure, and thus it can be more disastrous and will do no good to the real issue of the mitigation of "self-hatred". In this way an uneasy reconciliation between these opposing strands is forged through *hijra*s because not only their entire life, including their sex life, is structured primarily in a public domain but also their alternative family structure is quite different from the traditional heterosexual familial pattern. They have *guru* as a patriarch of the *hijra* family followed by *chela*s and *nati chela*s and they consider their *guru* as their father or mother figure and *chela*s or *nati chela*s are being considered as grandchildren. Though they have *panthi* (a substitute for husband), when the *guru* is dead they observe all rituals of widowhood and at times there is a sexual and deep emotional bonding between *guru* and *chela*, and thus the stringent boundaries and specific role play of husband and wife are constantly framed and reframed. In this sense they give impetus to the re-evaluation of the confines of familial sexual citizenship. By dint of their androgynous anatomy and a constant visibility in public domain (either through *danda* work or begging), they unwittingly bring about a reconciliation between these divergent impulses and inadvertently perpetuate the "moment of transgression" (to quote Jeffrey Weeks' term). Their alternative family dispensation along with their specific offspring bonds in the form of *chela*s and *nati chela*s creates that third space where the pro and anti-familial sexual citizenship rights claims are beautifully reconciled because their liminal identity breaks the opportunities/limitations framework of familial sexual citizenship rights. When in *Seven Steps around the Fire*, the inspector rebuts Anarkali for calling Uma her sister and states that there is nothing like sisterhood for *hijra*s, Anarkali retorts at the conventional system of blood ties and depicts the unique *hijra*s' ways of family dispensation and bonds that serve as a critique of heteropatriarchal family pattern. She lays emphasis on inherent love as a uniting tool rather than the overemphasis on loveless blood-ties. She states:

> We make our relations with our eyes. With our love, I look at him, he looks at me, and he is my brother. (*Munuswami looks away.*) I look at you, you look at me, and we are mother and daughter. — Dattani 2000: 240

No wonder whenever they try to relocate their identity within the heteropatriarchal family, they are invariably oppressed and suffer excruciating pain as is evident from Revathi's autobiography, *The Truth about Me* in which she describes the gory details of her horrible marriage to a man with whom she wants to duplicate the heteropatriachal family life as opposed to the alternative *hijra* family structure. Similarly in *Seven Steps around the Fire* Kamla, who is transformed into a beautiful woman (and appears so feminine that even priest cannot recognize that she is not a woman) and marries a minister's son by following all the rituals, suffers immensely for entering into heteropatriarchal family pattern and is burnt alive for tying knot with her lover. Apropos of this *hijra*, Champa cogitates: "she would not have been happy in the outside world" (Dattani 2000: 260). This symbolically reinstates the value of alternative *hijra* family (which certainly is not devoid of its own hegemonic power operations) as opposed to the traditional marriage and heteronormative family structure. Thus the very unique androgynous identity of *hijra* is not always a source of biphobia and suppression but at times subverts the existing power patterns and creates fissures and fractures in the notion that the so-called radical transfiguration through same-sex marriage is only possible at periphery and will not be able to destabilize the centre at all. The *hijras*' unique marital disposition questions and destabilizes the very core of heteropatriarchal marriage system. It not only questions the defacing effects of existing family patterns as in the case of Kamla and her lover's marriage, but also brings about a reconciliation between the two extremely contradictory positions. Thus *hijra* family structure symbolically makes an interesting intervention in viewing citizenship question from the lens of familial space.

In order to counter this clear-cut division of male or female category Bhaswati Chakravorty employs a very interesting linguistic strategy of coining pronoun "hir" (which is a combination of his and her) to address eunuchs. Throughout in her essay, "Right for the Third Gender", she has used the pronoun "hir" instead of his and her. However, despite horrible subjugation, due to the patronage of religion and myth there is a certain kind of awe mixed with phobia in the public memory. She observes:

> Mystification and aggressiveness are, at least in part, a deliberate strategy of survival. Differences give the *hijras* an aura that cows heterosexual society into propitiation. . . . It is an alternative society with its own economic dispensation.
>
> — Chakravorty 2007: 376

Hence the biphobia, encountered by *hijras*, transgenders, transvestites and bisexuals, is of very different nature to some extent. And thus it can be mitigated only by assigning them their unique identity as a third gender rather than the forceful mutilation and appropriation of them into a twofold gender division. This incurs horrid violence on their body, culture, genetic and physical make-up in the name of assimilating them into the mainstream of society. Their "intentional ambiguity" (see Trawick) needs to be preserved and highlighted because as Gayatri Reddy contends that it helps them to work as troubling agents that can help the theorists in general to go "beyond the aporia of the structure/agency debate undergirding much sociological and feminist analysis and to capture the fundamental, if elusive, quality of ambiguity — with respect to gender as well as religion, kinship, and class — that constitutes *hijras*' sense of self and relationship to wider society" (2006: 141). All the literary texts discussed in this chapter present both the effects of biphobia and countering strategies to counter them — such as the queering of the nation in terms of juxtaposing of Bhagmati and Delhi, the highlighting of the need to valorize distinct *hijra* body and consequently negating the requirement for sex reassignment surgery as in "I Hate Wet Tissues", the cultural biases prevalent on account of criminal tribes act coupled with the state's transpanic as shown in *Seven Steps around the Fire*, and the unmasking of the terrible violence and techniques of silencing as depicted in "Incomplete Human". They have potently challenged the dichotomous model of sexual studies where hetero and homo are mutually exclusive categories. Interestingly enough, *hijras*, more than any gender theorists, are aware of this complexity and ambiguity. As Munira *hijra* once said to Gayatri Reddy:

> We are neither men nor women, but at the same time we are both. *Hijras* are *adha-bic* (half in the middle) people and that is why we are both feared and respected at the same time.
>
> — 2006: 141

3

Lesbian Fabulation in Suniti Namjoshi's Poetry

A Tool to Familiarize or a Means to Escape?

POETRY APPEARS to be a more suitable genre than prose for the articulation of transgressive desires because the oblique mode of expression, the inherent gaps and the fluidity of poetic narration provide a fertile ground for blurring the boundaries of sexualities and gender which consequently gives impetus to plural interpretations. This polyvalence of poetic expression erases the definite closures, and the deviant sexuality is all about negating fixities and celebrating pansexuality. Hence the fluidity and fantasy, inherent in poetic technique, are apt to negotiate the multiple valencies that can be attributed to the varied axes of sexual identity. No wonder the famous (not so openly lesbian) poet May Swenson in her essay, "The Experience of Poetry in a Scientific Age", highlights the dynamic and organic aspects of poetry and talks about the cartographic nature of poetry that helps in forming the map of that globe which is viewed by the "naked eye" as a disk-like and one-dimensional formation but with the help of poetic map surprisingly enlarges and reveals its amazing topography, and traversing through this world our senses are transformed and undergo dilation. Inevitably poetry is one of the most apt genres for destabilizing the stringent heterosexist assumptions.

The recuperation of ancestral lesbian voices in Indian poetry can be traced back to the nineteenth-century Urdu *rekhti* poetry by Rangin, Insha and Jan Sahib as has been systematically examined by Ruth Vanita in *Same-Sex Love in India* (2002), *Love's Rite* (2005) and more recently in *Gender, Sex and the City* (2012). According to her, a few women also wrote *rekhti* but almost none of that survived. Rangin's *Chaptinama* depicts explicit same-sex love between women where lovers decide the male–female genders of the partners (butch/femme) on the basis of breaking an *ilaichi* or a meat bone depending upon the even and odd numbers of *ilaichi dana*s found inside the *ilaichi* or the larger or smaller part of the bone. (A detailed description of it can be found in Ruth's *Gender Sex and the City: Urdu Rekhti Poetry*, 1780–1870). The lesbian partners were known as *dogana* or *janana*. Thus various exclusive rituals and linguistic patterns surrounding the lesbians are catalogued in Rangin's *Chaptinama* and give an insight into the world of lesbians in the nineteenth century through Urdu poetry. And these are counter-productive of the assumption that homoeroticism is a Western import and has no Indian roots. This is specially significant since the Urdu poetic tradition is distinctly public in its production and reception as it is primarily meant for gatherings or *mushaira*s for the exhibition of the poetic prowess. Thus *rekhti*, an offshoot of *ghazal*, occupies a public sphere for the exploration of lesbian desire which in a way brings forth the homoerotic longings of women from the all-women private spaces of domestic households or the courtesans' homes to the public domain.

However, the visibility accorded through *rekhti* is marred by the lesbophobic anxiety and the male voyeuristic pleasure emanating from the lesbian double bonanza, which leads to the explicit depiction of sexual and romantic encounters between *dogana*s (female lovers), and thus there is a very little play of fantasy or myth making in *rekhti*. Similarly locating it primarily within courtesan household further erases the need to make it more suggestive and symbolic. But as Ruth argues, the distinction between courtesans and respectable women was blurred when the *nawab*s of Lucknow married some courtesans and employed others at court.

> Second the domestication of the figure of woman is partially undone. Much of the *rekhti* is set in the home but it is a home that seethes with female emotions not directed to husbands and children. Wifehood and motherhood is relegated to the margins, while the desire to experience moves to the centre.
>
> — Ruth Vanita 2012: 10

The re-sexualization of female desire without rioting through the procreative need is one of the marked features of *rekhti* and is quite radical in that sense.

> Neither buds nor flowers interest me/Young lady, I'm interested only in your alley. . ./Listen, neither cardamom nor betel pleases me/I long for something you have chewed/ I have come here, Insha, just for a pleasure outing/I have no interest in either fruit or the fruitful. — Ibid.: 140

But despite some sort of domestication of homoerotic desire the tone is always lesbophobic. In fact, in one of the poems, Rangin (as quoted by Ruth Vanita in *Love's Rite*) has gone to the extent of curing these homosexual women by ceaselessly forcing himself on these lesbian lovers till he feels that he has cured them of the same-sex desire. In this fashion the engagement of the poet with the popular belief that lesbianism is a deviation that emerges out of the unbridled desire of over-sexed woman is revealed. Under the garb of endorsing such accepted notions, the *rekhti* poets are able to create a free traffic between the straight and the queer readers because of which they do not feel the need for the overtly symbolic representation of the same-sex desire.

Thus the methods such as creating fables, revising or using symbols to justify the lesbian longing are countered not only by the lesbophobic preaching of the male narrator (even if for poetic production he has assumed the role of poetess) but also by the depiction of explicit sexual intimacies to titillate the male audience at public *mushairas*. Instead of poetic suggestiveness the familiarization is adopted by reinvesting the domestic and marketplaces with deviant desire and also through exchange of food and jewellery. All these serve as normalizing techniques for acceptance of transgressive desire by showcasing that the same-sex relationships operate on the same normative sphere and hence somewhat as natural as heteronormativity. The heteropatriarchal didacticism and lack of identity politics (for there is no "coming out" stories, which are invariably oblique in nature, involved due to the male narrator), coupled with the erotic pleasure to stimulate the male audience, at one level cease the need for symbolic expression of homoeroticism. Since the male writers writing about lesbian love have different connotative meanings, their challenges and adaptation techniques are also different as demonstrated by citing the examples of *rekhti* poets. But the immediate question is can the suggestiveness of lesbian poetry be seen as a tool to camouflage transgressive desire in order to enable a straight reader to pioneer spaces beyond hetero-normativity or is it only a way of adding a new dimension to exclusive "queer aesthetics" (to quote Raj Rao's term)? This chapter attempts to answer this question by a close analysis of the works of India's first lesbian poet, Suniti Namjoshi who has used poetry to come out of closet and hence her challenges and counter-strategies are bound to be different from those of her precursors, specially *rekhti* male-poets writing about sexual minorities.

After a long period of oblivion due to the colonial rule, much later after Independence, the poetic articulation of lesbian desire once again finds its manifestation in the writings of the first Indian lesbian writer Suniti Namjoshi who had to leave Indian Administrative Services to find shelter in the West due to her homosexual leanings. As opposed to the familiarization techniques (through food, space and ornaments as used in the *rekhti* poetry), Namjoshi employs the tools of myth, fantasy and technique of inversion to unmask the arbitrary and manoeuvrable constructs of the heteropatriarchal world. She, in fact, creates *Maya Diip*, a mythic island which is inhabited only by women and instead of reclaiming the space within heteronormative society like *rekhti* that shows lovers within heteropatriarchal homes (on roofs and in bedrooms) and cities (in terms of marketplaces where these lovers meet), Namjoshi creates a completely isolated space to evince radical discontinuity from the straight world. On the one hand it can be viewed as an escapist route, but on the other it is reflective of her practical understanding that the lesbian appropriation of heteropatriarchal space is only possible through the mutations at boundary and that the actual displacement of heterosexuality is still a distant dream. Her decision to leave country for foreign shores due to her deviant desire further contributed to this sort of understanding. Also the constant interplay between utopia and dystopia helps in both envisioning hyper-reality (that may extrapolate the ills of the so-called real world and thereby expose them) and presenting an altogether counter-alternative world to question the perceived notion of patriarchal reality. Namjoshi time and again talks about finding a secluded place where the reconfiguring of all-women space can be negotiated. There is a recurring image of appropriation of space through "queer only family" where there is a complete exclusion of men as in "Mainakah's Sister". In it the protagonist understands that being a female mountain is an impossible proposition and that is too with wings. So she folds her wings and thinks of going to mars where she will produce only female mountains and in this way can completely inhabit that place with women. To quote from the text:

> . . . one of these days I shall fly to Mars. Once there, out of

> fragments of myself I shall generate other mountains and then will swoop and soar and range over the landscape and rest where we like without bothering anyone. And we'll rival the rings of Saturn in our beauty and freedom. Earth, I do not think, is ready for us. — Namjoshi 2006: 66

Interestingly despite pointing to the subjugation of women in heterosexual family — as in her *Jackass and the Lady* she argues that "Lady, since I have behaved badly you can/Whip me in public with my shirt off/or my pants down. Undoubtedly I shall/make a ludicrous figure. But were you aware?/Such barbarisms occur only in your homes" (Namjoshi 1980: 37) — her all-woman space is also not egalitarian in structure as women form different sort of hierarchy due to the class division even among themselves. In *Maya Diip* where notwithstanding an all-women space the hierarchy is based on motherhood and they are divided as grade "A" mothers (official mothers), grade "B" (biological mothers) and grade "C" (caretakers of children) mothers. This hegemonic structure of motherhood is directly proportional to the power operations at the island. Also the ambivalent cruelty to men in terms of reducing them to reproduction machines bears a close semblance with the state of women in heterosexual society but the non-egalitarian structure of the lesbian-island is also revealed when Asha the eldest daughter of the Matriarch opposes this cruelty and she is exiled from the kingdom. Thus at one level the myth of the lesbian utopia has been burst by her, but at the other the detailed and gory description of using pretty males for extracting semen and after that reducing boys to foam put question marks on the catholicity of the temper of the author. To quote the writer:

> Boys aren't the norm on Maya Diip. The Boys fight among themselves. The mothers of Maya let them. Eventually there is nothing left to fight, only the waves. So they fight the waves, turn into foam, so to speak. . . .
>
> — Namjoshi 1989: 160-61

This is in continuation to her belief that it is not always man who perpetuates patriarchy and it is the patriarchal mindset (that can be possessed by both man and woman) that needs to be rejected, for instance, in "And Then What Happened" she challenges the idea of reducing a man to a money-churning machine. It is an ingenious overturning of the story of Cinderella. After marriage the Prince accuses Cinderella of marrying him for money to which she retorts back by saying that he has married her for beauty. The Prince replies,

> "But your looks will fade, whereas my money will last. Not a fair bargain." "No," said Cinderella and simply walked out.
> — Namjoshi 1981: 112

Indeed Suniti objects to the monolithic notion of placing man always as a victimizer and unveils the fact that both man and woman can be victims of patriarchal subjugation depending upon the situation at the given moment. It endorses her belief that lesbianism is also not an ultimate panacea for heterosexual oppression because a different mode of power-operations works even in homosocial spaces as is evident in *Maya Diip*. Indeed her approach to the eclectic nature of sexuality and power-mechanisms is not lopsided.

Also *Maya Diip* raises two pertinent questions regarding lesbian motherhood and citizenship claim of lesbians through alternative family structure which are also the primary concerns in her "Snapshots of Caliban" and *Sycorax*. Caliban, the displaced native in both "Snapshots of Caliban" and Sycorax is a lesbian who has been turned into a racial and sexual minority by the colonizer (quite similar to Suniti's own position). And in *Sycorax*, interestingly, Sycorax is not dead (unlike in *The Tempest*) but returns back to claim her right on the land, and as a mother of a lesbian unwittingly she forms an alternative family structure, though by inversion — because she is a mother of a lesbian and not a lesbian who is a mother — and therefore it requires a nuanced understanding of the issue.

Sycorax returns to her lost native land and raises issues concerning motherhood and the consequent citizenship rights on the land. Critics such as Katrak H. Ketu in "Indian Nationalism, Gandhian 'Satyagraha', and Representations of Female Sexuality" talks about how the nationalist discourse projects the ideal Indian woman as a heterosexual monogamous mother as opposed to white woman and consequently her right on a land as a legitimate citizen is primarily by virtue of producing the future citizens, and in this way for women citizenship and motherhood are closely linked, specially in Indian context. No wonder the right to citizenship is always fraught with duty and hence brings about a certain sort of compromise. Apropos of this David Bell and Jon Binnie argue:

> . . . the twinning of rights with responsibilities in the logic of citizenship is another way of expressing compromise — *we will grant you certain rights if (and only if) you match these by taking on certain responsibilities.* Every entitlement is freighted with a duty. In our reading of sexual politics, rights claims articulated through appeals to citizenship carry the burden of compromise in particular way: this demands the circumscription of "acceptable" modes of being a sexual citizen.
>
> — 2000: 3

Family being the smallest unit of society is the most conspicuous site for claiming citizenship rights and the procreative sex inherent in the heterosexual family structure corroborates that, and in this fashion motherhood becomes a key to a woman's right on nation. In this manner the reversal of the paradigm — by rewriting the female body in such a manner that the alternative family structure becomes a possibility in terms of having a lesbian daughter in the form of Caliban — and the return of Sycorax to claim her native land lend a unique distinction to Namjoshi's poetry and lay bare a complex web of signification. The originally dead Sycorax resurrects and comes back, and she has "blue eyes" which has an ambivalent connection with pregnancy as Suniti states in her introduction to *Sycorax: New Fables and Poems*:

> . . . as for Sycorax not only did I resurrect her, but I also gave her blue eyes, when all the scholars tell us that the epithet "blue eyed" has very little to do with the colour of the eyes and much more to do with being pregnant.
>
> — Namjoshi 2006: xii

Significantly the juxtaposing of motherhood and lesbianism works as a primary signifier in the process of reclamation of the lost land by Sycorax and although it cuts across various other axes of differences as well but by and large becomes one of the most significant domains within which lesbian identity is constructed and evaluated.

Interestingly in a quite intriguing fashion Sycorax contemplates:

> Blue was always my colour, my blue eyes were my one claim to fame. But as I've walked through the world what I've seen around me is red and green. Even on this island, which is deserted, there is red and green. But it is muted. I can ignore it. — Ibid.: 8

She, with her unique family structure and consequently distinct world-view, challenges the heterosexual ordering of the world and comes back again to assert her right on the land as a mother who has given birth to a queer daughter and she seems to familiarize this so-called "queer family pattern". Sycorax inscribes her understanding as a female-colonial subject through and onto her relationships with Caliban and the land occupied by Prospero. At the very outset the blue-eyed Sycorax proclaims:

> . . . as I'm still here/I'm able to say clearly that when Prospero/said he took over an uninhabited island/save for Caliban and the enslaved/Ariel, he lied./I LIVED ON THAT ISLAND/it was my property (at least as much as it was anybody else's)./He drove me away, made himself king, set up/his props and bided his time/Now that they've

> gone/I may return, and ask myself, not who/they were, but who I was and what I mourn. —Ibid.: 1

Thus procuring citizenship rights despite having a lesbian daughter who has a non-procreative identity (due to lesbian mating) radicalizes the viewing of alternative sexualities through the lens of citizenship or vice versa. After Sycorax lesbian Caliban is going to be the next heir and in this mode of operation Suniti achieves what Lissa Duggan calls, "queering the state". Family is an important component for claiming citizenship right as Bell and Binnie in *The Sexual Citizen*:

> In current sexual rights claims, the struggle to define "families we choose" bears the mark of this privatization impulse, as the retreat into a family — space is a necessary strategy for claiming citizen status — sometimes that closes down ways of living and loving that don't accord with the model of family no matter how it is expanded. — 2000: 5

Hence producing an alternative family structure to have equal citizenship right on the land is a radical move towards claiming public and cultural sites in new imaginative ways. Suniti Namjoshi eloquently asks about the all female ancestry when she questions in *From the Bedside Book of Nightmares*:

> We loved those kindly gentlemen, I mean
> our own father, and your daughter's father
> But in our long ancestry,
> where are the women. — 1984: 13

Further the eclectic mapping of queer spaces in terms of Suniti's own lesbian diasporic identity — because she is a "sexual other" in her own country and "racial other" in the West — finds a complex manifestation in terms of overlapping of post-colonial and lesbian feminist readings of *Sycorax*: *New Fables and Poems* and "Snapshots of Caliban". In *Flesh and Paper* she categorically states:

> For us, love is not the same; sex is not the same; /parenting

> is not the same; work is not the same; /safety is not the same; respect is not the same;/trust is not the same. Only death might, perhaps, be the same. — Namjoshi 1986: 3

This reciprocal double bind of space and sexual identity is visible when the lesbian Caliban writes her own journal and tries to document the native history of land and her lesbian identity through her own perspective and is appreciated only till the time she endorses the colonizer's idea of land and does not reassert her right on the land by proclaiming her love for Miranda. Although the journal of Miranda and writings of Prospero are also mentioned in the poem but they appear to be used as tool to highlight the plight of Caliban by contrast.

In fact, both the notions of land and love have to be corroborated with the dominant discourse of patriarchy to be accepted and it has been demonstrated ingeniously through the metonymic figure of Caliban. The following is the passage from the Caliban's journal:

> These barriers are nice, those are not nice. This water is fresh. That water is salt. I learnt. I learnt all day by myself, and I told it to them. They were so pleased. But one day when I said to myself, "Miranda is nice," and told it to her she didn't like it. She told it to him. I was whipped afterwards. — Namjoshi 1984: 57

At times it is the heterosexuality of the space (as in case of Suniti's lesbian identity in India) and sometimes it is the whiteness of the space (Suniti's racial othering in the West) that perpetuate the marginalization of sexual and spatial diasporas. Quoting from Heidi Mirza and Creet, Rani Kawale in "A Kiss Is Just A Kiss. . . Or Is It? South Asian Lesbian and Bisexual Women and the Construction of Space" writes about this kind of sexual and spatial displacement:

> . . . whiteness is a powerful place that makes invisible, or re-appropriates things, people and places it does not want to

> see or hear, and then through misnaming, renaming or not naming at all, invents the truth — what we are told is "normal", neutral, universal, simply because the way it is. This applies to public places for lesbians, gay men and bisexuals too. A group or commercial venue does not need to specify that "white" people are welcome: this is assumed, because the term "lesbian" is racialized and usually refers to "white" lesbians. Hence lesbians and bisexual women's places that are not overtly racially assigned tend to have little room for "black" women to be "black" in them.
>
> — Kawale 2003: 183

She further elaborates the technique through which only white bodies are understood as the "somatic authentic lesbian norm". These techniques involve considering them primarily as heterosexuals or bisexuals rather than lesbians and consequently seen as inferior and exoticized "sex subjects". No wonder the white woman is considered more lesbian in queer spaces as compared to the South Asian woman.

Obviously first of all presenting Caliban as a female (instead of male) and then investing her, instead of Miranda, with lesbian identity are reversals of dominant culture in all possible ways. It presents an interesting post-colonial site for queer negotiation. The reversal of heterosexual love through the depiction of lesbian Caliban's infatuation for Miranda makes the heteropatriarchal boundaries porous at one level but at the other the aversion of Miranda for Caliban perpetuates the notion of lesbophobic anxiety and the intentions of the poet appear somewhat opaque in this fashion. But probably this contradictory double bind emanates primarily from the fact that Caliban has been used traditionally as a stoic symbol of "other" in multiple perspectives and this polyvalence creates a complex web of signification as has been suggested by George Lamming:

> Caliban is the excluded, that which is eternally below possibility. . . . He is seen as an occasion, a state of existence

> which can be appropriated and exploited to the purposes of another's own development. — Lamming 1984: 107

The native lesbian who has been displaced by her own land and has a living mother (thus has an alternative family) clearly reveals the clever juxtaposing of lesbian rights on the land through familial structure. In fact, just like Caliban, Miranda also writes poetry and exhibits her ambivalent homophobic anxieties through her hate poem on Caliban, the concluding line of which shows her subtle attraction towards Caliban and a reflection of lesbian continuum that transcends the racial boundaries. Importantly, when Caliban falls sick Miranda gets worried but she is surprised at her own concern for Caliban:

> Caliban is ill. I can't help wondering if she is going to die. I do not want her to die. I am surprised. This thought surprises me. — Namjoshi 1984: 61

Caliban's journal in which she records incidents from post-colonial queer perspective is an attempt to record lesbian history vis-à-vis land. She gives a poignant account of her sexual diasporic existence through the detailed descriptions of the modes of subjugation which result in the erasure of her identity. She has been deliberately kept out of intellectual endeavours such as game of chess which becomes a symbolic site for heterosexual privileges:

> They are playing chess I could learn too, I am not stupid. But they say it's a game intended for two. They have left me out. — Ibid.: 57

Similarly the red lining of dissident sexuality by the straight world is explicit when Caliban states that the physical labour done by Caliban is unnoticed but when Ferdinand picks up the log, Miranda feels miserable. Thus banishment and partiality meted out to queer people in contemporary work culture is apparent even in Caliban's island.

This anthropomorphic lesbian identity of Caliban is indeed

an important marker in decentering the notion of idealized-authentic citizen subject. Hoshang Merchant adds another dimension to the whole argument when he sees this effort of assigning lesbian identity to native Caliban as a double bonanza, for it not only negates the assumption that homosexuality is a Western import and questions the native perception of homosexuality — because in the whole discourse instead of the white Miranda it is the native Caliban who is queer and fights for the right of the native land — but also in a way tries to nativise the predominantly queer culture. To quote his words:

> While the hegemony of Europe or America is based on a subject's class, gender and ethnicity, in India it is a person's caste, gender, sexual preference, social and political affiliation and geographical location, which in many ways Namjoshi reminds us of. Identifying the diasporic lesbian self with the motherland then not only puts forward questions related to "indianising" queer culture and community, it also upsets "national" perception of homosexuality . . . it is in this sense Namjoshi, from the diaspora, is Indianising queer community.
>
> — Merchant 2009: 229

In fact, in "Cyclone in Pakistan" she connects the question of queer citizenship with other fluid identities when she proclaims that nations are emerging in all possible shades of black, brown, white, green, yellow, purple and blue, and compares them with the spinning confetti of carnival day. Undoubtedly, the assertion of the right of multiple fluid identities on the land has been her preoccupation since early days and the issue pertaining to queer citizenship has come under the ambit of this larger umbrella.

This recognition of the sexual and racial other indeed is a progressive move by Namjoshi but creating an isolated island in the form of Maya Diip is slightly ambivalent from the perspective of the citizenship rights. As one can notice that it indeed is a way of having a nation of one's own and of proclamation of lesbians as authentic citizens but it also clearly reveals that hetero and homo assumptions cannot coexist and in order to have a space of their own, the lesbians need to be banished to some exclusive remote island of their own. Although it is certainly opening up the issue of rights of lesbians over nation but it does not show the necessary displacement of heteronormativity within heterosexual structure to negotiate a queer space. In this regard Roshanabadi's "Vande Mataram" adds an interesting dimension because she uses the cult of patriotic song to reinvent a nation which is an all woman space. Quoting Sridevi K. Nair in chapter 1, I have affirmed that Roshanabadi tries to challenge the masculine cultural patriotism. She rewrites the "whole notion" of Mother India by using the same tool of subjugation and through the ingenious inversion of "Vande Mataram!" places woman's desire for another woman (irrespective of heterosexual mother image) at the centre of it. Thus she inscribes lesbianism at the very centre of the nation. In this poem she uses the trope of homoerotic desire to celebrate the independence of "the motherland" and reaffirms that lesbians are equal citizen subjects (because patriotism is seen as an obvious marker to claim the right on the land) by remoulding masculine desire for nation and woman. Interestingly in somewhat oblique fashion Caliban also expresses desire to occupy the island with people of her own choice but do these people share her same-sex proclivities or not is unclear? To quote from the text:

> Soon very soon. I shall people this island (with nice people).
>
> — Namjoshi 1984: 58

However, the reworking of myth and overturning of classic colonial patriarchal text, *The Tempest*, create a unique space for fantasy where tales of phallocentricism can be deconstructed. As Mary Daly in *Gyn/Ecology* asserts that "patriarchy perpetuates its deception through myths" (1978: 44), so the reworking and re-imagining of myths from the queer and feminist perspectives are not always efforts to camouflage homoeroticism through symbolic attire but are meant to rectify the value systems imposed by the compulsive heterosexuality. Adrienne Rich in her essay, "When We Dead Awaken: Writing as Revision", writes:

> Re-vision — the act of looking back, of seeing with fresh eyes, of entering an old text from a new critical direction — is for us more than a chapter in cultural history: it is an act of survival.
> — 1975: 90

Obviously this revisionist myth-telling should not be understood only in terms of escapist route but should be viewed as an attempt to re-order and re-imagine identities from queer perspective and as an effort to catalogue lesbian history through recreating a past — in which their presence has been systematically erased by the dominant heterosexual culture. In this way homosexual women record their existence through the inversion of age-old heteropatriarchal tales and infusing queer characters in them. C. Vijayasree in *The Artful Transgressor* asserts that in lesbian myth-making the project gains an additional edge of urgency since it is an important aspect of their attempt to create a lesbian identity and culture. It is interesting to recall here what one of the characters in Noretta Koertge's *Valley of the Amazon* (1984), Helen, says of the power of myths:

> 'Don't ever doubt the power of myths . . . I mean women's myth, not the bullshit stories we grew up with. We have to build a feminist mythology and recover woman's herstory'.
> — Koertge 1984: 75

Interestingly the "Beauty and the Beast" and "I See You What You Are" showcase the seemingly irreverent play with traditional tales to break the conditioned mindset. Reversing the paradigm she demonstrates how female beast loves beauty and tries to forge a lesbian bond but she has been jeered at. Likewise in re-conceptualization of the stock stories like *The Twelfth Night*, cross-dresser Viola and Olivia are placed within the space of homoerotic possibilities. Regarding the technique employed for this reversal, C. Vijayasree writes:

> Namjoshi retells these tales with careful but slight slippages, and gives them a subtly subversive twist which practically makes them stand on head, and lays open an unreasonably biased social order contained within them. — 2001: 78

Apart from overturning and revisionist myth making (to quote C. Vijayasree's term), the other interesting method used by Namjoshi to counter the heterosexual policing of homoerotic desire is the novel use of fables. The all-pervasive animal imagery is used deftly to blur the boundaries of gender and sexuality because when one sees an animal there sex is not evident, whereas in human beings the gender markers are quite explicit and consequently also the sexual choices. In "A Quiet Life" she writes:

> "I don't want to be a woman." "Do you want to be a man?" "No." "What do you want?" "I want to hide, to live in the bushes, to be a rabbit or a squirrel or a mythical animal. . . ." When there is nobody about, be what I am; and when people are present, disguise myself. "As what?" "As a fake woman."
> — Namjoshi 1981: 51

According to Ruth Vanita, Namjoshi calls it a fake woman for the disguises of dress, hairstyle and gender role camouflage the sameness of species and this produces a fake woman. In fact, in Suniti's *Conversation of the Cow*, the cow not only turns lesbian but magically changes gender and race by being white man Baddy intermittently and disrupts the fixities of sexual and gender roles. In "Her Form In Clear Water" Namjoshi topples the tale of fall of eve who prefers to mate with the snake rather than being in the bondage of Adam and creates a liminal space to produce counter discourse for negation of the taken for granted assumption of the heterosexual matrix. To quote from the text:

> Her form in clear water made him/raise his head/His length slid about her limbs. Eve/in her turn/encircled the snake, pressing her body/to him/Curious coupling, brown snake and Eve,/caught in a twist/of the blind green coil being Adam/and evil and Eve. — Namjoshi 1980: 13

In the same collection animal trope is used for exploring the themes like coercive nature of heterosexuality such as in "The Arbitrary Order" where the poet vehemently cries: "the arbitrary order: ducks/quenching in the pond/drakes mounting them" (p. 34). Likewise Namjoshi turns the mythical characters upside down and then juxtaposes them with animal imagery to circumvent heterosexual canonicity. In "Homage to Circe", Circe turns her lovers into animals and through a symbolic riddle the subtle undertones of dissident desire is being negotiated. The speaker in the following passage wants to get close to Circe and therefore pleads:

> I am all animals to you?
> I could sit cat-like and gaze/sisterly
> I am all animals to you
> could offer myself
> on a wide lily-pad. — Ibid.: 45

Though Namjoshi has used both the Western and Indian myth with equal potency to lay bear the multiple subversive patterns of homosexuality, the intermingling of animal and human in order to create a ceaseless continuum of pansexuality is a very Indian expression (as one can notice that in mythological tales and religious texts, there are constant transformations of humans into animals or vice versa; at times as a result of curse or due to some situational need) and helps in Indianizing the queer culture. In an invigorating interview given to C. Vijayasree, Namjoshi contemplates:

> . . . but rather to the use I made of the Hindu notion that there was not a clear cut division between human beings and animals in order to deal with my alienation from the male centered Western humanist tradition. This is too polysyllabic. I think all I meant was that if to be centrally human meant that one had to be an Anglo Saxon heterosexual male, then I personally would rather identify with the birds and the beasts. — Vijayasree 2001: 177

Namjoshi in *Because of India* stresses the point that "beast" for her does not mean "bestial" in the popular Western sense because "Hinduism" is after all saturated with pantheism "and the popular notion of reincarnation attributes a soul to everyone. This may sound odd to Western ears, but for me, it was as familiar as it was unconscious" (1989: 28).

The whole idea of Indian intervention in the development of queer theory takes a sharp turn when we scrutinize this ceaseless interspecies transformations in the light of nullifying sexual and gender hegemony. It ultimately helps in the formation of a very specific Indian queer literary technique. Importing a Western tool to give voice to subaltern sexualities is a common practice among many queer litterateurs, specially diasporic writers. But it has been strongly criticized by queer critics and activists on account of two concerns. First, because gay subculture is perceived as a Western import, which is popular only in upper-class English-speaking people and thus the Western queer literary theory framework used by LGBTQIA writers and critics (specially diasporic lesbian writers) further perpetuates the homophobic myth that tends to divorce Indianness from the queer aesthetics. Second, from the post-colonial perspective importing Western tool in the absence of exclusive Indian queer theory is indeed a backlash at the overall post-colonial literary agenda of Indian academia. In fact, these racialized and class-oriented aspects of the language of lesbians have been unveiled by KISS and KALI (two South Asian lesbian organization in England). Quoting

Puwar, Rani Kawale explains how speaking "legitimate" English especially in a profession is a way of erasing "ethnic differences" but the so-called impurities of dialects, accent and structure of native language, to some extent, help in locating an individual's native place within a larger space. It is precisely for this reason that

> the spoken English at KISS is often broken or with a South Asian accent — whether naturally or in fun. Some words, concepts and meanings do not directly translate from South Asian languages into English either, and so some women use different languages to express themselves. This particular "illegitimate" form of English in a white space for lesbians and bisexual women would place South Asian women on the margins; but at Kiss, it contributes to the construction of the space as South Asian and locates the members certainly within that space. — Kawale 2003: 190

This deliberate fractured use of language to create the much needed gap to assert native sexual identity is brilliantly used in lesbian Caliban's journal where she records her romantic proclivities in broken English and is able to create a sense of her geographical sexual identity. Thus Suniti's grotesque inversions of fables and use of fractured language (though very rarely) in her lesbian poetry is a strategic contribution to the development of the exclusive Indian queer theory. Miranda and Prospero's journals and their language as opposed to Caliban's journal make the issue of identity and language more conspicuous because Miranda's writing is a specimen of already established and respected identity of heterosexual white woman and hence the codes of language are not only existing but also are well defined. As opposed to this, Caliban's broken English and slippages are marks of deliberate erasure of native lesbian who has no language and therefore she struggles for words and reinvents her own language. It clearly brings forth the idea of developing an exclusive lesbian language specially for the South Asian women who are still the missing dykes in the entire discourse of queer literary activism. Suniti's Caliban indeed tries to invent lesbian-ecriture. This mutually reciprocal relationship of language and identity has been wonderfully elaborated by Judith Butler:

> We do things with language, produce effects with language, and we do things to language, but language is also the thing that we do. Language is a name for our doing: both "what" we do . . . and that which we affect, the act and its consequences. — 1990: 8

In the same vein it is interesting to note that Ruth Vanita suggests etymologically word *rekhta* from which the word *rekhti* is derived literally means "mixing or pouring different things into a mould to create a new compound" (2012: 28). Since language is fashioned only to give expression to accepted form of love, there is a complete lack of linguistic codes for lesbian-language and in the process of frantic search for exclusive lesbian vocabulary, there is a continuous linguistic hybridization and formation of novel linguistic structures. And this reinventing of queer language is visible even in nineteenth-century *rekhti* poetry. In fact, due to the all-pervasive dynamics of homoerotic desire across respectable *grihastha* (domesticated) woman and courtesans — both speak quite a different language from each other — there is a curious mixing of linguistic patterns which forms a unique queer language. Ruth Vanita by quoting Rangin succinctly charts out this aspect of *rekthi*:

> I do not restrict this to prostitutes (*kasbi*) or to domestic (*gharelu*) women/I am interested here only in women's speech (*zanani boli*). — 2012: 28

In fact, the blurring of this binary opposition between public and domesticated women and the negation of falsely associating dissident desire only with courtesans (this notion perpetuates monolithic linguistic structure without any distinctive feature) find an interesting manifestation in the language of *khangis*. *Khangis* were married women who were involved in sex-work (both with men and women) also and therefore their lesbian experience and its articulation had a distinct hybrid flavour. Ruth writes how Rangin used to pay special attention to the speech of *khangi*s to learn language for penning down women's specific sexual experiences that fall outside the boundary of patriarchal norm in every sense of the word. To quote Ruth:

> . . . he used to pay attention to the speech of every member of the group. Having spent some time thus, I acquire knowledge (*ilm*) of many of their idioms and sayings. . . . This fourth (*rekhti*) collection of poetry is in their language (*zuban*). — Ibid.: 28

In this light the imperfect language of Caliban's journal is not only a reflection of lack of lesbian vocabulary but also an example of formation of new queer language through the hybridity created by mixing of lesbian native language and the language learnt through the white, heterosexual colonizers.

In fact, like Suniti the use of animal trope to redefine desire is used by many writers as has been articulated by Ruth Vanita in her brilliant essay, "I'm an Excellent Animal". She reveals how animal imagery is being used to forge possibilities of alternative sexualities through texts like *Manu-Smriti*, the poems of Bahinabai and Rukun Advani's *Beethoven Among the Cows*. These symbolic riddles on the one hand open up loads of fluid space where pansexuality can be prescribed, but on the other they seem to camouflage the lesbian identity through suggestive ways of narration and unusual symbols. In fact, in her interview to C. Vijayasree she seems to admit that it is an "unhappy" choice because it accepts marginalization. She further states:

> A "happier" choice, which I made later, was to claim center stage for the dispossessed and to challenge the traditional assumptions. — Vijayasree 2001: 177

Little wonder in "Well, then let slip the masks" she blatantly pronounces lesbian eroticism:

> The curve of your breast is like the curve/of a wave: look, held, caught, each instant/caught, the wave tipping over and we in our bower/the two of us sheltered, my hands on your thighs,/your body, your back, my mouth on your mouth/and in the hollows of your jaws and your head/ nuzzling my breasts. — Namjoshi 1986: 7-13

She goes to the extent of asking her same sex lover: "will you let my tongue caress you? Will you lie in my arms? Will you rest" (ibid.: 14-18)? The unabashed exploration of lesbian longings may have emerged out more prominently in later poetry when she has been able to mitigate internalized homophobia more potently, but even her early poetry bears the mark of blatant exposition of subaltern sexualities bereft of any symbolic interpretation. Quite obviously in *From the Bedside Book of Nightmares* the usual accusation regarding the plausibility of lesbian's sex-encounters in the absence of penetrative sex (which is a possibility even in gay sex) is ironically turned upside down when she asks: "I wonder what those others/ — those lovers of men — do" (p. 34)? This is a fitting answer to the oft asked homophobic question as what the lesbians can do in bed.

Moreover a new twist to the entire discourse is being given by Ruth Vanita and which has been identified by Shohini Ghosh in her essay,"Bombay Cinema's Queer Vision" as "analogical identification". Quoting Ruth, Shohini argues that the idea of analogical identification has been first used by Ruth in her essay on Virginia Woolf's *Flush* about Brett Browning's pet dog whose despair emanates from its inability to fulfil Elizabeth's needs. Because of biological compulsion it is already an outsider in the domain of intimacies and this inter-species difference is effectively used by the writers in terms of social gap and sexual and gender hierarchies. In yet another essay,

"I'm an Excellent Animal" Ruth quoting Wittig affirms that the negation to remain heterosexual is being associated with the refusal to become a man or woman wittingly or unwittingly and "it is likely that every culture has fashioned spaces for such refusal; every written literature certainly has. The apparently uncrossable cultural gulf between human and non-human animals often functions as a metaphor for the equally uncrossable, although socially created, sexual gulf between human members of the same gender" (*Gandhi's Tiger and Sita's Smile,* Ruth Vanita 2005: 291). In this respect reviewing Suniti's method of incessant use of animals reveals that it is certainly not an "unhappy choice" as she calls it. It unwittingly unveils the multiple and interlinked complex systems of oppression which cannot be interpreted only as an escapist strategy of making homoeroticism palatable to a largely straight readers. Raj Rao twists the tale of the argument further by elaborating on Dollimore's notion of need of elusive "other" as a prerequisite for any romantic alliances. And since unlike cross-gender relationships the same-sex lovers have same gender (as per the stringent and limited notion of gender), the need of the other for sexual intimacies is compensated by reinventing the categories of otherness through "the dream of age, youth, equipment, animalism and so on" (Chanana 2012: 155). Thus the use of animal imagery cannot be interpreted as a monolithic regressive tool for hiding dissident sexuality only, rather it has to be understood in terms of dismantling closed, stable and unitary sexual identity. Indubitably the unabashed re-sexualization of transgressive desire in *Flesh and Paper* has its own advantages but revisiting myths and fables for the exploration of the lesbian desire also adds to the agenda of providing unique cultural spaces, which further contribute to the formation of the exclusive "queer aesthetics" (to quote Raj Rao's term).

The world of fantasy is supposedly believed to divorce us

from the hard-core realities of working-class underprivileged lesbians as has been catalogued by the contemporary lesbian poet, Maya Sharma's hard-hitting and below one's belt way of depicting the plights of working-class lesbians. As opposed to the use of symbols, myth and fables of Suniti, Maya Sharma's engagement with the lesbian world is expressed through concrete hard-hitting realistic style of narration. This style mostly emerges from her serious concern for the working-class lesbians, a sub-group which has been largely ignored in the lesbian discourse. In fact, her lesbian anthology *Loving Women* is a collection of tales told by exclusively working-class women. It deconstructs the notion that same-sex desire is whimsical, sexual experimentation of over-sexed and West-oriented rich women. She in her poem, "For You" highlights this aspect:

> How can I bear
> the weight of you
> so near to me?
> I, who am so used
> to carrying bricks,
> stones, mud.
> I turn my face,
> push your hand away
> Even then, you sit so near?
> Is the shelter you offer
> the truth or a dream?
> tell me. — Sharma 2006: 403

However, a close examination of lesbian Caliban's unpaid labour puts her into the category of working-class lesbian and is counter-productive of the conception that the world of fantasy and fables cannot portray the various marginalized identities within the oppressed groups. Therefore the use of concrete and hard-hitting language with the underplay of imagery is not the only means of articulating every aspect of the protean nature of desire.

Hence viewing Namjoshi's fantasy-laden lesbian world of poetry as a product of schizophrenic anxiety or a tool to perpetuate one step forward and two steps backward sort of movement, will be a serious misreading of her work. Raj Rao in his exclusive interview, given to me for the special number of *Indian Literature* on same-sex desire, talks about evolving a distinct "queer aesthetic" which should focus on "hybridization and corruption" of language by deliberately shunning the elegant English language in the line of "*dalit* literature" to shock the sensibility of the reader and thereby puncturing the very idea of "normalcy". This has been successfully adopted by the sensational use of the so-called crude language in Abha Dawesar's *Babyji* and Raj Rao's *The Boyfriend* and *Hostel Room 131*. On the contrary Namjoshi's deliberate hyper-elegance, constant lesbian fabulation, creation of fantastic lands where animals freely transform into multiple identities, fractured narration and employment of rich and evocative symbols also propound another extreme of queer aesthetics which equally helps in breaking all the conventions of heteronormative reality by evincing multiple possibilities through varied techniques and thereby celebrating queer inconsistencies. Suniti's incessant mixing of genres (poetry and prose) coupled with her photographic snapshots in "Snapshots of Caliban" give impetus to deliberately structured gaps which readers can fill according to their own subjective positions, and this helps the author in producing much needed plural interpretations. Thus by intentionally avoiding straightforward articulation of lesbian desires, specially in her early writings, she is not following an escapist route but is destabilizing the complex codes of stringent, monolithic, sensational and blunt sort of "queer aesthetics" which is certainly a potent tool to counter the heteronorm as a primary signifier, but this is not the only way of doing so. Through her distinct lesbian fabulation, Suniti presents an alternative way of achieving the much desired aim of queer aesthetics. In the light of the inherent celebration of plural sexual subjectivities that queer literature aims at, the employment of multiple polyvalent techniques is a necessity and Suniti accomplishes this brilliantly. Her own sense of liminal identity further contributes to the development of this unique, experimental lesbian style (which is a representation of authorial and ontological realities and an answer to the well-established literary writings of the custodians of patriarchy) in the absence of any accepted codes for queer articulation. She points out the spatial schisms that are equally applicable to fissures in lesbian literature, and both these require not only an urgent attention but also a novel method to fill them up. In this context she writes:

> I had thought once that I felt most at home in a plane in mid-air; but that isn't true. I belong to India and to the West. Both belong to me and both reject me. I have to make sense of what has been and what there is.
>
> — Vijayasree 2001: 181

Also I believe that her lesbian anxiety which bears a close semblance with her spatial dilemma prompts her to devise methods of overturning the myths so that the lesbian characters may inhabit the fantasy land. To conclude, we must take her work as an explication of new mode of queer aesthetics, and hence it will be erroneous to brand it as an escapist strategy.

4

The Polyvalent Power Structures in the Gay Writings of Contemporary Indian English Writers

With Special Reference to R. Raj Rao and Hoshang Merchant

Family Members
From England, America and Canada
Visit you at Bombay.
Some of them are sex tourists,
You their post-colonial pimp
Hungry for pounds and dollars

— R. Raj Rao, "Bomgay", *Yarana*, p. 100

ALTHOUGH THE collective character of the homosexual life tends to blunt the multidimensional plurality, pervasive in the gay subculture, but any inquiry into the dynamics of same-sex union should be sensitive to types of privileges and deprivation occurring on account of class, gender, race and sex. No wonder the already outcast gay identity is further complicated by the overlapping of issues of class, ethnicity, race, cast, gay rape, implementation of Section 377, epidemic of AIDS, marginalization of women in gay subculture, gay lingo and binary oppositions between *koti/panthi*, active/passive, M.S.M. (men having sex with men)/gay/bisexual/bi-curious (one of the identities that have social encounter with same-sex but do not consider themselves as a gay or vice versa).

In Foucauldian terms power elicits its own resistance and this shifting paradigm of the oppressor and the oppressed in this already marginalized gay identity makes it all the more a malleable force that operates at contradictory levels and consequently produces uneven polyvalent power structures. Apropos of this Joseph Bristow states:

> The very discourse that sought to produce a regulative order managed to empower those it sought to subjugate.
>
> — 2007: 178

The fluidity of the outcast gay culture challenges the already existing hegemonic structure and this eclectic dynamism is effectively portrayed in the contemporary gay writings of Raj Rao's *The Boyfriend, Six Inches,* "Moonlight Tandoori" and Hoshang Merchant's "The Slaves". Though the texts under discussion are of disparate nature yet the fact that makes them of equal valency is the depiction of margins within margins in gay subculture which illustrates the plurality of power operations and in a way unwittingly dismantles the already existing hegemonic patterns of the heteronormative society.

Raj Rao's *The Boyfriend* is a story of same-sex love between a middle-aged, middle-class educated brahmin Yudi with a young twenty something, working-class, illiterate, *dalit* boy, Miland. Hence whether the power structures are dismantled here or different sorts of hegemonic patterns are re-established is debatable, for on account of class, education and caste Yudi has a superiority but on the basis of youth Miland has an upper hand and he very successfully plays this card throughout the text. So the question whether the class trumps over sexuality or vice versa remains ambiguous because in the end Yudi has to pay directly for the sexual rendezvous with Miland and it becomes mutually beneficial for both of them. To quote from the text:

> In his place Miland had found a sugar-daddy! That was

> what gay men all over the world looked for anyway: Sugar daddies: So why should Yudi be surprised or sad?
>
> — Rao 2013: 113

Similarly on another occasion when they both have beer at a nearby café and Miland pretends to pay:

> Yudi told Miland not to be silly and put away his wallet. This was the first and last time such a thing would happen; henceforth it would be assumed that Yudi was the treasurer with an endless supply of easy money. — Ibid.: 80

Regarding the complex matrix of class and homosexuality and the effects of market forces on shaping the individual sexual orientation John D'Emilio argues in his classic essay, "Capitalism and Gay Identity" that the emergence of the queer identity is largely associated with the rise of capitalism because with the gradual rise of family as an institution that offered "emotional satisfaction and happiness" rather than an institution that provided goods, there is an undermining of the significance of family's "economic rationale" and this automatically gives impetus to the growing opportunities to sell one's labour outside the self-supporting family. It meant that the alternative sexual styles of living became available to many more people than before, especially in urban centres. Emilio affirms:

> The relationship between capitalism and the family is fundamentally contradictory. On the one hand, capitalism continually weakens the material foundation of family life, making it possible for the individuals to live outside the family, and for a lesbian and gay male identity to develop. On the other, it needs to push men and women into families, at least long enough to reproduce the next generation of workers. The elevation of the family to ideological pre-eminence guarantees that a capitalist society will reproduce not just children but heterosexism and homophobia.
>
> — 1992: 13

Inevitably the changing circumstances allow sexual minorities to emerge, but these situations also help in consolidating the pressure on the family to reproduce itself. So on the one hand it gives rise to the homosexual encounters, but on the other it gives impetus to internalized homophobia and consequently the availability of partners are reduced and gay men are compelled to transcend the boundaries of class and caste. Their being outcast make them align with other marginalized entities. Therefore the more down and out Miland was the more they would click.

> Outcastes, after all can only expect to be friends with outcastes.
> — Rao 2003: 75

No wonder the liaison between *dalit* Miland and Yudi has been depicted by the author as a panacea for annihilating the caste and class discrimination. On one occasion Miland asks Yudi to eat his *jootha*. He eats it and says,

> "Homos are no different from *bhangi*s. Both are untouchables. So why should I have a problem eating your *jootha*?" "But you are a brahmin, aren't you?" "No, I am a homosexual. Gay by caste. Gay by religion." . . . "What I am saying is that homosexuals have no caste or religion. They have only their homosexuality." "How can that be?" "That's how it is straight people are brahmins, gays shudras. So you see, both you and I are shudras. That's why we are best friends."
> — Ibid.: 82

Hence the differential treatment that they get at the hands of the society as a sexual minority makes them come together as a cohesive unit and consequently among them the differences on the basis of class and caste get mitigated. So the margins within the gays get dissolved at one level in this fashion and in a very complex manner their subservient identity works as a potent tool to dissolve the existing powerful hegemonic structures of class and caste. As Yudi asks to kiss Miland on his face,

> It was his way of demonstrating that he cared two fucks if Miland was a brahmin or a *bhangi*, whose ancestors cleaned the shit of others. — Ibid.: 74

Likewise in a play, *Do the Needful* by Mahesh Dattani, the Goda brahmin boy copulates with the shudra *mali* boy. On another occasion when Yudi is entertained by his cousin at Taj and Miland has to wait outside the hotel Yudi exclaims: "This was India after all and Miland was a working class *dalit*" (Rao 2003: 98). By quoting Dollimore, Raj Rao speculates that the queer sexuality reverses the idea of sameness and difference in terms of gender. Hence the need for the "other" (a primary requisite for attraction) is satiated in queer intimacies on the basis of the "otherness" in the terms age and class for unlike the heterosexual relationship, here the constant "other" on the basis of gender is altered and becomes "same". Unmistakably we notice that in "The Slaves", "Moonlight Tandoori" and *The Boyfriend* there is huge difference in the age and class of the partners. In fact, on one of the occasions Gauri questions Yudi as why he has such fascination for working class? Similarly one of the clients at A.K. Modelling Agencies tells Miland that working-class type turns him on. The romantic notion of the working-class "other" is heightened so much in Yudi's mind that he goes to the extent of writing a sexually surcharged poem on Chinchpokli:

> Lizards crawl over my religion,
> spiders infest my politics.
> I itch. I become horny.
> I booze. I want to get smashed.
> And I do.
> It comes easy at Chinchpokli,
> Where like a minor Hindu god, I am stoned
> By the misery of my worshippers and by my own
> Triumphant impotence. — Rao 2003: 162

In fact, when the "otherness" is not there on account of class and age, Yudi finds it in physically challenged men. He calls them unusual men. To quote from the text:

> Men who were physically disabled, for instance, turned him on. It could be any handicap: blindness, lameness, a hunchback; he was ready to give anything to sleep with them. — Ibid.: 30

Thus the dissolved hierarchy of class is not only on the basis of lack of availability of the partners due to the heteronormativity and their recognition of themselves as larger marginalized gay identity in which the distinctions of class, caste and age get blunted out, but also due to the significant and deep-rooted need for the "other" in the sexual relationships. Regarding the complex dynamics of class and caste in gay world the scene from *My Beautiful Laundrette* by British Pakistani screen writer Hanif Kureishi is specially significant, as depicted by Gayatri Gopinath in her book *Impossible Desires*. In it the white, working-class gay boy Johnny tries to get intimate with the upper-class, Pakistani-born Omar. Omar initially responds to his advances but suddenly snubs him for he is suddenly reminded of a boyhood scene of standing with his immigrant father and witnessing a march by whites to abhor the Asians and Johnny being a part of it. He tells Johnny that he has seen him in that march, at which Johnny first feels ashamed but then gradually goes to him and embraces Omar. Commenting on this scene Gayatri Gopinath pertinently remarks that

> the scene eloquently speaks to how the queer racialized body becomes a historical archive for both individuals and communities, one that is excavated through the very act of desiring the racial Other. For Omar, desiring Johnny is irrevocably intertwined with the legacies of British colonialism in South Asia. — 2007: 1

Hence despite their racial prejudices they come together. The coalition politics of assimilation of the already outcast gay world works in favour of breaking the existing established power structures in more ways than one. However, the whole "cleansing scene" where Yudi bathes Miland puts question marks on the catholicity of the temper of the writer, for he calls it "purification rites". Though it can be adduced to the poor upkeep and unhygienic and unpalatable appearance of the boy.

There is another dimension of the whole issue of class dynamics when viewed from the perspective of male prostitution, and then the utopian world of classless and casteless gay world seems to crumble. Miland when thrown out of the job goes to the extent of becoming a male prostitute for ageing rich elite gay men. There is a chilling description of the male brothel and the amount of exploitation that young poverty-ridden boys have to bear.

> Besides being gay or bisexual, all the clients were wealthy, with huge disposable incomes. The customer profile of the agency revealed that most of them were men in their fifties and sixties. About one half were married, while the others were bachelors. Ninety per cent of them were businessmen. They alone could hire boys at prices ranging from one thousand to ten thousand rupees at night, depending on the overall smartness and the dick size of the boy in question, of which the boy got to keep 25 per cent. — Rao 2003: 180

However, the idea of falsified notion of masculinity and the passive/active dichotomy follow the reverse module and make the whole issue more eclectic as opposed to the unilateral power structure of the ruler and the ruled. In the gay culture due to patriarchal notion of "masculinity" the passive partner is considered womanly and the active one can resort to his manly pride by virtue of being a penetrator rather than being penetrated. This is the reason why the writer while describing the logistics of gay prostitution states:

> On the whole, penetrators had to pay much more than penetrates. As the agency's C.E.O. had a penchant for hunks

> (rather than queens), he had to put up with the hostility of those who were made to perform "womanly" acts in bed. A survey showed that most of his boys didn't think they were abnormal or perverted as long as they were "active". They couldn't care less whether what they inserted their organs into was a man's backside or a woman's front side.
>
> — Ibid.: 180

As Manohar Shitole, one of the gay men interviewed by R. Raj Rao in *Whistling in the Dark,* asserts that masculinity is prevalent everywhere and there is a perennial insistence on being a "top only guy". This leads him to conclude that there are only few men who are genuinely gay because for a real homosexual this dichotomy should not be a part of his scheme of things. "To most guys being 'bottom guys' challenges their masculinity" (Rao 2009: 80). For a homosexual man in India specially of the working class, being a gay and that too of the passive variety is synonymous with being eunuch. Little wonder, as the reversal of power dynamics, Yudi (an upper-class educated brahmin) has been shown as a "passive" as opposed to Miland (*dalit*), who is an "active". Miland always feels superior at the thought that it is he who fucks (active) and hence he is less effeminate and more masculine and this lessens his internalized homophobia.

In the marriage scene also the privileges of being an active partner is seen when they both decide to delve into a "mock marriage" at Yudi's home:

> They lit a fire in the fucking room, and were about to go round it seven times, when a major dispute arose between them. Each wanted to be the engine as they encircled the fire. Each had strong case. Miland's was that he was "active"... Yudi's that he was a breadwinner. In the end, of course, Yudi capitulated.... He fished out a chiffon that his mother had once left behind, draped himself in it, and became the bride. — Rao 2003: 107

In fact, whenever Miland feels overpowered and subjugated

on account of Yudi's class and education, he consoles himself by believing that it is he who fucks rather than being fucked. To quote from the text:

> Milya continued to be in bad mood. He had been called an "illiterate" and a "slave" by a man who went down on his knees before him like a whore. — Ibid.: 127

This notion of being "passive" as effeminate and hence being condemnable has a deep-rooted cultural biases and conditioning emanating from slave tradition where slaves by and large were seen as passive sex objects to their masters. As Paul Veyne has suggested in his essay titled "Homosexuality in Ancient Rome" that in a slave owing society the master had a sexual dominance so the moral stands varied with the social status:

> To be "*impudicus*" (that is passive) is disgraceful for a free man wrote the leader Seneca but it is the slaves absolute obligations towards his master, and the freed man owes a moral duty of compliance. — 1985: 31

Paul Veyne further argues that utter scorn was heaped on the freeborn adult male if he was a homosexual of the passive variety *impudicus* or *diatithemenos*. Hence in ancient Rome the passive homosexual was not rejected on account of his homosexuality but due to his passivity, a very serious moral, or rather political infirmity. In India the relationship between Malik Kafur (the castrated passive gay) and his master Ala-ud-din Khalji is a classic example where Kafur, was forcefully castrated to become a passive gay and it was an accepted norm, the reference of which we find in John Keay's *India: A History*. Thus an egalitarian paradigm is established by reversing the pattern when Yudi, the provider becomes passive and this enables Miland to counter his homophobic hatred. In fact, whenever Yudi picks up strangers and takes them home, he gladly offers them the active role for his years of experience has taught him that as long as men are allowed to penetrate there was no fear of their returning afterwards to demand money or beat him up:

> Some even thought it beneath their dignity to accept cash from someone they had buggered. — Raj Rao, 2003: 12

Nevertheless Miland's indulgence in male prostitution dismantles this privileged superiority of active over passive. He suffers from severe anxiety and even being "active" is no solace:

> Yet Miland was pissed off with himself and with everyone around him. He hated his work, was "sick and tired" of it, as he frequently told himself, in English. No matter how many Esteems he rode in, his self-esteem was annihilated. He thought of himself as a *dhandhewala*, a whore, and in his scheme of things it was women who were whores, not men. In other words, he was doing womanly work, like sewing and cooking, not manly work as his brothers did. So what if the men he served spoke in passive voice and gave him a chance to speak in the active? It didn't take away from the fact that he was selling his body. — Raj Rao 2003: 201

The eclectic nature of passive/active dichotomy in Hoshang Merchant's "The Slaves" takes a unique tangent when Mazhar, who usually fucks (an active) his menial servants and prostitutes because it gives boost to his perception of masculinity and makes him less effeminate, becomes passive for the upper-class narrator, primarily due to his economic condition. In fact, in order to combat the inherent homophobia that he suffers due to his passivity, he employs various methods. One day he brings a famished Christian girl to assert his masculinity:

> One night Mazhar bought a Christian girl to my home. . . . The girl dressed. A cross glistened on her impossibly lean frame. She probably needed food. Mazhar paid her fifty rupees. He felt like a man. She looked like a poor girl. I felt bad for her. — Merchant 1999: 49-50

Mazhar was fatherless and was used and exploited by his maternal uncle and all male boarders started using Mazhar.

> When he grew up, he started using the servant girls. He felt like a master. They were his sex slaves. — Ibid.: 50

This is his way to counter his rage against his own notion of homophobic effeminacy. In fact, the misconception of active masculine man is so complicated in his mind that it becomes claustrophobic for him to be a passive partner to the narrator but he could not disrupt the internalized hierarchy of class superiority of the narrator though there is no exchange of money for sexual favours in their relationship.

Once he brings a boy home and becomes an active partner and insists that the narrator should watch it so that he could assert his active masculinity, though in implicit form, before the narrator:

> He came inside the boy. Once. Twice. Thrice. Then the boy begged mercy to let him go. I gave the boy ten rupees out of pity. The boy asked Mazhar too for an equal amount . "Don't teach him bad habits," Mazhar admonished me. — Ibid.: 51

Now this whole incident gives Mazhar a way to get out of his crippled sense of helplessness at being passive before the socially superior narrator. Mazhar is perennially puzzled by the fact that he penetrates prostitutes and servants and he lets the narrator penetrate him. He asks: "It's I who fucks everyone why is it that I let you fuck me?" (ibid.) After one sexual encounter with the author Mazhar leaves a ten rupees note on the grass. This is his way to get even with the narrator, and this clearly lays bare the complex polyvalent overlapping of class and gay subculture that constantly regulates each other and creates a perennial flux.

Similarly in Raj Rao's "Moonlight Tandoori", the story revolves around the intimacy between a university graduate living in a rundown restaurant and its cook who pays heed to narrator's advances due to his lure for good T-Shirts, and other materialistic benefits. Just like Mazhar in "The Slaves" the cook has also been exploited sexually by his uncle because of his economically inferior position:

> Then confiding in me he'd tell me how Ahmed, his uncle and employer, owner of Moonlight Tandoori, exploited him, and I would feel helplessly sorry and my feelings would show. — Raj Rao 1999: 78

This sort of oppressive sexual slavery finds its manifestation in the form of power assertion over prostitutes whom he can buy out in the same way as his uncle and others economically rich would do to him. So the sexual coercion he suffers, on account of poverty-ridden life, gets translated into the subjugation of economically weak fairer sex or servants and thus the apparent utopia of classless and casteless same-sex union has its own fishers. And one such fisher is when many straight men act as gay and trick their partners for money and then blackmail them. This constantly puts doubt in the minds of their gay partners which over all weakens the cause of gay activism. On one such occasions Yudi contemplates:

> Perhaps the boy wasn't innocent after all, and harboured similar ideas of trying to track him down — the difference in age and income between the boy and himself made him a fit candidate for the post. — Rao 2003: 22

In fact in a very humorous and comic way Raj Rao's play, *Six Inches*, explores how class trumps over sexuality and many times straight men pose as gays to gain benefits from the sugar daddies. In this play Rashid and Ashok are in same-sex union. Ashok enjoys living in Rashid's well-furnished home and this fact emerges time and again in their conversation:

> Ashok: "You think I'm your slave."
>
> Rashid: "No"
>
> Ashok: "You keep me in your flat, allow me to drive your

> car, so you can control my will."
>
> Rashid: "No. No." — Raj Rao 1999: 134

Rashid on his part accuses Ashok of being straight and faking as a gay, so that he can enjoy benefits provided by Rashid. He calls Ashok a liar and states:

> Liar. Voyeur. I know what you were up to in my flat when I was away in US. You're not even queer. You pose as one because it's trendy. — Ibid.: 136-37

But the tables are turned when Rashid has got a photographic assignment through the contacts of Ashok in which he has to click few Indian men in action without being overtly pornographic for a very famous men's magazine, "Six Inches". Now like Ashok (whom he accuses of being straight and faking as gay for materialistic comforts) he too manipulates the straight men busy in innocent day-to-day activities to appear as being indulgent in same-sex activities through his cleverly clicked photographs. This is highly symbolic of the manipulation that many straight men do to appear as gay for money. For the first photograph they go to Chowpatty beach where many men have gathered sitting together and holding hands. They clicked the picture of the two boys in such a manner as it appears that instead of the waist they are holding the arse of each other. The boys think them to be foreign tourists and consider it to be an innocent photograph without doubting their intentions.

Likewise for the second picture they go to Nariman Point.

> They stop before two collegians, one of whom has his leg on his friend's. Ashok physically rearranges the lads in such a way that one's knee is almost on the other's crotch.
>
> — Ibid.: 135

And when one of them asks whether they are from press they blatantly lie and nod in affirmation. They affirm that they are doing a feature on different facets of Marine Drive. For the next picture he clicks two men squatting while facing each other. He stealthily clicks the photograph which appears highly erotic from the perspective of gay rendezvous. For the fourth photograph they select a second-class compartment of a train which is so overpacked that it appears to be a sight of orgy (everyone looks like on the top of other when clicked from a specific camera angle) when viewed from a twisted queer gaze.

For their last snap they cleverly manipulate the picture of wet male bodies falling at one another at *Dahihandi* festival. All these photographs have been shot skilfully with such angles that these straight men indulged in non-sexual activities appear as gay men engrossed in homosexual mating. Hence Ashok's act of faking as a gay (if it is true) is synonymous with Rashid's cunning distortion of pictures of straight men to satisfy gay fantasy because both of them are doing it for economic benefits. Little wonder Rashid calls it a "cunning Alibi" and tries to break the camera in a fit of rage. Thus in a very humorous manner the author is able to present a very dubious side and heart wrenching agony of a homosexual man who is compelled to be constantly in doubt whether his partner is actually a gay and it's a mutually satisfying same-sex activity that he is engaged in or his mate is merely faking it for money. This pretention of being gay and cheating is also apparent in the story, "The Jungle" by Madhav G. Gawankar. In it the protagonist cries vehemently:

> Many guys have deceived me. They cheated me. They pretended to be gay. Now, many of them are married. Please don't do that. — Gawankar 1999: 47

All these examples bear witness to the fact that the subject queer/economy/gender is too sprawling and contradictory to be a single comprehensive and linear monograph.

Another interesting dimension of the intersection of class and homosexuality is the effect of class on internalized homophobia. Though the working-class men are exposed to same-sex activity at a much younger age and they tend to indulge in it more frequently (because they are less guarded), homophobia is more internalized and heteronormativity is more deep-rooted in this class. Thus homophobic anxiety is much more apparent and acceptability of their own alternative sexuality is extremely hard for them. Apropos of this Michael Pollak in his essay, "Male Homosexuality – or Happiness in the Ghetto", asserts:

> Class origin has different effect on sexual behaviour on one hand, and on the guilt feelings caused by homosexuality on the other. The higher one climbs in social hierarchy, the fewer becomes one's sexual contacts and with increasing age they diminish more rapidly in the higher classes than in the world of the working class. . . . However, much stronger feeling of guilt seems to be experienced by the working classes than by the higher executive class. . . . Socialization in the lower classes is very rigid and clearly defined in terms of restrictions and demands. At the same time the techniques of inculcation are less insidious than in higher classes, and the children are not endlessly supervised.
> — 1985: 49

The consequence is that the strict norms, peculiar to lower-class socialization, are often followed without internalization and this results in the lower degree of inhibition regarding the same-sex liaison and the higher degree of guilt and internalized homophobia in working-class men. There is a constant rage against their own self which finds manifestation in the form of their reflected hatred for their gay partner. That is why when after a long time Yudi meets Miland and tries to hug him he is repulsed and yells:

> You are the one who has ruined my life. It's because of you that I became homo. Had it not been you and your perverse ways, I would never have landed up at a place like that A.K. Modelling Agency and become a prostitute. Shame on you! I wonder whether I will now be able to lead a normal married life.
> — Rao 2003: 210

The contradiction in lower classes is persistent for yet another reason and that is their negation of the myth of youth — since the rules of the milieu are also less internalized, and the myth of youth that produces a diminution of sexual activity towards the age of forty affects them much less, their sex life in its full intensity lasts a good deal beyond that age. Thus as Reich and Dannecker state that they have a more prolonged sex life (because of the negation of the myth of youth), and also a greater hostility to homosexuality in their class, with the result the feeling of guilt persists in them for a longer period. This obliges working-class homosexuals to keep two sides of their lives much more strictly apart and to feign a heterosexual lifestyle especially at their workplace because fear of losing a job is much more heightened in their psyche. That is why Miland in *Boyfriend* is extremely annoyed and anxious at the presence of Yudi in his marriage and is greatly perturbed that everybody will think him to be a *chhakka* like Yudi. He urges Yudi in anger to get out of his marriage venue as early as possible. Time and again he accuses Yudi of being responsible for his initiation into gay world. He does not want Yudi to drop at his workplace and expose his gay identity there because of which he might lose his job. Then Yudi says that if he looses his job he will take care of him, to which Miland retorts: "I do not want to be your gulam" (p. 116).

In fact, the guilt-complex is so intensified in Miland that throughout the text he has been shown as someone who is constantly depreciating himself for his homoerotic passion. When Miland comes back after his stint with A.K. Modelling Agency and faces various questions regarding his whereabouts, he thinks:

> Could he tell them he was busy doing *randibazi*, being a whore for six months? They would say he was better off dead.
>
> — Ibid.: 203

Similarly in "Moonlight Tandoori", the lower-class cook is

extremely confused and uncomfortable about his alternate sexuality and at one level he refutes his university graduate upper-class mate's advances, whereas on the other he in a coquettish way asks him to handle him as gently as a man would do to a woman. He reacts:

> Bhaisaab, it's okay if one of us was a woman, he said with some hesitation. I pinched his cheeks. He shrieked and implored me to handle him gently as a man would a woman.
>
> — Raj Rao 1999: 80

At times they try to resolve their homophobic anxiety by resorting to heterosexual marriage. In "Moonlight Tandori" the cook is aghast at the unabashed exploration of the narrator's same sex leanings and suggests that he must engage in heterosexual relationships: "He did not resist but spoke of my need to have a girlfriend" (p. 81). It's much more easier for an upper-class person to come out of his closet and become comfortable with his sexuality without the persistent anxiety and this notion finds its articulation in the passionate outburst of one of the characters in Dattani's *Night Queen*. When the narrator accuses Ash for being hypocrite in hiding his gay identity Ash vehemently cries:

> Who are you to feel superior? You think you have it easy? Just because you have this — (gesturing to the room and bed) this arrangement, this set up. . . . Just because you are smart enough to defend yourself, you have a sister who understands you, you have a secure job and all that, it doesn't make you an . . . (stopping) Yes. It does make you superior somehow. You can tell the world to fuck off.
>
> — Dattani 1999: 68

Moreover at times the overlapping of guilt complex and class consciousness is much more ambivalent and reverses the stereotype module of the ruler and the ruled. Sometimes despite their guilt they thoroughly enjoys the act but pretends to be a sexual slave for if they exhibit their pleasure then they cannot ask for money in return. Hinting at this Kamlesh in Mahesh Dattani's *On a Muggy Night in Mumbai* asks the guard:

> You do enjoy it. What you do to me, what I do to you. Don't you? . . . But we will have to pretend you do it only for the money.
> — Dattani 2000: 51

So whether the guilt complex is actually so heightened in Miland or a product of clever manipulation in order to extract more and more money from Yudi is debatable.

Eugenics or false science has also contributed a great deal to the perpetuation of the guilt complex regarding homosexuality specially in the Indian context. Whereas the "disease" model of homosexuality has been dismantled by American Psychiatric Association long back in 1973 when they removed homosexuality as an illness from the Diagnostic and Statistical Manual of Mental Disorders (DSM-3), in contrast the Indian Medical Establishment has followed the WHO system of classification of mental and behavioural disorders known as ICD-10. This system classifies homosexuality into two groups — ego-syntonic and ego-dystonic homosexuality. This system considers ego-dystonic homosexuality as psychiatric disorder. In ego-syntonic disorder they are comfortable with their sexuality and thus no treatment is warranted whereas in ego dysyntonic they are not comfortable with their sexuality and hence treatment is required. The upper class on account of more internalized education system and liberal attitude is prone to embrace ego-syntonic sexuality whereas the working class on account of persistent guilt complex, by and large suffer from ego-dystonic homosexuality. But this sort of distinction is obviously problematic because considering any sort of homosexuality a pathological disease, endorses heteronormativity and perpetuates psychiatric abuse. In fact, Freud's interpretation of same sex desire has given an impetus to psychiatric abuse. He has seen homosexuality as the result of having a domineering mother/absent father and a pathological condition to be cured. It was one of Freud's follower Sandor Rado, who invented reparative therapies that are designed to change the sexual orientation of the patient. Reparative therapies are aimed at changing the sexual orientation of the patient through a variety of techniques, including the administration of "nausea-inducing" drugs, "shock therapy" and "behavioural therapy".

Thus Yudi, who is an ego-syntonic homosexual and despite being comfortable with his same-sex desire has to go through these therapies, though symbolically, when he has been constantly chased by Gauri who thinks that coercive heterosexuality can cure him of his homosexuality. It suggestively represents Sandor Rado's nausea-inducing therapy, for he reacts to her advances by vomiting constantly and it has been cleared by Gauri with her bare hands.

> She opened her hand bag fished out a roll of tissue and passed it on to Yudi to clean himself up. She also parted with her bottle of mineral water. . . . Gauri cleaned up her man-friend. She freely used her tissue roll to wipe off the specs of vomit on the tinted glasses. — Raj Rao 2003: 55

Yudi later on calls his puking, "a cathartic discharge". Similarly when he was yearning for Miland and vomiting in the wash room, Gauri rang,

> he was in the loo, vomiting into the shit pot when Gauri rang. He managed to hobble towards the instrument and pick it up. "Are you all right" Gauri asked, and Yudi wondered what karmic connection the lady bore to his vomiting. Many months ago she was present when he threw up in horny educator's car. Now when he was sick she was there again. — Ibid.: 190

In fact, he pokes fun at her futile efforts to cure him of his homoerotic passion by enticing him. She continues to think of him as a possible husband. In his private lingo, she is the "backbay reclaimation kind". At times even the usual depression faced by a gay man is misjudged as a product of an ego-dystonic homosexuality and in the process at times creates doubt, fear and anxiety in the mind of a gay man who otherwise seems to be comfortable with his sexuality. As in *On a Muggy Night in Mumbai* by Mahesh Dattani, Prakash who has gone for the treatment of usual depression is misguided by the doctor and becomes the victim of psychiatric abuse:

> for the first time in my life, I wished I wasn't gay. . . . I realized where that feeling was coming from. The psychiatrist I was seeing. . . . I chose the psychiatrist out of yellow pages. He pretended to understand. Until he began to tell me about aversion therapy. For a while, I believed him. Because medication helped me cope with my depression better. Until he said I would never be happy as a gay man. It is impossible to change society, he said, but it may be possible for you to reorient yourself. . . . I tried explaining to him that I needed his help to overcome my anxiety and fears, not to be something I am not.
>
> — Dattani 2000: 69

Likewise making fun of medical doctors who claim to cure people of homosexuality as if it's a disease and assumes the role of moral police, Raj Rao in *Boyfriend* describes a scene in which in order to get the treatment of S.T.D. Yudi and Miland visit an insensitive doctor.

> The doctor to whom Yudi and Miland jointly went for treatment was disgusted. How could two men be so shameless as to openly admit they had contracted the warts through anal intercourse? "No unnatural sex, no warts," he kept telling them as he injected them, assuming the manner of a high school master. It was only because he was the friend of a friend that Yudi resisted the urge to ask him to fuck off and mind his own business! Miland understood him better. Can't you see, "he told Yudi," that he wants one of us to have unnatural sex with him? — Raj Rao 2003: 152

Hence the myopic point of view of medical science also

endorses heteronormativity and by proving it unnatural perpetuates guilt complex and internalized homophobia.

The lower class becomes more of its victim on account of more embedded guilt complex along with larger hostility at uneducated working environment and it's these difficulties which make them more prone to medical abuse as Ankleswaria, a gay man, interviewed by Raj Rao in *Whistling in the Dark* averts:

> If there were therapies that could cure or rid me of my homosexuality, I'd be the first one to enroll for the treatment. Being a homosexual is messy. It leads to unnecessary problems, and to needless pain and suffering for all concerned. It's a curse to be born homosexual, and I wouldn't wish it for anyone. — Raj Rao and Sarma 2009: 206

Another onslaught of medical science on gay activism is the way it has hijacked queer movement by extrapolation of AIDS as an incurable fatal disease and categorizing M.S.M. (man having sex with man) as the most vulnerable category. Apropos of this Raj Rao asserts: "The AIDS endemic has played a major role in the appropriation of queerness by heteronormativity" (*Whistling in the Dark*, p. xv) and thanks to the worldwide propaganda AIDS is being synonymous with homosexuality and once again the most vulnerable group is the working class due to lack of knowledge, inadequate medical facilities and early exposure to sex of all varieties and child abuse. Patently the oppression on account of AIDS epidemic is far more accentuated in the working class and it makes them doubly marginalized. Seeing two working-class men indulged in unprotected sex Yudi cries:

> "Idiot, haven't you heard of HIV?" He said to the man who was still on his knees. "*Kuchh nahi hota hai*, nothing will happen", the chap replied, waving him away. "Fools," Yudi thought to himself. "They'll never learn". — Rao 2003: 3-4

The class dynamics and the knowledge about AIDS precautions are explored by the author in yet another scene when during the act with Miland condom is torn and Yudi exclaims:

> "God! Yudi exclaimed. "Don't you even know how to use a condom? How old are you? Nineteen, isn't it?" "We'll do it without a condom", the boy suggested, instantly reminding Yudi of the suicidal fool at Churchgate who swallowed a stranger's cum. But Yudi did not argue with the boy. He did not want to play teacher all the time. As it was obvious to him that the boy would never succeed in fucking him, there was no danger. The semen would merely trickle down his buttocks. That's all. — Ibid.: 12

Hence from both the incidents it's clear that the lack of knowledge in working class makes people much more vulnerable to this disease. On account of his educated upbringing Yudi knows that sexually transmitted diseases are not big issues and can be cured with a shot of penicillin whereas the lack of clear knowledge of sexually transmitted diseases creates unnecessary phobia in the minds of working-class uneducated youths and make them all the more homophobic and gives a setback to the gay visibility:

> His other worry was AIDS. STD, HIV, AIDS, these acronyms were freely used by everyone in the agency. None of the boys clearly knew what they meant. . . . He still hadn't learnt to wear his condoms. . . . Milya had little use for rubbers. All rubbers to him were Nirodhs. They were useless. He was sure he would die of AIDS. — Ibid.: 201

In yet another instance the heterosexist nature of the prevalent condoms is exposed:

> The ones available in the market, they believed, were heterosexist: they assumed that dicks entered only cunts. When A.K. boys used them, they tore half way through and exposed both user and the used to grave risk. — Ibid.

As Chandraratne, a Sri Lankan gay man, in *Whistling in the*

Dark affirms that due to the awareness and medical development AIDS manufactured panic ceases to exist and it is precisely for this reason that the people in the West are not that scared of AIDS as they used to be when the desease first broke out thirty years ago. Although there is no definitive cure of AIDS, people can go on living endlessly with anti retroviral therapy (ART). But the basic knowledge ai awareness of primary precautions regarding the use oi condoms are still available to educated middle class, and thus the class dynamics operates on this issue as well.

Yet another form of subjugation from which the gay world suffers is on account of the implementation of Section 377, a draconian law that makes even two male adults having consensual sex a criminal offence. Ashwini Sukthankar has argued in *Facing the Mirror* that the Section 377 is applicable only to male homosexuality because it considers only penetrable sex as an offence and lesbianism by and large does not come in its preview. Although this according to her is a "silencing technique", because in a way it is a non-acceptance that something like lesbianism exists, but at the other level it makes gay men extremely susceptible for police atrocities and gay bashing. Hence here is also the *kothi*s (the ones that have mannerism of more effeminate kinds and look explicitly gay) are more prone to such oppressions as compared to the *panthi* (the more masculine kinds whose physical features do not betray their sexuality). It is precisely for this reason that effeminate sort of Yudi is always in a fear of being locked up and bashed up by the police. In fact, on a given day Dnyaneshwar (the policewallaha) first has sex with him and then tries to blackmail him and extorts a huge amount from him. But Yudi turns the table and reverses the stereotype by making the gay queens ravish Dnyaneshwar's modesty publicly at a gay bar:

> Dnyaneshwar looked like Gulliver in the land of Lilliput.

> While his friends manhandled the chap who'd blackmailed him scarcely twenty-four hours ago, Yudi sat on "The Wall" and smoked cigarette after cigarette in hailing the refreshing sea air. — Raj Rao 2003: 30

Dismantling the power structure and making a mockery of Section 377, Dnyaneshwar, the homophobic blackmailer is shown being bashed up by "gay queens". The reference to sitting on the "wall" is suggestive of "Stonewall Movement". Yudi contemplates at the end of the episode that operation Stonewall was a spectacular success. Similarly the policemen in *Six Inches* harass the photographers for clicking the so-called sexually explicit pictures and demand money, but Rashid and Ashok trick them to become their gay partners and heteronormativity has been appropriated by homosexuality. Apropos of this Ashok contemplates:

> Whether he and Rashid seduced the policemen or the policemen seduced them. — Raj Rao 1999: 144

Another category among gay men who is more oppressed than *kothis* is the one who has not come out publicly. The closet gay is doubly oppressed by the police for violating law and as well as being blackmailed on account of exposure of his gay identity. As Arvind Narrain argues:

> The police capitalize on the fears of the queer community of being outed as well as the deeper societal homophobia to blatantly subject queer people to all forms of harassment and violence. — Narrain and Gupta 2011: 76

That is why when Dnyaneswar states that he will spill the beans and tell everyone at his workplace it does not bother Yudi as much, for he has been an open gay. Thus being *panthi* and open gay have obvious advantages in gay subculture from the point of view of police atrocities.

The marginalization suffered by sexual minorities can be seen in the way they use certain codes in the language. They are forced to use the coded and secretive language for fear of "outing" which can cost them their jobs and social acceptance. The sense of extinction makes them learn to adapt themselves to the situations, as Michael Pollak writes:

> Shape your surroundings and your own way of life to accord with your sexual desires. — 1985: 56

Further throwing light on the issues of distinct lingo of the gay world Michael Pollak writes that

> secrecy is responsible for the two outstanding features of homosexual culture — its language and its humour. The two are closely connected. The dictionary of homosexual slang produced in the United States gives hundred of examples of a vocabulary that is full of variations on the theme of love, pick ups, timidity, grief and joy, aggressive cynicism . . . in the game of social hide and seek.
>
> — Ibid.: 52-53

But in language also, like any other aspect of homosexuals, the exclusive gay lingo is more prominent in the working class because as has been discussed earlier that the fear of "outing" is more conspicuous in that class. No wonder Raj Rao's *The Boyfriend* is saturated with working-class lingos whereas since the upper-class Yudi is comfortable in his skin there is hardly any trace of coded language in his conversation. There are numerous references to coded words such as *kothi/panthi* or cat and pigeon or plug and socket for active and passive dichotomy. To quote from the text:

> Yudi knew all the slang of working-class homos. "Dhakka start" was gay. "Biryani khayega" was rimming.
>
> — Rao 2003: 30

In the same fashion another tool used by homosexuals for the social hide and seek is projecting themselves as quintessential comic caricatures and this is a result of deep-rooted psychological conditioning. One such example is the "crazy old queen", the figure that constantly pops up in jokes and music hall acts. At times to counter the extreme hostility of the heteronormative world, they carefully cultivate these humorous traits as a survival and adaptation technique, for by doing so they make themselves more acceptable to the straight world.

Referring to this ironic and sad adaptation technique of homosexuals Michael Pollak observes:

> By such behaviour he hopes to mitigate the aggression he anticipates from his heterosexual companions by making them laugh and by fulfilling all the expectations expressed in the heterosexual view of homosexuality. — 1985: 53

However, in this context also the worst sufferers are the *kothi*s because of their obvious physical attributes that make it difficult for them not to expose their gay identity, and hence they are compelled to resort to these kinds of demeaning coping strategies. But at times the upper-class gays cruising on internet, which is also not foolproof and a written medium and so in one way more dangerous, also use lot of coded language. As has been mentioned by Chandraranate, a Sri Lankan gay man interviewed by Raj Rao. Chandraranate in one of his interviews affirms that one to one interactions are better than letters, phone calls and e-mails, for they are not fraught with risk. He states:

> I cruise a lot on internet. But we use a guarded, coded language understood only by us. We follow this approach even in the chat rooms. Your e-mails, on the other hand, used standard language understood by all.
>
> — Rao and Sarma 2009: 180

One speculates that probably it is precisely for this reason that the serious issues such as gay rape, instability, heart break, joblessness due to gay identity, and the police atrocities have been depicted by Rao both in *The Boyfriend* and *Six Inches* in an extremely humorous and farcical manner so that they become more palatable for a straight reader. Likewise Shyam Selvadurai (the Shri Lankan diasporic writer) who depicts the serious theme of the effect of racism on homosexuality, titles his novel *Funny Boy*.

However, oppression of women in gay subculture gives an interesting twist to gender and sexual dichotomy. Though gays themselves are sexual minority, in the patriarchal society even heterosexual women are subjugated by them. Thus the position of the victim and the victimizer interchanges here as despite being queers in a hostile heteronormative society gay men are capable of ostracizing straight women and hence in these cases sexuality trumps over gender and makes the notion of unified gay subjugation problematic. As throughout in *The Boyfriend* Gauri has been shown as a caricature who is all out to entice Yudi and she has been portrayed by Yudi as someone who takes great relish in even clearing Yudi's puke with her bare hands as it gives her an opportunity to be with Yudi. She has been seen as a competition and has been constantly mocked at. There is a sharp satire on Gauri's eco-feminist society, though Yudi's boyfriend gets job there.

> Yudi found women, even if they were Madhuri Dixit (who this one certainly was not) so much like uncooked brinjals (that is to say insipid), that he could not bring himself to look them in eye. — Rao 2003: 44

He has gone to the extent of calling her a nymphomanic. Yudi describes her as someone who is all out to hook Yudi and even tries to look masculine to catch his fancy:

> Gauri looking rather corpulent in the T-shirt and jeans she wore in a bid to look like the men who turned Yudi on.
> — Ibid.: 110

One reason that can be adduced to this hatred for women is that they are competition for gay men because both of them are vying for the attention of the straight men. A very interesting parallel can be traced in Namita Gokhale's *A Himalayan Love Story* in which Lalit, a gay man, when discovers that his childhood fancy Mukul is attracted to his wife, becomes all the more abusive to his wife both physically and verbally. But the portrayal of Gauri as a nymphomanic caricature is a mockery of women in general and a dig at heterosexuals is debatable, for in the end Gauri is shown as a friend to Yudi and someone who hints at experimenting with lesbianism.

> "You know, hear you go on and on, I have started feeling attracted to women!"
>
> "Really!" Yudi exclaimed. The news made him laugh! as if tickled to death in armpits.
>
> "I am not joking," Gauri continued, her face growing serious. "I mean it. For starters, how about introducing me to Miland's wife? I've even done a painting depicting the four of us." "Perfect arrangement," declared Yudi. "While Miland entertains me, you can humour his wife! Keep her busy so she won't miss her husband". — Ibid.: 232

Time and again throughout the text Yudi makes fun of heterosexual marriage. When Miland and his brother get married to identical twins Sheila and Leela and since in such cases mistaken identities could be hazardous, he suggests that each girl should inscribe her name on the bed sheet. The mockery of heterosexual marriage is not only a dig at compulsive heteronormativity but is also a revelation of the sad picture of the gay world where the non-acceptance of the gay marriage both by the society and the law is all-pervasive.

And this dire need to get recognition for their permanent union and the consequent pain at the rejection of it find their manifestation in the fake marriage that Miland and Yudi perform at Yudi's home, though it is laced with irony and bitter humour.

> *Shehnai* music from Yudi's collection of cassettes created the right mood. They lit the fire in the fucking room. He fished out a chiffon *sari* that his mother has once left behind, draped himself in it, and became the bride. Miland made up with Vicco turmeric paste, *bindi*, *kajal*, nail polish. Put *sindoor* in his *mang*. Tied the *pallu* of the *sari* to his *jabba*. When they were done, they went round the fire seven times.
>
> — Ibid.: 107

But many critics including Raj Rao believe that aping marriage is writing back to heteronormativity and when viewed from the Marxists point of view, the sinister design behind this becomes all the more conspicuous as Raj Rao states that the global capitalism gives fillip to such a viewpoint. According to him, it is a well-known fact that queer men and women have higher disposable incomes than heterosexuals and now the market force wants that money.

> One of the dubious ways in which this can be achieved is by co-opting queers into heteronormativity, so they live under the perpetual illusion that they are a family, and even start spending like a heteropatriarchal family. Advancements in science such as sex reassignment surgeries and test-tube baby and changes in adoption laws that permit queer people to adopt children, all lend their tacit support.
>
> — Rao and Sarma 2009: xv

And that is why at the end of their marriage ceremony Miland and Yudi have been shown making *rangoli* with krazy lines cockroach poison and the embedded irony and satire in depiction of their prospected pregnancy is quite conspicuous. So whether the intentions of the writer in the depiction of this whole scene, and the portrayal of oppressive marriage of Miland and Leela coupled with the dig at Gauri are deliberate efforts to exhibit the non-egalitarian nature of the heterosexual marriage or a manifestation of inherent hatred and consequent subjugation that women receive in the gay subculture, are debatable. Because when a gay man is married especially in a lower class the kind of treachery and falsehood these women suffer is unimaginable and the writer very effectively draws attention to it when Miland gets married to Leela. In one of the episodes after his marriage he asks the perennial question, whether she is virgin and he returns the question with compliments:

> Miland was in a fix. Did men who sleep with men lose their virginity, or was virginity merely a thing between men and women? He wasn't sure. After pondering the question for a whole week, he decided he was a virgin and said so to Leela. To his way of thinking, then, all that he had done at the A.K. Modelling Agency hadn't killed his virginity. Nor had his affair with Yudi. — Rao 2003: 222

Hence the issues of adultery and cheating do not crop in his mind. Again when his wife asks him to take help from his rich friend, he goes to Yudi's home and takes money from Yudi for sexual favours because after his assignment at modelling agency he will not allow anyone to touch his body for free.

> Not even his wife who paid for it by doing his cooking and washing. — Ibid.: 230

When he returns home, he decides to keep all the money for himself and even thinks that if she is so desperate for money she should wash dishes at someone's home and gets fucked by the owner of the home. He even contemplates of fogging her with belts:

> Must flog her with my belt again, he told himself. She should know her place; she didn't own him. No one did, not Yudi, not she. — Ibid.: 231

Many gay men in heterosexual marriage do not think their homosexual encounters as adultery and consequently cheat their wives without an iota of guilt. This theme is persistent in Mahesh Dattani's *Night Queen*, *On a Muggy Night in Mumbai*, and *Bravely Fought the Queen*. There is a repeated delineation of the theme where husband and brother are in homosexual affair and the brother gets his sister married to his gay lover to hide his same-sex leaning, and it acts as a comfortable mask to hide their homoerotic passion. This poignant situation of women in gay marriage is described through the passionate plea of a gay man in "Night Queen". He implores his mate not to get involved in such exploitative marriage and asks him to come out in open:

> Pretending that she turns you on. That you are in love with her. That everything will be alright after marriage. Such pretence! And when you sleep with her, you will be groaning extra loud with pleasure, shutting your eyes, thinking of your snake God or whatever, and penetrating her with those images in your mind. Pretending, pretending all the fucking way. That's really shitty ugly. And in case you cannot make those wonderful fountains erupt, she will look at you, questioning you, and you will be ugly enough to lead her to believe that she isn't good enough. That she doesn't satisfy you. You will say to her it's alright, you still love her. And she will be grateful to you! That's ugly! See that! See all that and tell me if that isn't ugly. — Dattani 1999: 61

Thus whether it's a heterosexual man or gay, women are suppressed by both and thus sexual minority trumps over gender identity. Though there is a counter-argument how the queer identity of gay men appropriates the patriarchal subjugation and indirectly champions the cause of feminism as Bersani states in *Homos* that same-sex passion is transformed through self-shattering, since its "privileging of sameness" now derives "from the perspective of a self already identified as different from itself", that is from "a desiring subject for whom the antagonism between the different and the same no longer exists". Sameness seems to have the capacity to absorb — or perhaps to neutralize — difference, disarming the threat of otherness. As Cora Coplan states in "Queering the Pitch" that identifying with women or incorporating "woman's otherness" into himself is part of a complex trajectory of desire in which nothing is fixed in advance. Bersani quotes in *Homos*,

> In a sense, then, the very maintaining of the couples man–woman, heterosexual–homosexual, serves to break down their oppositional distinctions. — 1995: 61

Interestingly we notice that in the end both Gauri and Yudi get reconciled and have the same wavelength because of being cohesive marginalized identity, and fully understand the need of coalition politics. Similarly in Dattani's *Do the Needful*, a gay man recognizes the oppression of a woman who is forced to marry while she is in love with someone else. They finally settle for a marriage of convenience where both of them work as a shield for each other and under the garb of which they fulfil their needs. Likewise in "The Slaves" the gay narrator feels sympathy for a prostitute who has a famished body and is selling her body to his partner for money.

Since it is difficult to jam homosexuals into already existing hegemonic structures of heterosexual framework, it provides paradoxically ambivalent fluid power patterns that dismantle one kind of privileges over the others and the monolithic dynamics of the ruler and the ruled dichotomy is constantly negotiated on the basis of age, race, ethnicity, caste, active/passive, bisexual/gay and hence creates a perennial flux. Significantly in one way it provides an entirely different sort of egalitarian framework and negates the absolute kind of "economic determinism" as is somewhat apparent in the case of Yudi and Miland. Apropos of this Ruth Vanita remarks:

> Thus in cross class relationships, it is not always . . . the subordinate who is exploited. When the social superior is single and the subordinate married, heterosexual privileges may triumph over class privilege and result in a transaction that is mutually useful but that downgrades the gay person.
> — 2005: 244

However, critics like Michael Pollak believe that since by and large homosexuality is identified as a middle-class phenomenon and hence there are not readymade available frameworks for working class through which they can assert their gay identity and consequently they are less likely to describe themselves as gays. As a result, they are more likely to have heterosexual experiences and the insistence on being active will be more in them on account of homophobic anxiety and the experiences of Miland (*The Boyfriend*), Mazhar ("The Slaves") and the cook in "Moonlight Tandoori" bear witness to it. They all have female mates, constantly feel guilty about their homosexual encounters and do not recognize themselves as explicitly gays. But overall in the larger framework the boundaries of class, caste and age are bound to be less conspicuous than what they are in the heteronormative society. And the primary reason for this is, as Yudi states, that as an outcast they come together irrespective of the differences of all sorts and the need for the elusive "other" in romantic liaison also gives impetus to the egalitarian format. This finds its manifestation in the form of embracing "otherness" by transgressing the stereotypical boundaries of compatibility because the constant "other" in heterosexual relationship, that is "gender", is same here. However, the gender at times is unable to trump over the subaltern sexualities and women are equally or even at times more marginalized in the gay culture across all classes and cultures as in the cases of Gauri and Leela. But in the process of coalition politics the gay men and women join hands against patriarchy as in Mahesh Dattani's *Do the Needful* in which a gay man indulges in a marriage of convenience with a woman who is in love with a man outside her community. As a result together they create a unique third space outside the domain of patriarchy where they can assert their sexual identity.

According to Raj Rao, anal penetration is a symbolic act of

resistance against oppression occurring on account of vaginal penetration. To him "anus is a political site, with all its implication of entry, surrender and feminization of the male body" (Rao and Sarma 2009: xvii). Thus the identities of the oppressor and the oppressed are constantly interchangeable and hence problematic. Obviously the polyvalence in gay subculture on the one hand contests the established power patterns, and on the other constantly re-establishes new hegemonic structures which are at times absent or less visible in the heterosexual matrix and provide a unique tool for critiquing the monolithic power operations of the heteronormative society.

5

Plurality of the Significance of Lesbian Existence in Modern Indian Writers

Geetanjali Shree, Manju Kapur and Rajkamal Chaudhary

Bound to my home and hearth,
Should I tell you
My hidden truth
Of years and centuries?
. . . I was smothered within the bride's red *chunni*,
Then I was bound to the yellow for my son.
Holding him, the family's lamp,
I melted away, turned to forth
and overflowed
Only burnt dregs of me remain.
Should I knot myself into a bundle
And find my way to you?

— Maya Sharma, "For You", *Facing the Mirror*, p. 404

WOMEN'S EXPERIENCE of sexual oppression is not homogeneous but it intersects with other patriarchal subjugation and hence lesbianism is a malleable force, which operates at multiple contradictory levels. This plurality of lesbian experience is defined by Cheryl Clarke in these words:

> However, there is no one kind of lesbian, no one kind of lesbian behaviour and no one kind of lesbian relationship.
>
> — 1996: 156

The absence of coding of lesbians, specially in the Indian

context, where despite the seminal works by Giti Thadani (*Sakhiyani*) and Ruth Vanita (*Same-Sex Love In india*) — these works illustrate the recovery and the discovery of the lesbian histories from archaeological sites and ancient texts — same-sex love is still considered an idea imported from the West, and there is greater need to redefine the inherent complexity of the lesbian experience through critically examining the Indian literary texts. The fluidity of the contradictory positions within lesbianism regarding both challenging and endorsing the heteronormative structure can be illustrated through the culturally diverse representations of the homoerotic passion. Manju Kapur's *A Married Woman*, Geetanjali Shree's *Tirohit* and Rajkamal Chaudhary's *Machali Mari Hui* explicitly exhibit it. *A Married Woman* has Astha as a protagonist who is an urban contemporary woman, whereas, *Tirohit* has a semi-rural setting with uneducated maid-servant Lalana as a central figure and *Machali Mari Hui* (written in Hindi by a male author, Rajkamal Chaudhary as early as in 1966 and still unexplored) revolves around a courtesan and the dancing girl Shiri. Though the texts under discussion are of disparate nature, the common thread that binds them is the effective portrayal of the eclectic nature of the lesbian longings of married Indian women. The issues of latent sexuality, instinctive bisexuality, lavender marriage, lesbianism as an act of resistance, lesbian motherhood, homosexuality of convenience and homophobia have been effectively addressed.

A Married Woman is a story of an artist Astha, who teaches in a school and has two children. She suffers from the usual Indian middle-class dilemma of identity crisis coupled with a passionless sexual life. She challenges the constrains of the middle-class existence by indulging into a lesbian relationship with a much younger Piplika Khan, but finally the relationship breaks down due to the difference of expectations in both the lovers and Astha has been left with no choice but to resort to her pseudo-marital bliss. *Tirohit* by Geetanjali Shree is one of the most radical novels written in Hindi. In it the Sapphic relationship of Chhacho, who has been ceaselessly denied the conjugal bliss, with her so-called promiscuous maid Lalana (who in turn gives birth to the son of Chhacho's husband) effectively documents the different dimensions of the homoerotic trajectory, especially in the semi-rural Indian context. The third novel in question is *Machali Mari Hui* which presents the perspective of an Indian male (living in 1960s) on lesbianism. Here the central figures are Shiri and Priya. Shiri is a society girl who has been married to the psychologically impotent Nirmal and consequently suffers from sexual starvation. It gets merged with her childhood fear of pregnancy and the consequent hatred for man. She has been initiated into the same-sex love by her own sister and later on finds its fullest exploration with Priya, daughter of her husband's former paramour, Kalyani. All these three characters Nirmal, Shiri and Priya are shown as aberrations and products of complexes. Thus the portrayal of lesbianism here appears to be a typical case of male heterosexual lesbophobia.

The first novel in question *Tirohit* by Geetanjali Shree is iconoclastic about lesbian relationships between the main protagonist Chhacho and her maid-servant Lalana, who is forced into an illicit relationship with Chhacho's husband and gives birth to a son who is brought up by both Lalana and Chhacho. The entire situation reveals the complicated layers of patriarchal oppression regarding lesbian invisibility, compulsive heterosexuality, lesbian motherhood, sexual oppression within marriage and class dynamics in homoerotic passion. The novel is remarkable for its depiction of the system of patriarchal domination buttressed by the subjugation of women through heterosexuality. Chhacho's husband who lives in Hong Kong and comes only in vacations refuses to resuscitate her sexually. Not only this he masturbates before her and states that he wants a "woman" and not her. This infuriates Chhacho beyond measures:

> Chacha pretends that he is fast asleep. Chhacho comes near him. Her breath is extremely warm. She is all heated up. She is touching Chacha with great pride. She is embracing him, goading him and Chacha continues to be fast asleep. Now he wakes up. He is irritated; feels repulsion and pushes her. The entire bed starts rocking. She has been thrown aside. Like a wounded animal she pounces upon him. Both of them are hissing in violent fashion. "Why not?" Chhacho asks in a humiliated tone. "Because I need a woman and not you". Chacha says. This is not the first time that I have heard something like this. Chhacho is fuming like a crushed snake. And then . . . my eyes are closed but I know where the hand of Chacha is and what is he doing to make Chhacho all the more jealous. The moment Chhacho starts sobbing; his hand starts moving all the more rigorously. And the entire bed will laugh boisterously over the victory of man over woman. — Geetanjali Shree 2001: 73

This description is replete with the oppressive nature of heterosexual liaison, which aims at the perverted satisfaction of the penis alone and leaves a woman wounded and dissatisfied both emotionally and physically. Another dimension of this stark reality is presented in the form of forceful sexual exploitation of Lalana by numerous men of the block, including Chacha. They both find solace in each other's arms. Thus the novel reveals the coercive nature of heterosexuality and the depiction of homoerotic passion as the only space available for the complete and unexploitative exploration of feminine sexuality. Hence at one level it valorizes lesbianism as a tool to free one's self from the bondages of penetrative sex and posits the possibility of showcasing it as a means of liberation, but at the other it exhibits the homoerotic passion as a substitute for dissatisfying heterosexual relationships, which indeed is a regressive move.

However, the author somehow mitigates herself from her anxiety by re-sexualizing lesbianism instead of emphasizing the romantic aspect of it only. Apropos of this Diane Richardson in "Constructing Lesbian Sexualities" asserts: "There is a tendency to see lesbian relationships as primarily emotional rather than sexual. Partially it can be understood in terms of the way woman's sexuality has traditionally been seen as primarily 'passive'" (1996: 281) in nature. No wonder Lillian Faderman's definition of lesbianism does not necessarily include genital contact. It can be interpreted in terms of dominant definitions of sex as Diane Richardson affirms:

> For if to the predominantly male "experts" what lesbians do isn't real sex, then it's perhaps not altogether surprising that studies of lesbian relationships have often focused on emotional attachment rather than sexual behavior. . . . Some lesbian writers echo this view in claiming that lesbians, as women, are sexually inhibited and repressed. — Ibid.

Obviously the writer in the unabashed portrayal of relentless physical passion presents herself as the true champion of lesbian cause. Chhacho and Lalana not only delve in *sakhi bhav* (companionship) which finds its manifestation in their exchange of clothes, garlands and singing together, but also engage in unadulterated sexual mating. To quote from the text:

> While Chhacho was sitting on the chair her body beneath the waist was constantly and rhythmically rocking at regular intervals. . . . I have also seen Lalana's back and head. Her head was bent before Chhacho's chair. She was tossing her head left and right and then right and left frequently. From her open hair light was reflected. Oye Hoy Paresh screamed and speak temptingly. 'See Lalana is licking it as if it is a chicken curry'.
>
> — Geetanjali Shree 2001: 71

However, the entire scene is viewed by an adolescent youth and his friend and the former thinks that instead of Chhacho there is her husband and it is a heterosexual encounter. It is unclear whether Paresh's this sort of assumption is the result of the fact that since childhood same-sex mating is unthinkable or it is the exclusive invisibility of lesbian relationships because Paresh thinks it to be obviously a male and female encounter but asks his male friend the child narrator to lick him beneath. The intention of the author is opaque, for on the one hand there is relentless portrayal of sexual gratification between the two women, whereas on the other there is also an indication of lesbian invisibility.

The invisibility of the lesbians finds its manifestation in the form of narrative technique of the "ghosting of lesbians" or "apparitional lesbianism", the terms used by Terry Castle in her work, *The Apparitional Lesbian: Female Homosexuality and Modern Culture* (1993). Terry castle has given the concept of "self-ghosting" through which a lesbian can invisibilize herself in order to secure a safe zone in this homophobic society. Not only this, as Shormishtha Panja rightly observes in her essay, "The Ghosts Who Talks: Terry Castle's *The Apparitional Lesbian* and Gender Discourse":

> The lesbian threatened the moral, sexual and psychic authority of men and the response of hostile men (and patriarchal women) was to "ghost" her. Hence, the conjunction between lesbians and apparitions seemed apt — they were both seen as diabolic. The ghost's image also drained the lesbian of her carnality and denied her erotic force. — 2006: 47

Quoting from Castle, Panja infers that Castle gives various examples such as in Gautier's Mademoiselle de Maupin, Rosette pursues Madelein like a "loving ghosts" not knowing that she is a female in male disguise. In Baudelaire's *The Flowers of Evil*, Delphine and Hippolyte are described as damned spirits. In James's *The Bostonians* the ascetic Olive Chancellor is the "ghost woman" floating through rooms and greeting strangers with a chill hand. Woolf's Orlando claims that she has been haunted ever since she was a child. Her Russian lover Sasha seems to appear like an "apparition in Grey fur". Castle calls it, "recognition through negation" (ibid.: 60). Panja rightly points out in this regard:

> Even though an apparition has no bodily existence, it nevertheless appears and makes its presence felt. Castle cites the gesture that recurs in many of these books — passing one's hand over one's eyes whenever it comes to the moment of acknowledgement of lesbianism. This she calls the "exorcism gesture", the gesture with which lesbians try to free their mind of the knowledge of their own sexual identity. — Ibid.: 48

Hence ghosting of lesbianism is eclectic in nature as at one level it gives them freedom to negotiate their own space without worrying about the prying eyes of the homophobic society, whereas at another level it is reflective of the complete annihilation and negation of their existence. Geetanjali Shree in *Tirohit* brings out the elusive dynamics of this connection between lesbianism and ghosting. Chhacho constantly states that Lalana who is a maidservant and hence has lesser restriction on her is like a ghost and can be invisible and do whatever she wants to do. Chhacho yearns and wishes that she could be a ghost like Lalana.

> Some people are like that, I told Paresh, who are invisible even in their visibility. Lalana very boldly walks before everybody on the roof and nobody comes to know about her. She is invisible where she actually exists and she is visible where she actually does not exist.
>
> — Geetanjali Shree 2001: 45

Once Chhacho tells Lalana,

> You are very lucky that you are invisible and can go any where. — Ibid.: 89

At which Lalana aptly remarks,

> I am not invisible. I have been deliberately evaporated.
>
> —Ibid.: 90

This conversation clearly brings out the two contradictory aspects of the lesbian ghosting. At one level Chhacho craves for this invisibility because it will provide her greater opportunity to meet her lover, but on the other Lalana's statement highlights that this ghosting is deliberately done by patriarchal society in order to make her lesbian leaning invisible. Later on, they discover the joys of this annihilation because it gives them their own private and unique space. They both talk about their itching. It is the same sort of sexual itching that used to bother Begum Jan in "Lihaf" and she tries to get rid of it by Rabbu's rubbing. This juxtaposing of sensual itching and orgasmic pleasure of a woman is also there in *Kamasutra*:

> She has an itch. . . . Combined with the erotic arousal of foreplay, this generates a different kind of feeling in her sense of pleasure. — Vatsyayana 2011: 30

Similarly Chhacho states:

> Whenever there is craving I itch desperately on thigh; this is ridiculous; why should I not itch, when I feel like doing it; why should I die for getting a false respect; when I am not visible then why should my itching becomes visible.
>
> — Geetanjali Shree 2001: 90

At this Lalana reacts:

> let me make you also invisible. Now you can come with me and none of us will be visible. —Ibid.

Thus there is a constant mention of the word ghosting throughout the text. Their sexual mating is invariably saturated with ghost images:

> the two changes clothes like a ghost in the bushes . . . why

> shouldn't the ghosts of the two meet at the roof. —Ibid.: 96

Interestingly at another place the writer poignantly mentions the silencing of lesbian love by lesbophobic society through the strategy of deliberate ghosting:

> These two girls had attained youth together . . . grew old together but people despite seeing them together were unable to see them. — Ibid.: 126

In this manner, the dichotomy of lesbian ghosting is quite effectively portrayed by Geetanjali Shree.

The novel is also remarkable for its effective delineation of yet another dimension of the same-sex love and that is overlapping of class and gender identities. Many times the same-sex relation across class becomes economically beneficial for a partner who belongs to the lower economic strata and hence at times the class precedes the sexuality. The classic example of it is Raj Rao's novel, *The Boyfriend*, in which the rich Yudi is able to get sexual favour from the poor Miland in exchange of economic help. This aspect of the same-sex love is also obliquely present in "Lihaf" in which Begum Jan showers lavish gifts on Rabbu. Same dynamics are implicitly present in *Tirohit* between Lalana (maidservant) and Chhacho. She asks Chhacho about her silk *saris* and wears Chhacho's gold bangles after her death and keeps the money earned by selling waste newspaper. Lalana states that Chhacho asks her to forget her previous husband and asserts:

> Forget that scoundrel who does not marry you. She gives me one more cheque to submit in my separate account. . . . Till the time Om Babu gets suspicious, I have already made Chhacho sign joint fixed deposits in my name.
> — Geetanjali Shree 2001: 114

Nevertheless the entire discussion may appear to veer around to an entirely different domain if viewed from Ruth Vanita's perspective as expressed in *Love's Rite*. She gives example of a medieval Indian poet, Maulvi Mukarram Baksh, who has given his entire property to his same-sex companion Mukkaram. Mukkaram observes *iddat* for the Maulvi. *Iddat* is a period of sexual abstinence and mourning that a widow observes for her husband. Ruth opines that

> Today, it is taken for granted, at least among the middle classes, that husbands and wives should share property and finances, which leads government to bestow joint financial benefits on them. But earlier Indian and Western ideals of friendship assumed that one's close same-sex friend was one's second self and therefore shared all one's worldly goods. — Ruth Vanita 2005: 27

Though Lalana does not observe the mourning in the conventional sense, she feels the presence of Chhacho with her all the time. And even her son, who does not appreciate Lalana otherwise, notices the constant presence of Chhacho with Lalana, almost like a Siamese twins. He states that it is very strange that "mourning is of Chhacho and it is Lalana who is roaming here and there like a ghost" (Geetanjali Shree 2001: 22). At another instance the narrator observes that Lalana has taken out all the costly *saris* of Chhacho and keeps them carefully in a systematic manner. He questions that "by doing so is she securing her own future or reliving the memories of Chhacho" (ibid.: 15). It is debatable whether this whole situation is a backlash at the egalitarian ideal of the unexploitative nature of the same-sex love and a manifestation of the fact that no relationship (whether the cross-sexed or the same-sex) can be bereft of hierarchal dispositions, or it is indicative of bestowing the same-sex couple with an equal right on their partner's belongings as is automatically given to husband and wife. As one can notice that in a heteronormative society nobody questions the appropriation of the property by a husband of wife or the vice versa, but when it comes to the same-sex lovers there are lot of question marks on the credibility of their affection. They are immediately labelled as gold-diggers as has been in the case of Lalana. In fact, the writer's stance whether she is asking for the same right as is available in the heteronormative structure or colluding with the dominant heteropatriarchal ideology is ambivalent.

The complexity of the issue of "lesbian motherhood" with its underlying multiplicity is explored in this text. It is a very complicated identity because there is a merging of the main stream identity of "mother" with the marginalized identity of a "lesbian". Sara Warn in her insightful essay, "TV's Lesbian Baby Boom" asserts by giving numerous examples of American TV serials such as "What Makes a Family" (2001), "Bobbie Girl" (2002) and "A Question of Love" that all these serials invariably start with the struggle of a girl with her lesbian identity and ultimately veer around the issue of motherhood. And the reason behind this is that the marginalized identity of lesbianism becomes palatable to a straight reader or audience only when it is merged with the mainstream identity of a mother. Thus in a way it becomes a subversive strategy and seems to inscribe the idea that sex is only revered when it is procreative in nature. Interestingly some academic scholars endorse the lesbian motherhood as a mechanism for overcoming heterosexual privileges and patriarchal oppression, as has been observed by J. Wald:

> They threaten the traditional structure of the family as the male role is deleted and the child-bearing becomes the result of purely female choice. — 1997: 1

No wonder the male narrator of *Tirohit* is reared by two mothers, Lalana and Chhacho, without knowing till late who is his real biological mother. The image of Krishna, who has two mothers, is woven throughout the text. Their family seems to be complete with a set of two parents and a son. And the role of the father is completely deleted in the sense that he has been shown in coma with no participation in household and is nothing more than a non-existing entity. Not only this, on the roof (a figurative house for the two same-sex lovers) the two lovers walk amorously while their son walks between them. Their son narrates the whole scene in this fashion that they get ready for each other like Damayanti and Shakuntala. He states:

> I have been made a small sage with the help of two *duppatas* . . . they put flowers in their pleats and took me in their arms and kiss me and say, "how charming we all look together" . . . they used to give me space between them and I used to walk with them holding their hand.
>
> — Geetanjali Shree 2001: 61

This completion of the family without the pernicious presence of the father bears a close semblance with the story of Bhagiratha's birth as depicted in *Krittivasa Ramayana* and popularized by Ruth Vanita. According to her, the most explicit case of the co-wives as partners and joint mothers is perhaps that of King Dilipa's co-widows. They produce a child by mutual sexual interaction. Ruth further explains that *bhagas* means vulvas and "Bhagiratha means born out of two vulvas" (Ruth Vanita 2005a: 199). Ruth also gives reference to Agni who is not only born of two mothers but is also nourished by a group of mothers. Hence there are historical and religious records of lesbian motherhood and alternative family structure and the efforts of Geetanjali Shree are indeed commendable for showcasing lesbian parenting as a viable choice and making possible the seemingly impossible. Another literary example of such lesbian parenting is in Suroopa Mukherjee's *Across the Mystic Shore* in which other than the mid-wife no one knows who is the biological mother out of the two same-sex lovers. The fulfilment at every level is provided by Lalana to Chhacho which is evident from this statement of hers that Chacha has given her only materialistic things which hold no value to her:

> This sort of providing is nothing, . . . what has he given me?

> Even child has been given to me by you.
>
> — Geetanjali Shree 2001: 61

But the whole endeavour is marred somewhat by showing a male progeny instead of a female, for our religious texts subvert lesbian reproduction under the garb of ennobling act of producing male heir (as in the case of Bhagiratha). Apropos of this Giti Thadani asserts that

> the focus is not on Usha (mother of Agni) . . . . the generating energy is no longer the nodal point; rather the appropriation and control of this point in its eventual production of male progeny becomes the centralizing factor. — 1996: 37

Now the big question is whether the depiction of lesbian motherhood in this text is an act of resistance by the author and an attempt to showcase that the so-called normal family with an offspring is quite a possibility within lesbian framework or is it an effort to subvert lesbian identity under the mask of the revered identity of the motherhood. Nevertheless the ease with which Geetanjali Shree is able to negotiate a specific space for lesbian parenting, which still suffers severe discriminating laws even in many developed countries, is commendable.

Geetanjali Shree's belief in lesbianism as a challenge to patriarchy and a very potent tool of feminism is apparent from her description of the marginalization of masculinity, symbolically represented in the form of Chacha's slipping into coma and being reduced to no more than a vegetable. Chhacho and Lalana secretly enjoy it and seek their revenge for all they have suffered either in the form of sexual starvation of Chhacho or forced physical relationship with Lalana. While he has been in coma Lalana asks:

> I am using razor before his dry lips. Just goad him with it. Let us see whether it will hurt him or not. Goad? Let us see. She gets tempted. "There will be blood." She presses my

> hand, while I am shaving him. Om Babu's head droops on one side.
> — 2001: 61

It suggests that only the complete annihilation of patriarchal structure provides a fertile ground for the exploration of lesbian leaning. It reminds the reader of the myth of Ashvamedha (sacrificial epoch), as has been depicted by Giti Thadani in *Sakhiyani*,

> where the queen unites with the dead horse in the presence of another queen. The dead horse represents the king but as absent-dead. In other words there is a lesbian exchange between the two queens, symbolizing also the death of the masculine as represented by the dead horse or king.
> — 1996: 62

Now the point of vintage is whether it is shown to describe that a sexual transaction between two women is possible only when the masculine structure is dead or to evince that it is through lesbian love that oppressive heterosexual structure could be thwarted. It is unclear whether the author tries to reveal lesbianism as an act of resistance and a means to validate it as a political ideology or to depict the sorry state of lesbians' lives where the co-existence of lesbianism with heterosexism is an impossibility and either of them has to be annihilated, but indubitably she is able to raise a very pertinent issue.

What distinguishes Manju Kapur's *A Married Woman* from the rest of the two novels under discussion is that in the process of tracing the evolution of the lesbian lover, the writer is able to catalogue the modern concept of sexual orientation, gaining association with romantic love and identity in addition to its original purely sexual meaning. The story revolves around an artist Astha, who teaches in a school and has two children. She suffers from usual Indian middle-class dilemma of identity crisis coupled with a passionless sexual life. She challenges the constrains of the middle-class existence by indulging into a lesbian relationship with much younger Piplika Khan. But finally the relationship breaks down due to the difference of expectations in both the lovers and Astha has been left with no choice but to resort to pseudo-blissful heteronormative structure. At the very outset of the novel Astha is described as a woman who has been brought up in a stringent middle-class environment that fills her with fear-psychosis and cripples her of any sort of self (sexual) exploration.

> Astha was brought up properly as befits a woman, with large supplement of fear. . . . The infinite ways in which she could be harmed were not specified, but Astha absorbed them through her skin, and ever after was drawn to the safe and secure. — Kapur 2002: 1

It is this false sense of security that prevents her from the final union with Piplika. Piplika wants a fuller life but the social conditioning of the overglorified sense of security inherent in heterosexual domesticity puts impervious impediments in Astha's realization of sexual identity. To quote from the text:

> Astha's mind boggled. What about their school, their routine, their friends in the colony, their grandparents, their father, despite his faults did love his kids? . . . The dynamics of domesticity did not include companionship and understanding was regrettable, but she had grown used to it. She saw herself as a bird pecking at a few leftover crumbs from the feast of life. — Ibid.: 242

At this Piplika remarks:

> And you do not want to change it that is the trouble with married people. — Ibid.: 243

Hence lesbian exploration is regulated not only by heteronormative conditioning, but also by the false sense of security that is considered to be the obvious outcome of such relations. A woman's false sense of feeling safe only in the company of a man (who is assigned a stereotypical role of a protector) is the result of continuous feeding of fear psychosis since childhood which in adults results in the perennial sense of insecurity in the company of female partners and consequently leads to the breach in the relationship between the lesbians. This is not the only reason for the gulf between the lovers, but undoubtedly a very significant one. Another such example can be cited from an incident where Astha's husband Hemant severely objects to her going to Ayodhya with Piplika Khan to a rally that supports secularism. The backdrop of communal violence serves as a stark symbol throughout the novel as the turbulence, conflict and opposition are ingrained in a homosexual relationship. In this way, Astha and Piplika's going to Ayodhya for a secular march is reflective of their search for unique space for their lesbian existence and Hemant's remark to stop Astha from going to Ayodhya is specially significant in this regard. He implicitly states that in the absence of a male company she can be raped. This enraged Piplika beyond measures and she retorts that this is his way of keeping Astha at home. So the writer assiduously evinces that this false sense of security regulates lesbian experience and shapes the opportunities for the homoerotic passion. No wonder Stevi Jackson in her essay, "The Social Construction of Female Sexuality", asserts that "sexual behaviour in this sense is socially scripted" (1996: 62) and operates through the culturally learnt meaning.

The novel demonstrates yet another instance that reveals the coercive notion of "romantic love" infused in the teenage girls as opposed to the "sexually inclined behaviour" of a man. This adds another dimension to compulsive heterosexuality. Apropos of this Stevi Jackson holds that

> the maintenance of a positive feminine self-concept depends on the successful management of romantic relationships, rather than on specifically sexual achievement. . . . Hence most girls pass into adulthood, still unsure of their sexual

> identity and with a romantic, passive and dependent orientation towards erotic activity. — Ibid.: 72

This statement is fully exemplified through Astha's affair with Rohan prior to her marriage. She has a romantic view of her relationship with Rohan and constantly urges him to marry, whereas Rohan wants to explore the sensual heights with her, for which she has been conditioned to restrict herself. She wants reassurance of marriage:

> "Do you want to marry me?" She asked breathlessly. . . . What! He asked distractedly. . . . She had to know how safe she was. Marriage, She persisted, "you know" she inched a little further away. "God! All right. We might get married One day." His mouth closed on hers, his tongue was exploring while Astha chocked and wriggled frantically.
> — Kapur 2002: 72

When asked whether she liked it or not,

> "I don't know," she mumbled non-committed. "Well! let us find out." Rohan was beginning to sound impatient.
> — Ibid.: 24

And finally Rohan leaves for Oxford without any commitment. She feels rejected because whereas Rohan's sexual longing is unmasked and has not been hampered by the ideal notion of love, her sexual urge is suppressed under the garb of romanticism and the so-called ennobling love, because it is unbecoming of a woman to feel sexually rejuvenated without the associated feelings of love. Hence the conditioned notion of romance stripped of sexuality hampers Astha's first chance of realizing her sexual identity. She twists herself into knots by overdetermined romantic view of sexuality.

The much debated issue of bisexuality is highlighted in this text with all its complexity and multiplicity. Adrienne Rich's advocacy for "instinctive bisexuality" as opposed to "compulsive heterosexuality" and Anne Koedt's scientific delineation of the fact that it is the clitoral sex instead of penetrative vaginal sex that provides orgasm make the case very strong for bisexuals, lesbians and pansexuals. Astha's partner Piplika Khan's first crush was on a girl known as Samira and then she married Aziz, which was followed by her homosexual relationship with Astha. Now whether her first love for Samira is the result of lesbian leaning or merely a homosexuality of convenience is debatable. Many girls in teenage, because of the lack of availability of the male partner, suffer from a case of terribly misplaced emotions which find manifestation in the form of mild romantic liaison with fellow girls because it is safe and convenient. However, as they mature, they outgrow it. Ismat Chughtai's *The Crooked Line* beautifully explores the "homosexuality of convenience" which is found in abundance in girls' hostel. Thus whether Piplika's relationship with Samira falls into the category of bisexuality, lesbianism of convenience or pansexuality is open to discussion and the following conversation between Aziz and Piplika fully bears witness to it. Piplika says to Aziz:

> "It was in school that I first fell in love, and now I am coming here on my honeymoon. I feel strange when I think about it, that's all. . . . Her name was Samira." Aziz asked, "You were in love with a woman?" Aziz thought, it must have been like those crushes that girls had on film stars or their teachers. She was young and inexperienced and imagined her feelings to be of love. — Kapur 2002: 129-30

Piplika's statement after the death of Aziz is especially significant in this respect. When Astha refuses to leave her family, Piplika says: "I thought it would be different with a woman" (ibid.: 243). It evinces an undertone of considering homosexuality a better option as compared to heterosexuality on account of better understanding between the same-sexes than the opposite ones. Inevitably the better compatibility and comfort level between the same-sexes become the reasons for their liaison rather than spontaneous attraction. At one point even Astha very pragmatically contemplates about the benefits of having a female partner for extramarital affair:

> Indeed had Pipee been a man, Astha would have found it impossible to stray so far down the road of intimacy, or be so comfortable in it. — Ibid.: 218

This *sakhi* space is quite eclectic, for on one hand, as has been suggested by Ashwini Sukthankar in *Facing the Mirror*, has a potential to purge the lesbian relationship of its eroticism and reshape it into harmless description of female friendship, on the other it provides greater mobility and opportunity for the lesbian experiences. Apropos of this Ashwini Sukthankar opines:

> The *sakhi* space where, in the gender-segregated Indian world, women can live and be together in relative freedom . . . can live with each other without being interrogated by any one. — 1999: 17

Patently extramarital relationship with same-sex lover is much more safe and convenient. Hence the relationships among Samira, Aziz and Astha put various question marks on the intention of the writer as whether she projects them as pansexuals, bisexuals, victims of coerced heterosexuality or advocates of homosexuality of convenience. Similarly Astha has been shown initially as a strictly heterosexual when at the age of sixteen, she envisages herself in the arms of a young man:

> Astha obediently closed her eyes to delicious images of romantics, somewhat shadowy young man holding her in his strong manly embrace. — Kapur 2002: 1

She has a physically intimate relationship with Rohan but her attachment with Rohan is initiated by her desire to fall into the esteemed category of girls who know the nuances of love.

> She brought out his name experimentally to show that she too had lived and knew what love was. —Ibid.: 15

Astha's initiation into heterosexuality is somewhat on account of imitating the norm followed by her heterosexual marriage with Hemant. In the initial period of her marriage she has been depicted as a woman completely intoxicated by the masculine charm of Hemant.

> Astha looked at him in admiration. Everything about him was so masculine, his decisiveness, his hairy blunt finger, his tall heavy set figure, his muscled limbs, his moustache that tickled, the bitter tobacco taste from his tongue.
> —Ibid.: 56

No matter, even if it is the social order that has shaped their heterosexual orientation, the portrayal of both Piplika and Astha as bisexuals and not strictly homosexual evinces the writer's somewhat regressive move, for as Cheryl Clarke remarks:

> Bisexual is a safer label than lesbian, for it posits the possibility of a relationship with a man regardless of how infrequent or non-existent the female bisexual relationships with men might be. —1966: 156

The valorization of the procreative-sex and motherhood also regulates the same-sex leanings. According to many lesbian feminists, it is one of the most potent tool for clitoral to vaginal transference and consequently for infusing compulsive heterosexuality. Let us illustrate it from the text:

> Loving Hemant as she did, Astha longed to get pregnant. During sex she imagined his seed spurting into her womb, later she would gather his wet shrivelled penis, adoring it strong, thick and hot, or wet, limp woebegone. "I want to have your baby". —Kapur 2002: 56

But after the childbirth, the burden of motherhood takes its toll and it becomes one of the main impediments for her self-actualization and the reason for her succumbing to subversive heterosexual domesticity. Thus, it is a vicious circle. The heterosexual oppression is all-pervasive in the text. Astha has been shown crushed between her duties as a mother and a housewife, having no time for her paintings or other interests such as social service. Despite working as a teacher, she has no access to her money. She toils relentlessly as a glorified maid and her turbulence is symbolically presented in the form of her frequent migraines which miraculously vanish in the company of Piplika. The predatory aspect of Astha's heterosexual domesticity reminds the reader of the popular slogan:

> It starts when you sink in his arms and ends with your arms in his sink. — Jackson 1996: 13

But despite getting no help from Hemant in the upbringing of children, Astha rejects Pippee's offer of an alternative lesbian family structure because the idea of lesbian-motherhood is unpalatable to her. In fact, the traditional family set-up that fosters the notion of ideal family consisting of father and mother regulates her desire to form a family with Pipee.

The eclectic nature of the homoerotic experience of Astha becomes all the more conspicuous when one views it from the perspective of the concept of "beauty myth". Naomi Wolf in her influential book, *The Beauty Myth* asserts that the constructed notion of over-glorification of beauty alters and regulates the sexual desire of woman.

> Beauty and sexuality are both commonly misunderstood as some transcendental inevitable fact; falsely interlocking the two makes it seem doubly true that a woman must be "beautiful" to be "sexual". That of course is not true at all. The definition of both "beautiful" and "sexual" constantly change to serve the social order. — Wolf 1991: 150

The ever-changing definitions of beauty are bound to make

everyone sexually unattractive at one point or another and are consequently instrumental in suppressing woman's own sexuality. In this novel the slim and attractive figure of Astha gets distorted after the childbirth and when she wants to wear a sensually appealing dress, she finds herself obnoxious. When she meets Pipee, the first seeds of lesbianism sprout in the form of eulogy of her looks by Pipee. This scene is highly evocative and soaked in multiple meanings. In it Piplika takes her to mirror and makes her aware of the sensual charm by showing Astha's beauty in the mirror.

> She pulled Astha by the hand and led her to the bathroom mirror. Are we going to do mirror, mirror on the wall/Who is the fairest of all? laughed Astha nervously. . . . A modern version of it, said Pipee putting on the light and pushing Astha's head gently forward , "look", Astha tried to turn away, "I don't like looking at my face especially so close." Then she felt Pipee's hands framing the oval of her face. Lightly from the behind she traced her eyebrows with her fingers, her nose, cheeks and mouth. The two women said nothing looking at their reflections in the small-water stained mirror. "See"? Whispered Pipee.
>
> — Kapur 2002: 221

The culturally scripted notion of feeling sexually stimulated only by having an aesthetically appealing self-image (because of overlapping of beauty and sexuality in woman) is evocatively expressed through the superimposition of images of Pipee and Astha. Pipee's young body becomes an extension of Astha's middle-aged haggard body and through her youth she internalizes her own aesthetic appeal and feels sexually rejuvenated. It finds manifestation in the admiration of Pipee's body. Again this narcissistic streak serves as a backlash against the instinctive lesbianism, for desire to own an aesthetically appealing self-image overpowers a genuine lesbian passion and adds a complex dimension to homoerotic trajectory.

The writer's belief in the fluidity of homosexuality is

evident from the fact that she has kept Astha and Piplika away from the "butch" and "femme" stereotypes that oversimplify complex identities into false dichotomies. "Butch" identity is often predicated upon a kind of androgynous powerful energy, whereas "femme" is modelled upon feminine attributes. However, Pip and Astha's relationship is based on "egalitarian structured" (a category given by Stephen O'Murray) model of lesbianism where hierarchy of class and gender are negated. Thus the writer carefully avoids the much debated and problematic issue of "butch" and "femme" identities which on the one hand is regressive because of its own underlying assumptions of heteronormative categories of masculine and feminine, and on the other hand is progressive because it evinces that all sorts of resignifying and parodic repetitions are possible within non-heterosexual frames, as has been suggested by Judith Butler in "Imitation and Gender Insubordination". By showing an "egalitarian structured" relationship rather than "gendered structure" Manju Kapur clearly shows her intentions of exhibiting the fluidity of homosexuality.

Homophobia, another issue pertaining to homosexuality, finds its fullest exposition in this text. Hemant, Astha's husband, feels deeply detested at the idea of Astha's desire to watch a "gay film" and vociferously rejects it:

> "Go with you and Piplika Khan to a gay film show? Are you out of your mind?" To which Astha replies, "well I am going with her. You can for once come to some thing, I am interested in." Hemant started, "I am not interested in homosexuals".
>
> — Kapur 2002: 236

This scene is also significant in this respect that Astha and Pipee's relationhip is limited to private sphere, but their going to watch a gay movie together is symbolic of transcending from private to public, however, the author's anxiety is visible when Astha leaves the film half way to return her home.

Despite exploring the wide spectrum of fluid homosexuality, the author fails to exhibit a permanent fruitful relationship between Astha and Pipee and homoerotic passion seems to be only an episode in the life of Astha, who returns to her colourless domesticity and Pipee abruptly leaves for USA to pursue her Ph.D. According to Subash Chandra, Pipee's leaving for USA is a narrative strategy known as "lesbian panic", a term used by Juliana Smith who defines lesbian panic thus:

> In terms of narrative, lesbian panic is, quite simply, the disruptive action or reaction that occurs when a character — or conceivably an author — is either unable or unwilling to confront or reveal her own lesbianism or lesbian desire. Caught in this state, the female character indulges in an action which causes "emotional or physical harm to her and others." . . . In an instance, the character is led by her sense of panic to commit irrational or illogical acts that inevitably work to the disadvantage or harm of her and others. — 1995: 567

According to Subash Chandra, apart from Pipee's sudden departure "lesbian panic" also manifests itself in the "neurasthenic" state Astha gets into after she returns home having rejected Pipee's offer of permanent union. She threw herself into a frenzy of house-cleaning. Anuradha, her daughter, has gone to the extent of stating that "mama has gone mad" (Kapur 2002: 285). In fact, when Pipee urges Astha to make a final decision, the writer explicitly states that "panic rose in Astha" (ibid.: 243).

What makes *Machali Mari Hui*, the third text in this study, a unique novel is that it presents the male perspective of the 1960s on lesbianism. Written in 1966, it is perhaps one of the first Hindi novels that depict the lesbianism both in public and private sphere with remarkable insight. Though imbued with lesbophobia, it deconstructs the strategy of "silence" employed by heterosexual constructs and makes lesbianism visible. Strangely at the very outset of the novel, the anxiety of the author is apparent when he affirms that "Lesbianism is not the subject of this novel, but only a subject proposal" (Chaudhary 1966: 11). This contradiction is pervasive throughout the text. The story revolves around a dancing girl Shiri who is married to Nirmal Padmavat. Nirmal has been shown in love with another society woman Kalyani and suffers from psychological impotence due to her rejection. Circumstances conspire in such a way as Shiri develops lesbian relationship with Priya, who is a daughter of Kalyani. The novel tells a poignant tale of these characters' struggle with their own sexuality and it ends with the rape of Priya by Nirmal and description of Shiri as someone who is contained by the heterosexual ordering of desire.

Written by a male author with great poignancy, the portrayal of the soul-crushing ill effects of heterosexual coercion in it makes it an interesting study. The novelist affirms that women's economic dependence and false sense of security become the root cause of their succumbing to heteronormative structures. He quotes Emily Dickinson in this regard:

> Woman does not give support/She needs it/Small but strong plank should always be beneath her arm/All the time.
>
> — Ibid.: 61

He asserts that Niyogi, a businessman, whenever angry with a girl, sends her to war front; likewise sexual exploitation of secretaries for economic favour is common. It is evident when a stenographer asks another one regarding her salary and then casually questions her about the number of abortions she has gone through. All female characters, Shiri, her sister, Kalyani and Priya exhibit lesbian leanings. They denounce penetrative sex and consider it an act of subjugation. Shiri's mother tells her:

> Everyman is a savage animal. Woman is forced to bow-down before his brutality. One should do it and at the same time hate it because man is horrifying and he can only give pain and not pleasure. —Ibid.: 111

No wonder Nirmal considers that it is his social, moral and religious right to explore Shiri's body:

> Shiri cannot say no. She wants to deny but Nirmal's hands are made of stone. —Ibid.: 105

The author's belief that satisfaction and peace are only illusions in heterosexual relationship is visible from the incident in which Shiri gets peace only after the death of her father.

> Both the sisters used to sleep in the night in the same bed. . . . No man could give her as much peace, excitement and such erotic sexual tension as her own sister. —Ibid.: 104

The author draws a parallel when a heterosexual liaison leaves her ignited and yet not satisfied and in the middle of this scene Priya enters and Nirmal throws Shiri like a garbage. Then Priya is forcibly taken away by Nirmal, who rapes her. This is height of heterosexual perversion because not only he is denying two women seek pleasure in each other, but also mutilating them physically, emotionally and psychically. Shiri is left alone and is forced to indulge in masturbation in the absence of Priya. Shiri has been shown masturbating.

> . . . She is lying on the bed completely naked; the primitive woman Shiri, does not need a man; she needs a woman like herself. . . . If she does not get another woman then what option does she have other than exploring her own body.
> —Ibid.: 108

The constant presence of a painting of the two naked women exploring each other's sexuality above Shiri and Nirmal's bed is indicative of the homoerotic negotiation within the heteronormative sphere. Significantly it is difficult to determine whether Nirmal's inability to satisfy Shiri is symbolic of general dissatisfaction that women encounter in vaginal sex rather than clitoral or is an attack on lesbians who marginalize straight men because Nirmal's impotence and the consequent rage are the results of Kalyani's rejection. None the less the writer is effectively able to evince patriarchy as the greatest impediment in the lesbian encounters.

Critics like Adrienne Rich and Lillian Faderman consider sexuality as a secondary aspect of same-sex love. This de-sexualization of lesbianism is vehemently opposed by A. Koedt, E. Levine and Diane Richardson. Little wonder Rajkamal Chaudhary shows Priya, Shiri and her sister indulged in explicit love-making without disguising these scenes under the garb of the romantic love and sisterhood. Not only this the writer breaks the incest-taboo, when he gives a detailed description of lovemaking between Shiri and her sister.

> She bites Shiri's breast. There were intoxication, madness and happiness. — Ibid.: 111

Many times this description is loaded with male voyeuristic pleasure that such a lesbian encounter provides. The Radha–Krishna tradition is saturated with this sort of male invasion for voyeuristic pleasure in women only space. Apropos of this Giti Thadani observes:

> The visual traditions often have very explicit lesbian depictions of Radha's *sakhi*s erotically playing together in water while Krishn(a), in the role of voyeur, looks on.
> — 1996: 72

A male writer's access to women only space carries subtle undertones of voyeurism. Hence re-sexualization of lesbianism is somewhat plagued with the male desire of getting titillating pleasure out of the lesbian double-bonanza.

Another way in which the de-sexualization of lesbianism takes place is the glorification of procreative sex. Alienating sex with reproduction is a measure to deconstruct the myth that the primary function of sexual intimacy is to procreate. In *Mahabarata*'s Shanti Parva, Bhishma emphasizes that a man, who copulates with a woman "for the sake of only offspring", can conquer any kind of difficulty (Ganguli, *Shanti Parva*, Rajadharmanusashana Parva CX.240). The dirt complex associated with sex is at times negated through the so-called ennobling act of procreation. According to Ruth Vanita, "such denigrations of sex and procreation are often read today, especially by some feminists, as evidence of misogyny and body-hating aestheticism" (Ruth and Kidwai 2000: 9). Thus amidst this sort of social and cultural background, where even men have been degraded if they seek only sexual pleasure bereft of desire to produce, creating a character like Shiri who vehemently rejects motherhood is indeed a progressive move by the author. Shiri has seen her mother dying in the child-birth and decides that she does not want children. Shiri's sister has told her that their mother has conceived a child due to sleeping with their father. And because of the child only the mother fell ill and died. Shiri started hating her father. In fact, she begins to hate every man and with the result starts loving her sister and not any man. Even when occasionally she contends that her sexual dissatisfaction with Nirmal is perhaps due to her fear of conceiving, she immediately contradicts herself by stating that she does not want to be a mother.

> The biggest fear of Shiri was that she might get pregnant that was why she deliberately avoided male company.
>
> — Chaudhary 1966: 111

Now this gives a slightly twisted and crippled turn to the whole issue and the dichotomy is apparent in the depiction of lesbianism as a product of fear psychosis rather than an instinctive choice. Nevertheless, avoiding pregnancy for the fear of pain and death is also a form of denouncing patriarchy, for as has been affirmed by Ruth Vanita that in "Judeo–Christian–Islamic Tradition", suffering in childbirth is God's curse to Eve. Ruth opines that

> Many European Christians took this curse so seriously that when anesthesia was first invented, they objected to its use in childbirth, because they believed women's labour pains were divinely ordained and should not be mitigated.
>
> — Ruth 2005a: 188-89

The somewhat liberal stand of the novelist is prominent in the manner in which he has brilliantly interwoven intertextuality, while recording a history of lesbian relationships through European novels across class and culture. He refers to Marquis D Sade's novel, *Justin and Juliet* (published in 1790, which depicts the same-sex love in public sphere such as hostels, prostitution, convents, etc.), and the novels of Balzac and Thomas Hardy's *Desperate Remedies* (that showcase the same-sex longings in the private sphere). Also the out of context mention of Radcliff Hall's *Well of Loneliness* and quoting lines from Stephen Gordon's impassioned plea can only be understood in terms of the writer's own desire to accommodate lesbians in the mainstream of society. Importantly the author quotes Stephen's prayer to God:

> We have not denied your existence God./Therefore please come and protect us/Give us acceptance/Give us a right to come out of closet/Accept our existence.
>
> — Chaudhary 1966: 129

"Ghosting of lesbians" is a very common mode used by the creative writers to counter their own anxieties regarding lesbophobia as has been mentioned earlier with reference to Terry Castle's article. No wonder in *Machali Mari Hui,* Priya has been compared to witch and ghost time and again. After seeing Nirmal for the first time, "she cries like a woman possessed by ghosts" (ibid.: 14). Likewise the pernicious intrusion of the straight mind is visible when after the rape, Priya has been seen "coming out of Nirmal's cottage after midnight as if a witch has come out of a cave of hell" (ibid.: 129). But the ghosting strategy becomes eclectic when Nirmal (a symbol of male supremacist imperialism) is described as a black ghost standing before Priya holding a riffle (again symbolic of penis, for in the end it is Nirmal who rapes Priya):

> There is a black negro standing like a ghost. His eyes are burning like a torch and he is holding a riffle in his hand and such brutal anger on his face. Now he will put riffle between Priya's legs and she will be reduced to a piece of flesh and blood will smear on the wall of her own house.
>
> —Ibid.: 15

Whether this sexually explicit imagery is indicative of the mutilating effects of patriarchal oppression or of just punishment for ignoring heteronormative structure is questionable because both the oppressed (Priya) and the oppressor (Nirmal who becomes the root cause of separation between Shiri and Priya) have been depicted as the invisible entities of ghosts.

The opaque intention of the author is apparent when despite showing the demonizing effects of the sexual starvation in penetrative sex, he represents lesbianism not as an instinctive choice, but as a substitute. The female characters in this novel have been initiated into the same-sex love in order to counter the fear of the oppressive heterosexuality and the pain of the childbirth. The author's homophobia is visible in the manner in which he punishes both Priya and Shiri. He sexually starves Shiri and rapes Priya for their lesbian liaison. Shiri has been shown desiring Nirmal and cries after he fails to consummate:

> Just this much you want. Just this much. . . . Tell me do you not care for me at all? Why do you not kill me? —Ibid.: 107

Only after a failed relationship with Nirmal, she wants Priya as a substitute and when she does not get her either she indulges in masturbation. Also the rape of Priya has been used as a metaphor to cure the lesbian leaning, and the lesbian tendency is seen purging out of the system in the form of vomiting after the brutal rape. The violence and torture inflicted upon Priya have been depicted as having medicinal properties:

> Nirmal used to put whisky on her lips and makes her conscious. After gaining consciousness, she used to laugh like an insane being and states "I am still alive (the lesbian in me), do it more, I am still conscious." — Ibid.: 130

The whole scene portrays forced heterosexual mating as a means to cure the so-called medical illness known as lesbianism. In fact, in a morbid and shocking scene Priya's father thanks Nirmal for the penile penetration because it cures his daughter of homoerotic passion which is a disease in his opinion. In a dramatic turn of events even Shiri has been described as a blissfully happy domesticated woman bereft of any lesbian leaning. This whole scene bears close semblance with Rangin's *Chaptinama*. Rangin is a mid-nineteenth-century Urdu poet and *Chaptinama* is a collection of writings devoted to lesbianism, where penile penetration is seen as a cure for lesbianism. According to Vanita, "it describes the anger of a man who witnesses two women's intimacy" (Ruth Vanita 2005: 266). Rangin remarks:

> They are "loose women" and are in search of a man. He then has sex with them by turn all night until worn out and bruised. . . . He then makes them promise never again to engage in *chapti*, otherwise he will continue intercourse with them as long as he has breath. — Ibid.

Since lesbianism is seen as an aberration rather than a natural choice, there is a constant tendency to find reasons for such inversions and one such explanation has been perceived in the form of woman's eternal desire to remain beautiful, for since childhood her self-worth is associated with beauty. Naomi Wolf in her work, *The Beauty Myth: How Images of Beauty Are Used Against Women*, argues that the rigid ideals of beauty are instruments of a backlash against feminism designed to lower women's self-esteem. She effectively shows how the constructed notion of beauty traps women within its confines and regulates their sexuality. A woman's beauty regulates her own sexuality and many a time the lesbian relationships are manifestations of the extension of the narcissistic streak. Shiri's obsession with her own looks is reflective of it:

> Shiri does not want to grow old and ugly. . . . She wants to hold on to her beauty. She stands before the huge mirror and appreciates herself and gets assured.
>
> — Chaudhary 1966: 90

This reassurance is further accentuated by the superimposition of images of Shiri and Priya in a mirror:

> Before the wash basin both Priya and Shiri are standing. Shiri is standing behind Priya. Two women in one frame of mirror . . . she embraces Priya and tells her with a slight hesitation, "You are very beautiful Priya." — Ibid.: 100

She ruminates that Nirmal has never appreciated her beauty and probably married her only to humiliate her previous husband, Vishavajeet. Thus reassurance of beauty by Priya becomes the root cause of their relationship. Therefore to some extent it inscribes the patriarchal notion that lesbian liaison emanates from the narcissistic streak, instead of spontaneous mutual attraction.

The very title, *Machali Mari Hui,* is loaded with symbolic significance. It fosters the notion that struggle with their own sexuality creates identity crisis in lesbians. They are like fish without water with no hands and feet, struggling to find their own space:

> There is a vacuum and two shadows of women. There is no man and there was no man. There is a vacuum and darkness and nothing holds a foundation. There is no reason, no religion, no identity and no form. There are only two shadows of women. There are no arms, no knees, no hands and fingers, no feet, only two fishes. Blue fishes and the sea

> of darkness. Fishes are floating in the darkness. They try to hold and catch each other, but there are no arms. They are craving to embrace each other, but do not have feet.
>
> — Ibid.: 121

This is reflective of the void and vacuum present in women only space, though, the author backtracks to bisexuality (which is for the author not a means for fluid sexuality or pansexuality) and evinces that heterosexual invasion and succumbing to "butch" and "femme" stereotypes make their consummation incomplete.

> Both the fishes (Shiri and Priya) remain alive despite dying. . . . Because both have a man in their heart, Nirmal Pdamavat. . . . The two lesbian women and both are having Nirmal in their heart and mind. — Ibid.: 80

They have to manipulate brutally the dimensions of who they are, in the absence of well-defined structure for homoerotic passion. No wonder Kalyani dies of mysterious mental ailment, Priya has to bear the brutal rape and Shiri is compelled to settle into a subversive heterosexual domesticity.

Thus the contradictory ambivalent positions adopted by these three novelists, regarding lesbianism exhibit that lesbianism in part is forged in the very heterosexual matrix, it displaces. It is revealed through various facets such as describing lesbianism as a pathological illness on the one hand and the depiction of the coercive nature of heterosexuality (as in the case of Astha, Shiri and Piplika) on the other hand. There is also an overlapping of an eagalitarian lesbian rendezvous (such as between Priya and Shiri, Piplika and Astha) and the "lesbian ghosting" through the characters of Lalana and Priya. Further the negation of the procreative sex is coupled with homophobia and lesbian panic (encountered by Priya, Astha and Shiri). Similarly at one level these texts document the regulation of the homoerotic passion through the false notion of "beauty myth" and at the other exhibit the alternative lesbian family structure (in the case of Lalana and Chhacho). These opposite stands are also revealed in considering lesbianism inconsistent with virtue by demonstrating both Shiri and Kalyani as prostitutes while highlighting the need for specific space for lesbians; sympathy with the character of Stephen Gordon (heroine of Ann Redcliff's *The Well of Loneliness*) at one level and showcasing lesbian mating for male voyeuristic pleasure on the other. Hence these books can be catalogued as valuable additions to lesbian discourse — despite showing that for a woman to be a lesbian, in a male supremacist, capitalist, misogynist, racist, homophobic society, is an act of resistance but it cannot substitute the heterosexual structure — for rendering visibility to the invisible and for raising the issues of the heterosexual coercion and the lack of the public space in lesbophobic society.

6

Lesbophobic Anxiety and the Contradictory Fissures in Modern Regional Women Short Story Writers

Shivani's "Manik" and Hiranmayee Mishra's "The Tale of a Rainy Night"

THAT LESBIAN existence has been hugely denied and marginalized within queer academia as well as in feminist concerns, especially in India, is a well-known fact. This has been vociferously argued through two brilliant lesbian anthologies namely *Facing the Mirror* and *Loving Women* by Ashwini Sukthankar and Maya Sharma respectively. The erasure of lesbian copulation as an offence on account of non-penetrative sex from Section 377 on the one hand provides legal protection to lesbians, but on the other it works as a potent silencing technique as has been catalogued by Ashwini Sukthankar:

> . . . The invisibility conferred on us by the law — our special share of the country's colonial legacy — does not necessarily result in lesbians being "legal" and therefore having legal recourse to fighting discrimination and harassment. On the contrary, invisibility means that the fact of our existence is employed to crush it out. — 1999: xiv

Thus the apparent exclusion from the Section 377 might appear as a respite and a privilege to lesbians but has a sinister motive of silencing by according invisibility to female homoerotic desire because if they cannot be tried under Section 377 then they can be tried under the obscenity law of Section 292. Not only in the LGBTQ circles, but also in the feminist forums lesbians face this sort of ostracization on the fallacious assumption that it is an upper middle-class Western import and does not concern majority of women in India. Quoting from Caleri Report and documenting the lesbian struggles within feminist circles such as National Federation of Indian Women (NFIW) and others that talk about the problems pertaining to the inclusion of lesbianism within the preview of larger feminist concerns on account of pitting women against women, causing confusion, considering it an utterly a private matter and a source of diverting attention, Maya Sharma affirms:

> The stand that lesbian issues and lesbians themselves not be made publicly visible within the women's movement has been based on the following arguments: it is for the greater good of the movement; the presence of the lesbians (since they are unacceptable publicly) will fragment whatever collectivity has been established over the years, fewer women will associate with the movement, fewer groups will participate, and mainstream and state support will be seriously compromised. — 2006: 25

Naturally this kind of phobic gaze by feminist movement and the step-sisterly treatment by queer activism have perpetuated the myth that lesbians are invisible category and the gory example of it is evident from the fact that in a very prestigious institutionalized seminar on gay subcultures organized by Indian Institute of Advanced Study (IIAS) held on 3-4 April 2012, there were speakers like Hoshang Merchant, Onir and Raj Rao but not a single open lesbian had given her presentation and this is a reflection of the sorry state of the Indian lesbians. Apparently the two short stories written in Oriya and Hindi hold a special place because despite the apparent lesbophobic anxieties of the authors, the homoerotic desires of women have been articulated in *bhasha* literature and this indubitably counters the myth that it is a phenomenon associated with the English-speaking Westernized individuals and thus representation of it is primarily limited to the English writings. Further despite the exhibition of homophobia these stories at least lend visibility to lesbian existence though in a somewhat regressive mode.

The first story in question is Oriya story, "The Tale of a Rainy Night" written by Hiranmayee Mishra and translated by Sumanyu Satpathy. It revolves around an unmarried writer who agrees to be interviewed by a young journalist and meets her at her home. During this meeting her lesbian tendencies have been exposed. The other is a Hindi story "Manik" by Shivani, which is still not translated. It focuses once again on the life of a middle-aged teacher who develops homoerotic longing for a younger woman who comes to stay with her and ultimately turns out to be a murderer. Despite being cast in different moulds, the two stories have common valency in terms of the exploration of the lesbian desire and the subsequent internalized lesbophobia of the writers. These aspects find manifestation in following the same pattern of showcasing the murder of one of the lesbians, creating a gothic environment around them in order to exhibit them as impersonal apparitions rather than real beings, exposition of sudden "lesbian panic" (to quote Juliana Smith's term) that aborts the transgressive relationship and the depiction of homoeroticism as an alternative choice in the absence of male partner and consequently portraying it as an aside to heterosexuality rather than an instinctive desire. Now the question arises: despite following this regressive module of feminine sexuality why do these stories require any attention. And the answer lies in the fact that these are the only few representations in *bhasha* literature by women writers who in spite of their lesbophobic anxieties accord visibility to lesbian existence and help in recording the history of lesbian literature that has been systematically erased from the queer and feminist struggles as has been mentioned earlier. Further irrespective of the homophobic tendencies, these stories create ruptures that are both problematic and progressive at the same time.

"The Tale of a Rainy Night", as the title suggests, starts with a rain-filled lonely night at a single journalist's home and the atmosphere continues till Sulagna reaches the writer Subarna's home where the environment gets all the more gothic in the absence of electricity and occasional lightening. In fact when Subarna embraces Sulagna,

> . . . her whole body shivered in terror. She felt robbed of her faculties as some vague apprehension gripped her. Yet she had no strength to resist and she began wondering whether the lady was homosexual. — Mishra 2007: 126

In the similar fashion in Shivani's "Manik" the middle-aged protagonist lives in a lonely huge villa at a secluded place which is far away from the city and there is a striking similarity between her body and the antique structure of her lonely abode. In fact, her own sister in a jocular fashion calls it "the grave of Tauta Khan". Thus both these stories create a haunted background and the reason for creating a ghostly backdrop lies in Terry Castle's interpretation of the narrative technique of the "ghosting of lesbians" or "apparitional lesbianism", the term used by her in *The Apparitional Lesbian: Female Homosexuality and Modern Culture*. Terry Castle has given the concept of "self-ghosting" through which a lesbian can disguise herself in her private space in this homophobic society. The detailed discussions regarding this idea is in Chapter 5. In this manner, the realities of the lesbian lives have been set against the much recognized diabolic environment. Obviously at one level the haunted backdrop is an ideal proposition for the anxiety-ridden self of these writers because it satisfies their need to invisibilize the deviant behaviour as abnormal, but at the other instead of portraying lesbian characters as ghosts (despite a fleeting reference to Subarna appearing as an apparition to Sulagna when she is embraced by her in a rain-filled night), they focus, by and large on just creating haunted environment and at the back drop of it the real characters are shown indulged in the same-sex desire. Hence the use of the narrative technique of "ghosting of lesbians" only to create an environment and not fully extending it to protagonists is indeed a progressive move and reveals a two-step forward and one-step backward technique that evinces much-needed fissures.

However, as the stories progress the heteronormative structures become prominent and hold the centre stage. Both the protagonists have been shown as unmarried not out of choice but due to the conspiring situations. Nalini Mishra in "Manik" remains unmarried because of the responsibility of a younger sister and has been shown in flashback having a desire to become a bride at the wedding of her relatives where she pictures herself in bridal attire with beautiful jewellery on her body. Her desire for motherhood is also highlighted in her excessive attachment to her nephew. Her sister constantly mentions that Nalini should adopt him although her insistence is in order to appropriate Nalini's property. Likewise Subarna in "The Tale of a Rainy Night" remains unmarried due to her breast removal because of cancer at the young age of twenty-five. She laments:

> When I was 25, cancer cells deprived me of the unique symbol of the female sex. One life-saving surgery removed the source of the elixir of possible motherhood. It is not that I had no lovers. But, can anyone be happily married by disowning the importance of the body. — Mishra 2007: 127

Thus there is indeed a stress on portraying these women deprived of usual pleasures of matrimony. The procreative sex as opposed to the mating for pleasure has always been valorized in Indian tradition and it is on account of the procreative nature of heterosexual relationship that it always seems to triumph over homosexual mating. This is the biggest argument in favour of heteropatriarchal society and the root of it lies in our religious texts and it can be illustrated from *Arthashastra* where the *ayoni* sex is considered a sin and it amounts to a punishable offence. In *Arthashastra* (4.12.20-22), it is stated that a woman deflowering a willing girl should pay 12 *panas* as a punishment and if the girl is not willing then the woman has to pay 100 *panas* and dowry. Referring to *Arthashastra*, Giti Thadani in *Sakhiyani* argues:

> Even within the heterosexual arrangement, if a man does not have sex with his wife after menstruation, this is seen as killing the foetus or developing embryo. — 1996: 57

But this linking of sexuality and motherhood has been seriously criticized by the feminist critics, for they argue that it is a tool to contain feminine sexuality because the over-glorification of motherhood is seen as an act of desexualizing female body and in this regard the non-procreative nature of the same-sex desire where the key focus is on pleasure and not on the reproduction is indeed an exploration of feminine sexuality. From this viewpoint it remains debatable whether the non-reproductive identity of the protagonist is an exposition of some kind of lack in her existence or the implicit suggestion that the non-procreative nature of same-sex desire unwittingly gives impetus to "pleasure principal" in sexual mating and consequently paves way for the exploration of unabashed feminine sexuality. Because as the Hindi story "Manik" progresses the subjugation within the heteropatriarchal family system becomes conspicuous, for Nalini's younger sister Rambha has to leave her lover and abort her unborn child and has to marry a money-minded patriarch who has a glad eye for women and who constantly forces her to be in good terms with her sister in order to get her property. Even her son is being used as a tool to extract money from Nalini.

Although all these Machiavellian efforts have been demonstrated in a very subtle fashion, the message is loud and clear that the oppression of woman in heterosexual marriage despite following the so-called "normalcy" and experiencing much valorized motherhood are a common reality.

The anxieties of the writers once again hold the centre stage when homosexuality is shown as a pathological illness. Rambha's husband describes how Nalini's constant association with younger teachers and students evokes doubts. To quote from the text:

> First there was this Nepalese *mastarni*, Miss Rana. I used to wonder how she pampered her. At times they were eating in the same plate then she had given her wrist watch and gold bangles. Then when she had tiff with miss Rana, she made an orphan beautiful young student her companion. On her wedding day how hysterically your sister was crying! I really consider this sort of *friendship* a sick friendship. Make her understand that people laugh at her due to all this.
> — Shivani 2007: 50

Similarly in "The Tale of a Rainy Night" when Sulagna is hugged by Subarna she feels terrified and suffocated and wonders whether Subarna is a homosexual and contemplates:

> What did she expect of her . . . what did she want from her . . . in this state . . . some unnatural bodily pleasure.
> — Mishra 2007: 126

Not only the transgressive desire is seen as a pathological illness, but also the element of criminality is being attached to it when Nalini is shown murdered by her paramour mercilessly for money. Patently it evinces the author's desire to exhibit same-sex liaison as a punishable offence for which the homosexual person should be punished and it reminds the murders of the queer characters in Lawrence's *The Fox* and *The Prussian Officer*. Similarly the dross of the lesbian longing of Subarna is seen being purged by the chanting of *shloka*s and the fragrance of the incense sticks early in the morning as if the repentance through religious rituals is being undertaken. Likewise despite Sulagna's comforting of Subarna after her breakdown, the possibility of their next meeting is abruptly cut short by Subarna herself when she in a state of remorse and lesbian panic tells Sulagna:

> I have one request to make. Please forget yesterday's rainy night, your question, my being beside yourself. Please do not try to see me again. — Ibid.: 128

Further the female homoerotic passion between an old and young woman is perceived as an extension of her longing for diminished youth and beauty because women in our society are culturally trained to get explored in sexual mating rather than exploring the charms of the masculine body. Hence the self-assurance through implicit autoeroticism is a part of the conditioned training and a tool to control the feminine sexuality as otherwise there will be larger demands on male body to appear attractive to female gaze. In this fashion, the female gaze is directed towards her own body. In one way it makes easier for women to find the codes of lesbianism within their body, but on the other it perpetuates the notion of regulation through "beauty myth" (to quote Naomi Wolf's term). Naomi argues cogently in her book, *The Beauty Myth* that women are trained to get sexually surcharged only when they feel that they are beautiful as has been suggested in Chapter 5. Obviously the regulation of feminine sexuality through beauty myth is a much debated issue in feminist circles and a relationship between an older lesbian with younger woman is seen by many critics as an effort to reclaim her lost beauty rather than an instinctive desire for the female partner. Apropos of this Deepa Gahlot in her article, "Gay Is a Sad Word" argues that the "naturally narcissistic streak in women makes them admire other women and their bodies, as an extension of themselves" (1992). This sort of argument has been vociferously rejected by lesbian feminists like Ashwini Sukthankar who finds this kind of approach extremely regressive. Little wonder both these stories exhibit relationship of older and not so good-looking women with younger women as if it is a compensation for their lost beauty. In fact, in a heart-wrenching scene, the agony of Subarna on account of her lost breasts and the compensation of it through the appropriation of the healthy body of Sulagna are poignantly depicted when Subarna puts Sulagna's hand on her chest. To quote from the text:

> In that total darkness the lady took her hand in hers and gently placed it on her bare breasts. A terrible thought shook Sulagna's body. Her hands touched something unnaturally rough, something jagged. Goodness! They were nothing but dried scars and stitches! Sulagna felt miserable. Out of fear she ran her hands over her own body. — Mishra 2007: 127

Similarly the butch/femme stereotypical degenerative model (where one female looks less feminine or to be precise masculine in order to ape heterosexual pattern) has been used by Shivani in "Manik" because when Rambha sees Nalini's lover for the first time she gets confused due to her androgynous appearance. She cogitates that

> indeed Dina Bataliwala is beautiful like a goddess but Rambha does not like the fact that her face betrays some strange signs of impertinent teen-aged boy. Is she not an imposter who is actually a boy and pretending to be a woman. — Shivani 2007: 43

Her incessant cigarette-smoking habits and over all persona put doubts even in the mind of the domestic-help and she thinks that Dina is a male-cheat from Bombay who is wearing a *sari* to deceive her owner. At this Rambha immediately introspects that Laxmi (the domestic-help of Nalini) is voicing her own opinion:

> Till now Rambha was also feeling the same way but there were some solid proofs of Dina's femininity that put Rambha's doubts at rest. No . . . she is indeed a woman but something must be lacking. — Ibid.

She further remunerated that when her sister hugged her and tried to kiss her then the way Dina laughed was reminiscent of the laughter of a boy. All theses recollections remind her of the chapter she has read in a book entitled *Water Gypsies* in which the two lesbian women discard their marital bliss and commit suicide. She shudders and thinks that since her sister has challenged nature by remaining unmarried, it is the turn of the nature to seek revenge by filling her heart with unnatural desire. This sort of demeaning interpretation in terms of associating lesbianism with a certain sort of incomplete womanhood and a constant linking with death and disastrous suicide indubitably put the writer's internalized homophobia at the forefront.

But once again fissures appear amidst endorsement of patriarchy when instead of locating homoeroticism into the de-sexualized and safe zone of *sakhi* space and associating the lesbian longing with emotional gratification only, the writers have revealed the very sensuous and physical aspects of lesbian intimacies. Quoting Thadani, Sukthankar talks about the perils of restricting the transgressive desires among women within the confines of spiritual and emotional love only. She affirms that Thadani points out that

> the terms historically used to describe women who love women — such as *sakhi* and *saheli* — have been purged of their eroticism over time and reshaped into harmless descriptions of female friendship, so today we find ourselves banished from language itself, literally at loss of words.
> — Sukthankar 1999: xvi

Despite critics like Adrienne Rich and Lillian Faderman's rendering sexuality subservient to emotional and intellectual bonding, the de-sexualization of lesbianism is vociferously rejected by A. Koedt and E. Levine. They affirm that

> until women see in each other the possibility of primal commitment which includes sexual love, they will be denying themselves the love and value they readily accord men, thus affirming their second class status.
>
> — Radicallesbians: 243

Diane Richardson in her essay, "Constructing Lesbian Sexualities" has gone to the extent of saying that "Lesbianism stripped of its sexual element was better described as political celibacy" (Richardson 1996: 283). Thus evincing an overt physical intimacy between lovers, though for fleeting moments, is no doubt an attempt to negate the heterosexual ordering of desire. Also a close scrutiny of these scenes and the language that has been used to portray them highlight another significant aspect, that is, the deliberate erasure of over sensationalization. The sensational language is used by some writers to titillate male readers. And this is a fault one finds in many contemporary writers due to the internalization of the male gaze (to quote Laura Mulvey's term) by the female authors. In a very sensuous fashion physical intimacies between the lovers have been described without bordering on to the voyeuristic pleasures of male fantasies of seeing two female bodies indulged in love-making and giving pornographic pleasures to the male readers as has been there in the writings of many male writers who depict lesbianism and one such example is Rajkamal Chaudhary's *Machali Mari Hui*.

Another progressive aspect of these stories is the constant portrayal of exclusive homosocial spaces. The very opening scene of the Oriya short story describes the home of Sulagna, where four women live and the husbands of the two of them live in the different cities. Likewise Subarna's home betrays no sign of male presence even in the form of a male domestic help. In the same vein Shivani's "Manik" shows Nalini Mishra as a principal of girls' college and she lives in a secluded *vila* with a female domestic help, Laxmi and the only male presence in this story is Rambha's husband whose presence in Nalini's home is marked only after her death. The correlationship between the homosocial spaces and homoeroticism has been widely discussed by the feminist writer E. Kosofsky Sedgwick who recognizes a continuum between homosociality and homosexuality. She states that

> it is precisely this broad spectrum of women's homosocial loyalties that Adrienne Rich has referred to and celebrated as the "lesbian continuum"
>
> — J. Childers and G. Hentiz 1995: 139

Hence both these stories, despite their apparent lesbophobia and presenting a crisis around the inevitability of heterosexuality — in terms of evincing deviant desire as an aside to heteronorm, exposition of lesbian panic, demonstrating elements of lesbian ghosting and murdering of one of the lesbians by the other — exhibit radical ruptures on account of the visibilizing of transgressive desire, re-sexualizing lesbianism, demonstrating potent homosocial places and depicting an equally oppressive heterosexual structure. This ambivalent dichotomy is inevitable as has been suggested by Pramod K. Nayar in "Queering Cultural Studies", who by quoting Judith Butler argues that

> lesbian sexuality is a process that reinscribes the power domain it resists. That is, lesbian sexuality is itself constituted partly from a heterosexual matrix. Therefore, the specificity of lesbian sexuality has to be established not outside but within the modalities of the discourse. . . . The term queer, which may be produced due to homophobia, may itself be cited as the discursive basis of opposition. The citation/repetition of the queer identity may be used to destabilize the very discourse of heterosexuality. Butler is

> here suggesting an *aporetic* condition where one needs to both reaffirm and reject the identity "queer" as both acceptance of a certain subject-position and as the site of prospective resistance. — 2007: 126-27

No wonder these stories constantly negotiate and try to bring about a reconciliation between the contradictory positions regarding lesbianism and endorsement of heteronormativity. In one way they are specimen of meaningful mediocrity because they not only help in documenting Indian literary lesbian history but also expose the fact that the injunctions against lesbianism are also part of a wider framework of regulating feminine sexuality that threatens the heteropatriarchal structure. Thus the complex unequivocal positions adopted by the writers make these stories a useful addition to Indian queer literature, and discarding them as mere homophobic tales can be considered a negligence to the eclectic dimension of these works and a sheer injustice to the LGBTQ cause.

7

Queer Identity and Homosexualization of Spaces in Contemporary Indian Literary Texts

IN THE LAST decade there has been a huge spurt in the radical researches regarding the reinventing and reinvesting of the idea of space. The study of "space" intersects with various other disciplines ushering in larger shifts across the different branches of knowledge. The earliest theorization of space can be traced in the works of geographers of ancient times like Polybius (*c.* 200 – *c.* 118 BCE), Posidonius (*c.* 135 BCE – 51 BCE) and Strabo (64/63 BCE – *c.* CE 24). These geographers (specially Polybius in *History*) have tried to emphasize that time is the primary marker in constructing history and space is subordinate to it. However, both Isaac Newton through his "Absolute Theory" and Gottfried Wilhelm Leibniz by "Relational Theory" have propounded concepts that have defined "space" independent of time. Thus in this fashion the temporality is replaced by spatiality. After that the major intervention came in the form of Immanuel Kant's theory of "Transcendental Idealism" in which he has negotiated the subjective nature of "space". None the less, according to Heidegger, space is both objective and subjective. His concept of "dasein" in *Being and Time* is about the essence of existence and the sense of belongingness, which is instrumental in transforming space into place. Similarly Henri Lefebvre in his *The Production of Space* argues that space is humanly constructed and consequently is a means of control and power. Adding another tangent to this idea, Yi fu Tuan has given the concept of "topophilia" to express the concept of affective bond between places and people. Likewise Michel Foucault (1967) in "Of Other Spaces, Heterotopias" speaks of the overlapping of identity and space through the notion of liminal space which he calls heterotopias. Elaborating it further, Edward Soja has developed the theory of "third space" in which "everything comes together . . . subjectivity and objectivity, the abstract and the concrete, the real and the imagined, the knowable and the unimaginable, the repetitive and the differential, structure and agency, mind and body, consciousness and the unconscious, the disciplined and the transdisciplinary, everyday life and unending history" (1996: 57). Thus the symbiotic relationship between "space" and "identity" has been the key area in the recent scholarly researches, for identity is not only determined by just the fact that *who* you are but by *where* you are, as has been mentioned by Africa Tylor in "A Queer Geography" (1997).

"Queer Geography" as a self-reflexive academic research area primarily emerged in 1990s. It attempts to outline the dodging nature of desire at a particular space and how it does not obey the obligation of the identity. Patently the eclectic overlapping of sexual identity and space (through which desire is constituted and practised) and its radicalizing effects on each other become the major concern of non-normative geographies. Naturally issues pertaining to gender, work and space (McDowell 1997), class and space (Bourdieu 1984), race and space (Allman 1996), queer identity and citizenship (Bell and Binnie 2000), bisexuality and space (Hemmings 2002) and domestic spaces and lesbian identity (Valentine 1989) have fired the imagination of the academics. The interdisciplinary prominence of space and sexual identity gained momentum after the publication of Manuel Castell's *The City and the*

Grassroots. However, the lesbian marginalization in these works is visible in their siding with the issues concerning gays mainly, and the construction of spaces in the context of lesbian women has been largely ignored in this discourse. This kind of partial treatment meted out to lesbians, specially the South Asian dykes, is argued brilliantly by Rani Kawale in her article, "A Kiss Is Just a Kiss . . . Or Is It? South Asian Lesbian and Bisexual Women and the Construction of Space". Moreover this chapter not only aims at showcasing the mutual interaction of sexual identity and space in the specific Indian context and the consequent spatial anxiety arising out of it, but also at the techniques of erasure which are universally applicable for silencing sexual minorities. In this context a special emphasis has been laid on the specific modes of surveillance of transgenders and lesbians in terms of (re)appropriation of spaces in Indian literary texts. Unlike America — where a considerable work has been done in terms of easily identifiable gay and lesbian residential areas as in "Gender and Space: Lesbian and Gay Men in the City" by S. Adler and J. Brenner (1992), Rothenburg's "And She Told Two Friends", and in Britain where due to the lack of explicit gay or lesbian neighbourhood, the researches are primarily centred around the consumption of public spaces by subaltern sexualities such as in the works of Hindle (1994) and Binnie (1995) — the Indian sexual minorities are still struggling with the issues of visibility at any space. Hence the re-orientation of the space, whether it is a private/public or domestic one, through homosexual identity is of paramount importance in the Indian context because the queer movement is still at a nascent stage in India as compared to the West.

Since space and sexual identity are mutually reciprocal and constantly evolving dynamic entities, there is a constant shaping and reshaping of the one by the other specially in the context of LGBTQ identity in Indian literary spaces. The ever evolving concepts of gender and sexuality alter the spaces and how in turn spaces produce gendered and sexed bodies, and both reinforce and challenge at the same time the stereotypical concept of sexual identity. Nancy Duncan in *Body Space: Destablizing Geographies of Gender and Sexuality* states that anxiety, apparently caused by space–time compression, is not gender specific. For many sexual minorities, the decentring of the local and the consequent redefining of the spatial horizons may have liberating effect, but it can also give rise to new anxieties. Significantly the interlocking of these networks of complex and eclectic spatial anxieties constantly and simultaneously forms, reforms, stabilizes and destabilizes sexual identities at the same time. Thus in the Indian context, with its unusually complex societal structure and conservatism at one level and the global impact and resistance to it on the other, the simultaneous coexistence of homo and hetero at a given space and their mutual displacement and appropriation produce ambivalent and multilayered relationship between space and sexual identity, and it can be critiqued at various levels. Indeed the focus in this chapter is also on the familiarization of homoeroticism through the appropriation of conventional heterosexual spaces and its various effects on the larger framework of queer activism.

The normalization of the same-sex desire by locating it within the familial heterosexual spaces is a potent tool of inversion in terms of homosexualization of spaces and subsequently it endorses the acceptance of homosexuality. This aspect of mutually reciprocal symbiotic relationship between space and sexual identity has been admirably handled by Aneeta Rajendran in her paper, "(Un)Familiar Spaces: The Erotic Geographies of the Contemporary Lesbian Indian Novel". She argues that lesbianism is domesticated in India as the lesbian writers try to situate the homoerotic passion in the life-spaces of ordinary household within the very reassuring, traditional and familiar spaces of a home, especially the kitchen and bedroom which are conventionally and almost exclusively regarded as female spaces in India. She states:

> By placing these intimacies and the very "domesticated" strategies — such as writing about cooking, gardening, washing clothes — employed by these writers in delineating this eros, within the larger, more theoretical context of how Thadani, Vanita, Kidwai and Sukthankar have domesticated the same eros by demonstrating through their scholarly work that a lesbian tradition, in terms of textual production and cultural visibility, exists/used to exist in India, and that it was not a foreign import.
>
> — <http//www.interdisplinary.net/critical-issues/transformations/persons-and sexuality/project-archives/4th/session-1-representations/>

In it she talks about the normalizing of non-normative relationships by placing them within heterosexual matrix which can help in displacing heteronormativity. The sexual rendezvous between Astha and Piplika in the bathroom in Manju Kapur's *A Married Woman* and between Chhacho and Lalana, the two lesbian lovers in Geetanjali Shree's *Tirohit*, in Chhacho's bedroom in which she sleeps with her husband bear witness to it. In Manju Kapur's *A Married Woman*, both Astha and Piplika created a home at Piplika's flat in the same city and lived for some days as a married couple with domesticity setting in. In fact, Astha has gone to the extent of visualizing a homoerotic zone within her own heterosexual home when she states in a symbolic scene:

> I have a fantasy, listen my love, and do not laugh. . . . I have a room, small but private, where my family pass before my eyes. It is very light, before me is a wall which divides the house, but I can see my children, that satisfies me, though to them I am invisible, that satisfies me too. This room will be our room, you with me, living in harmony.
>
> — Kapur 2002: 241

Though Astha's desire to remain invisible to her children refers to Terry Castle's concept of "ghosting of lesbians" which aims at unmasking the author's or character's lesbophobic anxiety through the constant ghosting of lesbian characters, yet the coexistence of homoerotic spaces and heteronormativity is indeed a progressive move. Likewise the love-making between Chhacho and her female partner Lalana in her bedroom has been wrongly interpreted as a heterosexual encounter by Paresh because only the backside of Chhacho has been visible to him. Thus on the one hand this scene reflects the unthinkability of the lesbian desire, but on the other it evinces the overlapping of hetero and homosexual passion and fluid negotiation of sexuality irrespective of fixed binary division, for there is a clear-cut appropriation of heteropatriarchal space (the bedroom of married Chhacho) by relentless and unadulterated sexual rendezvous between the two lesbian lovers. Similarly the sexual relationship between Marikolanthu and Sujata Akka in *Ladies Coupé* by Anita Nair takes place in the very bedroom of Sujata Akka on her conjugal heterosexual bed. In fact, in Dawesar's *Babyji*, the use of "kitchen", the sexual gaze of Anamika over Rani's body while she is washing utensils and the sexual mating between the two on Anamika's bed within the heterosexual home clearly reflect the author's intentions of familiarizing and normalizing lesbianism within the traditional familial spaces. To quote from *Babyji:*

> At home the servant was stooped over the kitchen sink doing the dishes. When she did the dishes in my presence she always squatted with her *sari* hitched half way up, and I could see her legs. Her legs were covered now.
>
> — Dawesar 2005: 258

In yet another text in Hindi, *Machali Mari Hui* (1966) by Rajkamal Chaudhary, the constant presence of the lesbian desire within the heterosexual familial structure is exhibited by frequent references to a painting of the two naked women exploring each other. This painting is hung just above the bed of the married heterosexual couple, Nirmal and Shiri, who are sexually incompatible. Though the text is saturated with lesbophobic anxiety, the negation of the heterosexual desire is documented by showing the two sisters indulging in passionate exploring of each other right inside their conventional patriarchal home. This domestication of lesbian desire is also very useful because the researchers like Valentine in "Negotiating and Managing Multiple Sexual Identities: Lesbian Time–Space Strategies" have incessantly argued that it is a firmly established fact that all kinds of spaces are primarily heterosexualized and therefore the need for a separate space is almost an existential need for homosexuals so that they may not be falsely understood as straight people in these spaces and get subsumed within heterosexual matrix. But Binnie and Brown counter this argument of creating a separate space because at times it endorses the separatist ideology that gay, lesbians and transgenders need to be pushed outside the heterosexual spaces so that they do not threaten the dominant heteropatriarchal structure. In this light, instead of pushing homonormativity to a separate exclusive domain, the consumption of the centre space through showing erotic relationships flourishing in traditional straight spaces is indeed a potent strategy in a way. None the less the basic problem with this sort of argument is that despite visibility of one kind, the act is described as largely hidden from the prying eyes of the heterosexual characters and therefore the spatial anxiety and displacement occur only at a very miniscule level in one way.

No wonder even in Mridula Koshy's short story, "A Large Girl", the lesbian paramour of the much-married narrator keeps a family picture of her lover and also wants her husband's picture to be decorated in her flat. Interestingly a beautiful reconciliation is brought out in the Punjabi story,

"The Home", by Sukirath in which a gay couple forms a perfect gay household with an almost adopted daughter, who is a niece of one of the partners. By naming the story as "Home" and drawing a close parallel between a gay household and a heterosexual home, the author tries to convince the readers that there appears to be no distinction between the two familial spaces. The setting of an exclusive gay household in the larger heterosexual city space unmasks the presence of the homoerotic spaces hidden within heterosexual matrix. It reveals an elusive desire on the part of the author to create the third space where homo and hetero identities can coexist without any antagonism. It is in stark contrast to the use of *chhat* (roof) in Geetanjali Shree's *Tirohit* in which the lesbian mating takes place only on the *chhat*, outside the heteronormative home. The writer in a very interesting manner presents *chhat* as a private space for lesbian love, outside the heteronormative boundaries of the house, for the open space of *chhat* without any boundaries is apt for fluid sexual intimacies. In this particular novel the roof assumes the form of that unique space where the sexual rendezvous between the two main characters, Chhacho and Lalana takes place. The author symbolically presents the fact that it is the roof that connects all houses of that block and hence indicative of the all-pervasive nature of the lesbian longing. It also postulates the idea that Chhacho and Lalana are able to create their own private space of unique disposition within the public space. After coding their sexual mating as "programme", they meet at the roof holding two sets of clothes. They dress up for each other.

> They put their bare feet on roof. They will have the entire roof under their feet. The touch is extremely pleasurable. . . . On it the ghosts of the two girls meet. They come alive at every touch, every taste, shiver and smell . . . they exchange clothes. They speak how beautiful are they. And how

> beautiful is the roof . . . whether they come to meet on the roof or to meet the roof. — Geetanjali Shree 2001: 96

Hence they and the roof become one and their mating on the roof is an extension and a symbol of the infinite free space which is possible only in the egalitarian same-sex love. Nevertheless this free space of roof is only possible outside the domesticated heteronormative structure of the house. Apropos of this the fictionist writes:

> Whenever she reaches at the doorstep of the roof her heart beats ceaselessly. The roof is beyond the door. This is not a roof, this is a wide sea. It asks and whispers in her ears to come . . . it is spread over like a sea all over Laberan house . . . it has a wet and dark attraction. It enables her to lift her sensuous arms up in the sky in order to touch the stars.
>
> — Ibid.: 17

She further states that

> roof is sympathetic to all kinds of relationships. It is bereft of any compulsions. It can even cross the limits of the infinite . . . it is easy to be invisible at the roof. — Ibid.: 32

At another place, the roof serves as a symbol of the fact that it is only at such places which are at the periphery of the accepted structure that something as unacceptable as the same-sex love is possible. This dichotomy of public space (*chhat*) being a private space is depicted effectively by Ruth Vanita through *rekhti* poetry:

> In *rekhti* the speaker and her *dogana* visit each other by night on the rooftop, a situation both exciting and dangerous. Sometimes both women belong to the same household and the danger then is that the sounds of their lovemaking may awaken other sleepers. At other times, they climb on to one another's rooftops, and creaking doors may betray them. Meeting in the day is also difficult because other women are around. — 2005: 258

To quote from *rekhti* poetry:

> Lady love is digression/That has uprooted thousands of home/. . . At night I scaled your roof with a ladder/And hid behind parapet. — Ibid.: 258

The representation of the roof as a symbol of the marginalization of the homoerotic relationships becomes conspicuous when Geetanjali Shree affirms:

> When there is roof under your feet and the sky above your head then there is no compulsion. Ghalib would not have been able to utter the golden words that *ishk per jor nahi*, had he been not living on the roofs in Agra and Delhi. . . . And only a fool will not understand the fact that at roof anything and everything can happen. At roof no one is upper and lower and no one is anyone's husband or wife. Everything can vanish at roof. Which means everything is possible at roof. — Geetanjali Shree 2001: 37

Thus the ambivalence in the symbolic interpretation of *chhat* is quite explicit, as at one level it is reflective of the infinite space and possibilities that it provides for Sapphic relationships, while on the other this space is at the periphery of the accepted heteronormative household structure. Also there is a constant mention of their being invisible at roof. In the similar fashion in Mridula Koshy's "A Large Girl", the roof becomes a metonymic sphere for exploring all kinds of forbidden desires like smoking and the same-sex mating. To quote from the text:

> But my girlfriends and I always smoke when we get together. We do it on the roof. I keep a mat rolled up on the stairs . . . The mat serves to soften crumbling concrete on which we have to crouch to prevent nearby tenants from invading our privacy. The mat is where I and Janet first kiss. The first time we kiss, she lights a cigarette and passes it to me, and then she lights another one. We are talking, but not easily . . . She is subdued downstairs, but loud enough on the roof, so I am

> relieved when finally we sit quietly, leaning back on the short wall. . . . My shoulder is touching hers and she slides down and rests her head on my lap and from there squints up at me.
>
> — Koshy 2007: 167

Throughout the text cigarette smoking and lovemaking have been juxtaposed as forbidden fruits, and in a suggestive way they both have been aborted when unexpectedly the daughter of the narrator has caught them smoking just after caressing each other. Consequently, the "lesbian panic" strikes the narrator and she abruptly leaves both smoking and the relationship.

> I leave her for many reasons. The first time when Rohini comes up the stairs to the roof one afternoon, and the metal stairs, instead of clattering as I had expected, absorb her Keds tread silently, and suddenly she is there — looking at us, "mummy", she says. She is wearing a stricken smile. She is saying with her eyes, "I don't see you with a cigarette in your hand", . . . shamefaced with the discovery she has made.
>
> — Ibid.: 168

Patently the roof throughout plays a significant part in the shaping and reshaping of transgressive desires and the whole scene mirrors the fear that one can be easily caught even at roof as described in *rekhti* poetry. The fear of the lesbian lovers that they might be caught at roof (as mentioned in *rekhti* poetry also) because it is outside home and yet a part of the home and has been dubiously located in this fashion (or could be called in Foucauldian term the "heterotopias of crisis"), comes true. According to Foucault,

> There are also, probably in every culture, in every civilization, real places — places that do not exist and that are formed in the very founding of society — which are something like counter-sites, a kind of effectively enacted utopia in which the real sites, all the other real sites that can be found within the culture, are simultaneously represented, contested and inverted. Places of this kind are outside of all

> places, even though it may be possible to indicate their location in reality. Because these places are absolutely different from all the sites that they reflect and speak about, I shall call them, by way of contrast to utopias, heterotopias. I believe that between utopias and these quiet other sites, these heterotopias, there might be a sort of mixed, joint experience. . . . — http://www.foucaullt.info/doc/documents/heterotopia/foucault.heterotopia.en.html

In this manner the spatial anxiety, arising out of this peculiar liminal position of roof, emphatically and constantly reconfigures the positions of the sexual outsiders in contradictory measures and once again demonstrates the significant interconnections between space and sexual leanings.

Likewise in *Impossible Desires*, Gayatri Gopinath also talks about this sort of slippages by locating lesbianism outside the household and lays bare the intricate connections between homoeroticism and homosociality. Referring to the two Bollywood movies, *Utsav* (The Festival, directed by Girish Karnad, 1984) and *Subah/Umbartha* (Dawn/Threshold, directed by Jabbar Patel, 1981), she argues:

> *Utsav* takes place primarily in and around a brothel and *Subah* in a women's reformatory, and both hint at the alternative forms of sexuality that exist outside the middle-class home. — 2007: 104

Supporting the position that argues in favour of exclusive separate spaces for homoerotic encounters, Rani Kawale states that due to the all-pervasive heterosexual nature of spaces "lesbian and gay men have reconstituted a variety of separate spaces in order to avoid having constantly to 'pass' as heterosexual or being subjected to homophobia" (2003: 182).

So whether relocating the same-sex desire within a middle-class heterosexual household and that too on the conjugal bed of a married woman is indeed a progressive move by Abha Dawesar and Anita Nair or the hidden nature of these relationships is a backlash of its own kind despite homosexualization of spaces, is debatable. All the encounters of Anamika in *Babyji* and Marikolanthu in *Ladies Coupé* take place in bedroom right inside the patriarchal format. Hence till the time the queer acceptance of the patriarchal spaces does not take place, the ideal proposition will be to create a unique amalgam of homosexualization of heteropatriarchal places and forming of exclusive spaces for alternative sexuality (not to segregate homosexuals) in order to save queer individuals from being subsumed in straight identity and being victims of homophobia. But in the larger course, the spaces need to be of fluid nature where both homo and hetero desires could flourish without antagonism. Therefore the separate domains can only be stopgap arrangements and cannot tantamount to the ultimate revolutionizing of any space as an ideal sphere for pansexuality.

At times the deliberate placing of the same-sex passion in the public domain, outside the confines of the domesticity, also has a potential agenda to evince it as an all-pervasive, well-accepted form of desire. This can be illustrated from the examples of the showcasing of gay leanings in Raj Rao's *The Boyfriend* through the explicit gay messages like *biryani khayega* on the wall of a public toilet and the acts of gay copulation inside it. This clearly adds another dimension to this discussion. Investigating the issue of usage of language to reconstitute a space Rani Kawale talks about the strategy used by KISS, a group of primarily South Asian lesbians in Britain, that deliberately uses broken English or English with a particular kind of the so-called illegitimacy which divorces them from the exclusive white lesbian spaces and helps them in reconstructing a space of their own. Interestingly the exclusive gay lingo inscribed on the walls of the public toilets reorients and relocates the public space as a very specific site for asserting gay identity, because language is indeed a significant marker of the spatial identity. Importantly this sort of overt reclaiming of public spaces by lesbians and transgenders are largely invisible. Instead of whispers only in couches as in lesbian domestication of desire, the very vocal sexual gestures in public domain (public toilets and parks as in Dattani's "Night Queen", etc.) demonstrate the public and the all-pervasive nature of the gay desire which is missing in lesbian representations. In fact, there is a full-fledged poem entitled "Gandu Bagicha" by Namdeo Dhasal dedicated to the exploration of the varied aspects of the so-called gay parks:

> I/No flower/No leaf/No tree/No bird/Only *kama's* play/ Musk scent/The sound of dry leaves underfoot/O my love, O the beauty of gardens! . . . The destroyed jungle of a pained heart/Gandu Bagicha Gay Gardens/What sorrow shall you sing/Boys have become that way now/Praise and blame/Consciousness and torpor/The darkness of doom/ The golden shore. — Dhasal 1999: 72-73

Moreover considering the public parks and gay bars as exclusive public sites has been criticized by many critics like Lynda Johnston, Gill Valentine and Michael Brown because access to both public parks and gay bars is often available only to certain people (gay bars thrive on the entry fees and the liquor-purchasing power of the clients, and thus class comes into the picture) and at certain times (as public parks for homoerotic activities can be used primarily at night). In fact, Tatiana Matejskova in "Straights in a Gay Bar: Negotiating Boundaries through Time–Spaces" redefines the concept of privacy and consequently alters the notion that gay bars are exclusive public places. She contends:

> I prefer to think about the nominally private and public spaces through the concept of privacy. Privacy here can be conceptualized as the realm of subjects' personal sexual identity and the performance of that identity, that is, as something that can be had and lost. And while privacy is

> certainly one of the attributes of an ideal private space, for many gays and lesbians privacy is often lacking in nominally private places, such as their (parental) home. In contrast, a gay bar, while not a private place, is often just such a *space of privacy* for gay customers, where their sexual identities, which are out of place in other (semi)-public spaces, can be enacted and performed. — Matejskova 2007: 138-39

Therefore the inhibition-free socialization, availability of partners and the safety from public opprobrium add the quotient of privacy to the so-called public gay bars. Endorsing further the notion of privacy of gay bars Michael Brown has gone to the extent of calling them as a kind of "extended closet" because many times a customer who has maintained a straight identity outside to gain heterosexual privileges can enter the bar and can be "out" temporarily in that space. Thus it is safe to assume it as a semi-public space. However, even if we do not consider it to be a strictly public domain, these spaces are not available, specially in India, for lesbians and therefore there is a severe dearth of such sites in Indian literary representations. None the less there are exceptions like the story, "Pity that Blush" by Annie Dykstra in which the public swimming pool and changing rooms have been reoriented as lesbian mating grounds in full public view. The narrator who is a lesbian through her queer gaze alters the complexion of the homosocial environment of changing rooms and uses shower-room for her sexual rendezvous:

> Usually I slip into the corner to avoid feeling like a voyeur and unexpected guests in their assumed sexless zone. This time I relish the play and the opportunity to look from body to body to search you out. One woman catches my gaze roaming the scores of half-naked bodies and tightens her eyes. I'm breaking the changing room code. Cruising at the club. — Dykstra 2012: 5-6

She suggestively invites a fellow swimmer to a shower-room in the presence of the attendants and other club members:

> I back into the shower cubicle. The curtain is just wide enough to fill the space. The cold tiles on the back wall make me gasp as I lean against them. I wait for a second to see if you will follow me in. You do. I see two of the other women lift an eyebrow together to wonder. The changing-room attendant stares, confused.
>
> —Ibid.: 8

But such literary representations of lesbian lovemaking at public spaces are very few and that is why it is not a matter of much surprise that in *A Married Woman* when Piplika and Astha go to watch a movie at a lesbian and gay film festival — a very public place — it turns out to be a gay movie rather than a lesbian one and interestingly Astha leaves it in the middle on the pretext of her domestic duties. The whole process of watching a gay movie and identifying with the common concerns of the sexual minorities evoke various questions in the mind of Astha. Although there are common grounds of oppression, but the subsuming of lesbian concerns under the gay ambit reveals the fact that gender binary trumps over homo/hetero dichotomy. The theatre becomes a public platform for reconstituting space for gay encounters and specific lesbian problems remain ignored.

Moreover the use of cinema as a medium to articulate gay concerns is an effective tool because theatre works as "heterotopias" in Foucauldian term. Foucault divides heterotopias into "heterotopias of crisis" and "heterotopias of deviation". As these places are in crisis with their atmosphere, it is difficult to jam them into a fixed spatial position and hence the fluid position of these spaces is a fertile ground for the exploration of the dissident sexualities. In the third principle of heterotopias, he also considers cinema to be a heterotopic site because of the emergence of the two-dimensional screen on which one sees the projection of the three-dimensional space. And thus it creates an in-between liminal space which is suitable for queer articulation because deviation which cannot find exposition anywhere can be best expressed at these counter-utopias or nowhere places. Also cinema provides a break from the traditional time as "heterotopias are most often linked to slices in time" (http://www.foucaullt.info/doc/documents/heterotopia/foucault.heterotopia.en.html). Naturally the fluidity provided by the temporal closing and opening of cinematic spaces helps in the projection of the transgressive relationships. Obviously at one level the spatial dynamics of the theatre is quite suitable for the gay representations, but on the other the hyper-visibility of the medium requires judicious coping strategies to make it acceptable to straight audience, specially in India where Section 377 has been recently read down by the Supreme Court. Again in *A Married Woman*, the viewing of a gay movie by the two lesbian lovers creates an "oppositional gaze" (the concept given by Hooks in *Black Looks*: *Race and Representation*) and raises questions regarding the issues of subjectivity within queer activism. These thoughts find an echo when Piplika contemplates:

> Pipee's voice breathed through the craven recesses of her mind, "we have to struggle for acceptance and the right to love as we feel. Don't you think so Ant?" But try as Astha could, she could not connect to what she was seeing. Her own situation was different, though if Pipee didn't think so she would keep that information to herself.
>
> — Kapur 2002: 237

The public viewing of a movie encourages oppositional gaze that creates a specific third space of resistance/assimilation which helps in the reordering of spaces and hence the eclectic public viewing makes theatre a very significant political site. Apropos of this Rani Kawale records the experience of the deliberate screening of the South Asian lesbian and gay movies, *Sweet Like Burfi* and *Chutney Popcorn*, in London in 2000 to reconstitute a specific space for the South Asian queer activism, bereft of "whiteness". The frenzied attack on the screening of Deepa Mehta's *Fire* further accentuates the significance of the public viewing to counter a phobic gaze. Similarly the overtly heterosexual romantic movies such as *Sholey, Kala Patthar, Dostana* and *Janjeer* which are referred to in Raj Rao's *Hostel Room 131* have been turned by the two homosexual lovers into homoerotic tales. Both these lovers use the cinema hall for their sexual romping while discussing the latent desires of the two heroes, as projected on the Hindi cinema screen, who appear to be romancing the lady but in reality have a deeper passion for each other. To quote:

> Siddharth went on to make an inventory of heroes with whom Amitabh Bachchan had been romantically paired by producers, directors and script writers — Dharmendra, Rajesh Khanna, Shashi Kapoor, Vinod Khanna, Shatrughan Sinha and Rishi Kapoor. — Kawale 2003: 106

The song, *"yaari hai iman"* that Pran sings to Amitabh is considered a love lyric by Siddharth.

> Amitabh looks so coy as the manly Pathan sings to him. . . . You know, most of Amitabh's roles have been written by Salim–Javed, whom stardust bitchily refers to as Shaw–Shakespeare. It's possible that Salim and Javed are projecting their own yearnings on screen, by pairing Amitabh off with other heroes. — Ibid.

In this sense, the cinematic space becomes a mating ground in actual corporeal sense for these two lovers and it also initiates a mental cinematic voyage which opens new vistas of interpreting and understanding the homosexual longings forged within heterosexual matrix.

Shohini Ghosh has used classic queer gaze to re-read some conventional heterosexual tales to locate queer visibility by adopting various spectatorship techniques. According to Brett Farmer, due to the lack of obvious cultural codes and cinematic language, the queer gaze has to probe deep to find the homoerotic presence. To quote his words:

> This process of appropriating or "queering" film assumes various forms and uses multiple tactics. At a general level, glbtq spectators are acutely adept at appropriating film to their own frames of reference and imbuing it with specifically queer affect. Some critics suggest that glbtq spectators learn almost as habit to read film symptomatically, to scour texts for casual signs of queerness — a "colourful" supporting character; an ambiguous line of dialogue; a furtive glance between same-sex characters — that may seem insignificant to the film's immediate narrative function but that enable the production of coded queer subplots. Others claim that queer spectators prize film not so much for its stories, which are invariably heteronormative, but for its moments of spectacular transcendence and bewitching glamour.
>
> — http://www.glbtq.com/arts/film-spectatorhtml.

Thus the use of the cinema hall for the under-belt activities and the subsequent interpretations of the non-normative desires as transgressive relationships within seemingly innocent tales of man–woman love, as depicted on screen, colour the entire cinematic space (both imaginary and corporeal) with homoerotic longings. In yet another interesting manner, even the songs of *yaari* or *dosti* of the two heroes are shown being translated by the narrator and in this process there is not only a literal translation of the Hindi songs into English but also the translation of desire from hetero to homo. The famous song of *Janjeer*, *yaari hai iman mera* is interestingly translated into this fashion:

> *Yaari* is my religion/My *yaar* is my life./I won't regret/Dying for the sake of *yaari*/. . . Why does the flower of my garden look so sad?/Is he a victim of ill-will?/Have no qualms, friends, let me into your heart/Let me know the price of your smile. — Raj Rao 2010: 106

In a very insightful intervention through gay gaze, Muraleedharan produces counter-strategies to combat this marginal status ascribed to queer moments. According to him, Indian cinema rarely

> preserves the narrative unities that designate classic realism. Temporal and spatial continuities are frequently disrupted by the song and dance sequences that constitute a crucial component of Indian cinema's technology of pleasure. The action or "stunt" sequences, comic interludes and even the melodramatic episodes could be seen as having a similar, though not identical, narrative function — each of them signifying as seemingly independent narrative units or texts . . . all packed into the logic of a fragmented narrative which Ravi Vasudevan prefers to describe as "non-continuous" instead of "discontinuous".
>
> — Muraleedharan 2005: 80

He further elaborates the autonomous independent identities of these songs and dance-sequences because with the proliferation of the private channels these scenes and songs are telecast independent of films and

> when telecast separately, its queerness is no more erased by the heterosexist narrative resolutions within which it was encased while within the film text. Many people, who never saw the original film, would end up seeing and "enjoying" these sequences as they are telecast again and again for a long period of time. — Ibid.: 81

This fragmented structure of the specific mainstream cinema and the subsequent reproduction of it on television channels (which also cater to audience who may have never seen those visuals in the context of the entire film) with respect to the maintenance and consolidation of "safe structure" of normative desire, indubitably produce potent spectator strategies which revolutionize the diegetic space of cinema and enlarge the frontiers of the cinematic space to a much wider magnitude. This further redefines the idea that the sphere of cinema is not limited to the four walls only. In this connection the brilliant use of Deleuze's theory of "affect" to extend the boundaries of queer geographies by Jason Lim in his outstanding essay, "Queer Critique and the Politics of Affect", is worth mentioning. He tries to establish a linkage between erotic geography and Deleuze's theory of "affect" that talks about any event being an in-between entity between the actual and the virtual. This consequently presents diverse possibilities for multitude of actions and relations, and in turn it can be effectively used to revolutionize the queer spaces. He states that

> for Deleuze the "event" can be thought of as virtual (and hence as enveloping a multitude of virtual worlds), as distinct from the actual "states of affairs" by which events come to pass. Events are always (just) past or just about to come, but are never the present state of affairs, although they are contemporaneous with the present. Events are intimate to bodies (Deleuze 5) but not actually corporeal themselves . . . . This sense neither originates in the subjectivities of individuals nor is fixed in place by an objective reality.
>
> — Lim 2007: 56

It is clearly evident that it straddles the virtual and the actual and incorporates the process of actualization which in turn pose the possibilities of repetition (by constantly reliving and modifying the past experiences) and differences of experiences. Naturally the effect of any event cannot be scripted in advance because it is dynamic in nature. Now when it is applied to cinematic space which is inherently a virtual space consumed by actual bodies, the mutual effects of bodies and the virtual world of cinema gesture towards the endless possibilities. And it is specially true when this cinematic world is recreated through memory at the same and different spaces later on. A very conspicuous example of it is a scene in Mayur Patel's *Vivek and I* in which after seeing the movie, *Basic Instinct*, the main characters Kaushik and his friend Krishna return home and later recreate the particular scenes through memory and find that the talk of heterosexual liaison between Michael Douglas and Sharon Stone veers around bisexuality and lesbianism. This discussion further takes a very different turn when they talk in a sensuous fashion about the masculine charms of Richard Gere in *Pretty Woman* which is unmistakably a heterosexual love saga. This kind of wish fulfilment of possibilities of seeing Mel Gibson and Harrison Ford in an erotic fashion and the recreation of the past events of virtual world in actual space by gay bodies give rise to the multitude of homoerotic options. Michael Douglas has been shown nude from the back in the movie in the context of a heterosexual scene but this event is represented in such a manner as it postulates varied gay possibilities by mobilizing the liminal space between the past and the future hopes. To quote from the text:

> They showed Michael totally nude from the back. "I wish they'd shown him from the front," Krishna had said. Krishna had never spoken so boldly. That's the first time the thought struck me that he might be gay. I didn't say anything to that. His toe had been continually playing with mine. — Patel 2010: 86

This scene is followed by the "coming out" of Krishna, and the lovemaking between Kaushik and Krishna ensues. Indubitably it is a very significant example of the transformation of virtual world, that has immense possibilities in terms of interpreting an event, and its plural translations into the actual world. In this connection Jason Lim, while taking a clue from William Connolly, talks about the concept of "virtual memory" that incorporates the idea that the impact of previous events is stored within the body either as habits, pleasures or unconscious opposition towards certain things. Connolly cites the examples of daily soaps where we do not have the time to recall previous episodes in order to have a rational continuity for understanding a serial. In the midst of watching a serial we depend upon the "affect" and that is our bodies' memories (instead of active memory) which have a particular way of functioning at a given space. Hence the juxtaposing of bodily memory, space and corporeal sense of existence determine our understanding of an event. Jason Lim states:

> For human bodies (understood in a loose sense as shifting composites of matter and movement — biological, technological, and social), virtual memory subsists below explicit memory as a "repository of past cultural life" (Connolly 2002: 25). . . . It is part of a rapid process for subtracting from the multiplicity of things that can be sensed or done in any encounter. — Lim 2007: 61

In this fashion, speaking of "affect" in terms of virtual memory again stresses the point that the repetition of actions done before is not a matter of reliving the past, but of acting it out in new circumstances and spheres that colour both the bodies and the spaces as is evident in the case of Kaushik and Krishna in *Vivek and I*. So the cinema as a space has been used quite dynamically by many authors like Manju Kapur, Raj Rao and Mayur Patel (the writer of *Vivek and I*) in their writings where they have not restricted the physical space of cinema in terms of depicting it as a place for physical proximity only, but the joint viewing of a movie by the lovers and later the recreation of the scenes from movie through virtual memory in different spaces enlarge the diegetic space of the cinema. Further the inclusion of the mental landscapes of viewers as well makes the use of cinema in these texts an ever-evolving spatial phenomenon.

While talking about the consumption of public spaces by "sexual others", another dimension of the public spheres — viz. the use of public domain for activism — emerges. It is significant to note that the visibility at such spaces is an interesting strategy to combat the erasure techniques inherent within the movement. KALI and KISS, the two South Asian lesbian activist groups active in Britain, are two such platforms. Similarly in India, Maya Sharma's book, *Loving Women*, catalogues the long history of deliberate displacement of lesbians within feminist movement at public platforms and places. Thus amidst this kind of antagonism, the establishment of the lesbian tent in 1995 in the middle of the conference venue in Beijing at "The NGO Forum at Fourth World Conference on Women" was a radical move to capture the public sphere of feminist political movement that had for long shunned lesbians. Back to India, the restructuring of public feminist activist spaces by lesbians has been effectively depicted in the Caleri Report that talks about the protest by lesbians in an answer to *Fire* controversy. Quoting Caleri Report Maya Sharma argues:

> It just took one poster, one banner and a few scared but brave women in a public protest of eighty other slogans, posters and hundreds people, to generate all this public discussion and media glare. One brave act of holding up a placard that said "Indian and Lesbian" had caused such *hulchul*, such journalistic diarrhoea. —2006: 12

It is only after a fierce struggle that the political public space has been somewhat reoriented for queer visibility in the form of gay pride marches, Kinnar Sammelan and Aravani festival, but the individual assertion of homoerotic desire, specially the lesbian longing is still not acceptable at the public places. So the only form of recapturing the public spaces remains within the limited sphere of political activism. Indeed it is not a matter of great surprise that in Indian literary texts, there is hardly a fictional account of lesbians holding the centre stage and occupying a public space in an activist movement. It is only in Manju Kapur's *A Married Woman* that we get a faint glimpse of Piplika and Astha's participation in a protest march on account of Ayodhya demolition and in an oblique manner they occupy the public sphere of an activist movement, though the exposition of their lesbian identity in that public forum is debatable.

In a sharp contrast to the above argument, the empty space used for cruising in the novel, *The Boyfriend* is suggestively named as Azad Maidan. Paul Carter in *The Road to Botany Bay: An Essay in Spatial History* states that the personal interests and "ambitious principle" colour the inherent politics of the naming of places. Though Carter speaks of spatial history and at macro level, his concept that the act of naming the space as a place inscribes it with a character by which it can be referred to is particularly true in terms of renaming of a wall as Stonewall in Bombay near a gay bar in *The Boyfriend*. This process of renaming an insignificant wall as Stonewall connects a local event, that has taken place outside a gay bar which is adjacent to this particular wall, of ravaging a police man for blackmailing a gay man (thus a reversal of the power paradigm) with a global gay revolution known as Stonewall Movement. Hence an innocuous wall becomes the site of Indian and global linkage of gay activist movement by the simple act of naming at a particular junction, and this clearly exemplifies Carter's concept regarding naming of a place. But this sort of appropriation of public spaces by lesbians is significantly inconspicuous. The reason for it can be adduced to the facts that women have less mobility and financial independence, and consequently less accessibility to public sphere. Thus on the one hand, placing lesbian love within the heteronormative domesticity indeed "restructures, radicalizes and invest(s) these spaces with new dissident symbolism" (Aneeta Rajendran, in http://www.interdisplinary.net/critical-issues/transformations/persons-andsexuality/project-rchives/4th/session-1-representations/), while on the other this exclusion from public spaces appears to be a backlash against the representation of all-encompassing overt pervasiveness and public acceptance of lesbian and transgender intimacies. From this perspective in *Ladies Coupé* there is a unique combination of public and private spaces allocated to Sapphic desire, for in this text the lesbian encounter takes place in a train. *Ladies Coupé* revolves around the life stories of six women who narrate their tales of heterosexual subjugation in an all-female (due to the presence of ladies coupé) homosocial space. The very title of the novel *Ladies Coupé* is indicative of the all-women space which provides a conducive ground for six women to unfold unabashedly their stories of oppression and subjugation in a patriarchal structure and their incessant quest for identity outside the male-dominated space. There is an interesting symbolic dichotomy due to the presence of ladies coupé in a train, for the train which is not stationary suggestively represents the ever-moving all-pervasive homosocial domain (ladies coupé) within the heterosexual patriarchal (train) space. It is a public transport of a very heteronormative nature within which there is a deliberate locating of ladies coupé (an all-women sphere) which works as a fertile ground for the narration of an exclusive lesbian encounter. Apparently this is a very interesting intersection of public and private space.

While there are rampant depictions of gay clubs, parks (which during the day might have a very heterosexual character but at night change their complexion and turn out to be queer-friendly sites) and public toilets as convenient cruising places in Raj Rao's *The Boyfriend*, but such ephemeral experiences at transient sites are by and large absent in lesbian narratives as has been mentioned earlier in this chapter. The mutability of these fleeting experiences at an equally ephemeral sites has a very important advantage as has been charted out by Larry Knopp:

> Cruising is not so much tied to a fixed site but is all about the flows of movement and passings. Clubbing, meanwhile, is an ephemeral experience — both the ephemerality of erotic

> encounters with others on and off a dance floor, but also the ephemerality of the club night itself, coming together to use a space for one night a week or one night a month, congregating and then dispersing. Such queer experiences and practices might be understood in terms of Thrift's idea of an "ecology of place" as a "spectral gathering", in which various practices, meanings and "actants" are examined for their myriad and ephemeral interconnections. Similarly "placelessness" might be productively reconceptualised as an embodied and material practice, one that offers certain pleasures and other benefits (such as security) through its various perceived qualities (heterogeneity, temporariness, anonymity, cosmopolitanism), rather than just a lack.
>
> — 2007: 23

Interestingly in the story, "Conference Sex", there is a production of lesbian site in the form of a mutable space of conference because the very atmosphere of a conference is saturated with a certain sort of temporality and anonymity regarding both space and identities as people are there for a very short period of time bereft of any attachments. Little wonder the two lesbians meet at a conference, have sex and part without any ceremonial parting words. And the "placelessness" inherent in the conference sites helps in making them ideal places for the flourishing of transgressive desires as the protagonist contemplates:

> It was a conference, I reassured myself; no one expects anything like this, and there are no set rules for behaviour.
>
> — Ellen 2012: 183

Indeed the mutability of such places is indubitably not a "lack" in any sense of the word but contributes to the rewriting and bending of the rules of desire.

Coming back to the train as a site suitable for the flowering of transgressive desires, it appears that train is not only an interesting site of intersection of private and public sphere but also a fine example of Foucauldian heterotopias. According to Foucault, there are certain identities like adolescents, menstruating and pregnant women, who are in crisis with their environment. Foucault argues that boarding schools in its nineteenth-century form or military services for young man, the train and honeymoon hotels are all examples of "heterotopias of crisis" because

> first manifestations of sexual virility were in fact supposed to take place "elsewhere" than at home. For girls, there was, until the middle of the twentieth century, a tradition called the "honeymoon trip" which was an ancestral theme. The young woman's deflowering could take place "nowhere" and at the moment of its occurrence the train or honeymoon hotel was indeed the place of this nowhere, this heterotopias without geographical marker.
>
> — http://www.foucaullt.info/doc/documents/heterotopia/foucault.heterotopia.en.html

No wonder the train has been the centre space for sexual-encounters of queer people in Raj Rao's *The Boyfriend*, "Six Inches", Sarojini Sahoo's "Behind the Scene" and Abdul Khalid Rashid's "Incomplete Human". Giti Thadani in *Sakhiyani* by quoting Sonia Singh's article, "A Lesbian to Lean On" in the magazine *Chastity* (July 1994) states that there is growing anxiety regarding the development of lesbian relationships due to the easily available homosocial spaces at the ladies compartments of the local trains. Thadani observes that there is a growing demand to create heterosocial spaces as compared to homosocial spaces in order to eradicate lesbianism. Obviously the politics of subsuming exclusive homoerotic social places by creating more heterosexual spaces has a larger sinister agenda. To quote Sukthankar:

> the above constructs lesbian experiences as arising from the fact that homosociality is more easily accepted, leading to lesbian experimentation. The moment that heterosociality is accepted this "problem" supposedly will be eradicated.
>
> — 1999: 97

Thus unlike Nair's *Ladies Coupé*, Sarojini Sahoo's "Behind the Scene" takes a radical shift by not depicting lesbian lovemaking in an exclusive ladies' compartment but by placing it in a general compartment and that too before the married couple. Throughout the text the heterosexual desire is displaced and dismantled through lesbian love by appropriating the spatial dimensions in all possible forms, and consequently it bursts the myth of the ultimate pleasures of heteronormative desire by the constant caressing and passionate physical intimacies between the two women (one married and another unmarried) before Pooja. It creates significant doubts regarding heterosexual conjugal bliss in the mind of the married onlooker Pooja, who is travelling with her husband and is seated before them. By seeing them indulged in a passionate embrace, Pooja constantly contrasts her drab and passionless marriage with the joyous and intense lovemaking between the two lesbian lovers. To quote from the story:

> The "girl" in jeans kissed her partner's red face. The whole scene reminded Pooja of how Radha was stricken and prostrated by the witty arrows shot by her *sakhi* Lalita, such was the overwhelming nature of her abashment at those. Their amorous play reminded Pooja of Radha and Lalita's love-frolic in the *Kunjaban*. — Sahoo 2007: 79

This is followed by her recollection of her mundane and routine dull married life:

> All this and much more of such routine life: twenty years of her married life had whirled past. When could she have enjoyed her life. — Ibid.: 80

While Pooja and her husband slept on the separate berths, she noticed that the two women were interlocked in each other's embrace oblivious to the world. They appear to her like a two flowers in a single stalk. This observation is further followed by her recollection of the fact that over a period of time, she and her husband have become unaware of each other's body:

> . . . After that they became unaware of each other. The same familiar bodies, the same limbs, hands, face, and spots. Besides, they had got tired shopping, and at last lay on the bed turning their backs to each other. —Ibid.: 82

No doubt the presence of the same-sex lovers and their unabashed caressing and kissing in a general compartment of heteronormative nature, which is viewed by a straight woman who after seeing them questions her own heterosexual marriage, are indeed attempts to reverse the heteronormative paradigm by displacing heterosexual space through all-pervasive lesbian lovemaking in the train. Suggestively one of the lesbian women fills up the entire vacant space with her luggage and then captures the place of married Pooja's birth.

> After packing the space below their seat with their luggage, she shoved the rest into the empty space below Pooja's berth. She pushed aside Pooja's bottles with a karate chop and placed her own jug there. —Ibid.: 75

The overlap between space and identity has been negotiated explicitly in the very first paragraph of the story:

> Why do people make so much fuss over this two-day affair? As if the space belonged to them eternally. —Ibid.: 74

Little wonder one of the most ostracized identities within queer academia and the obvious corporeal marker of liminal existence, a *hijra* (who is otherwise largely invisible in the literary representations) expresses the pathetic and the inhuman condition of his/her life inside a train compartment in "Adhura Insaan" or "Incomplete Human". It is but natural that the chosen space for this transgender intersexed identity can only be a moving fluid nowhere space of a train. The spatial anxiety and chaoss, which are necessary requisites for any kind of politics, germinate in a moving scene where the male co-traveller insists that since only men have occupied a particular compartment s/he should sit somewhere else. The transgender in question remains adamant and sits in that very compartment and changes the spatial dynamic of the location and in turn the sexual crisis of his/her existence gets highlighted and discussed at length. Similarly the fluid dimension of the boat is used in the short story, "Dreams and Desires in Srinagar". This story revolves around the sex escapades of a Kashmiri youth with a Delhi-based professional on a boat, and all the sex encounters are described along with the vivid depiction of a floating boat which serves the unique purpose of providing a fluid heterotopia for the sexual negotiations of the two extremely different men — one a Kashmiri youth with a traditional upbringing and the other a middle-aged educated professional from Delhi. The improbable propositions in terms of gay encounter, class and cultural disparity find reconciliation only in the fluid nowhere space of boat, for it signifies the complete blurring of binaries because the boat belongs to nowhere and has no geographical marker, and consequently relationships that fit nowhere can easily find their exploration in this heterotopic site. To quote from the text:

> We moved back to the rear deck and onto the threadbare sofa that faced the water. We sat side by side, with legs touching. What had played out between us moments before didn't now mean that we had to keep space between skin. . . . For me the musk of crystallized sweat on a man is pure sex.
>
> — Malik 2012: 22-23

Significantly just after this scene the narrator recollects another memory of his gay encounter that has taken place in yet another heterotopic site — metro train in Delhi. So the immediate constant shifting from one fluid space (boat) to another (metro train) together with the overlapping of the same type of gay experiences clearly evinces the writer's intention of showcasing the fact as why and how such sites are chosen for forbidden desires. Similarly in Ugra's story,

"Chocolate Charcha" or "Discussing Chocolate" published in 1924, a self-reflexive discussion on Ugra's gay writings takes place in the train itself. The entire story starts with a moving train and ends within a train. The whole story is a debate about whether writing about gay sex perpetuates homosexuality or it is just an act of exposing this hidden aspect of sexuality. In fact as early as in 1924, the use of moving train for homoerotic articulation was made visible. The additional ontologies that include placelessness and movement, and help in creating a queer-friendly environment are explored through this story effectively. In this regard Larry Knopp's observation in "From Lesbian and Gay Prospects to Queer Geographies: Pasts, Prospects and Possibilities" is quite pertinent. He observes:

> The visibility that placement brings can make us vulnerable to violence as well as facilitate our marginalization and exclusion from the security and pleasures that placement typically brings members of dominant social groups. It is no surprise then that queers are frequently suspicious, fearful and unable to relate easily to the fixity and certainty inhering in most dominant ontologies of "place". Indeed, many queers find a certain amount of solace, safety and pleasures being in motion or nowhere at all. Social and sexual encounters with other queers can feel safer in such contexts — on the move, passing through, inhabiting a space for a short amount of time — and a certain erotic (or just social) solidarity can ironically emerge from the transient and semi-anonymous nature of such experiences.
>
> — Knopp 2007: 23

Likewise in a quite humorous fashion Raj Rao in "Six Inches", through the homosexual gaze of the two photographers who have to click pictures of men in action without being overtly pornographic, appropriates the usual heteronormative spaces. The eye of the camera turns the usual sexually innocent acts into sensuously surcharged activities with sexual undertones, and this implicitly implies that every straight space is saturated with latent homoerotic passion and a gay gaze can catch it and turn it upside down as these two photographers do. Brett Farmer in *Spectacular Passions*: *Cinema, Fantasy, Gay Male Spectatorships* discusses the psychoanalytic concept of "fantasmic spectatorship", and uses fantasy to explore the uniqueness of gay men's social and psychic positioning that

> functions not only structurally, in that it positions the subject within pre-existing paradigms of desire and meaning, but also contingently, in that the realization of fantasmic imperatives always depends on the determinate conditions of the subject's cultural and historical particularity.
>
> — http://www.glbtq.com/arts/film-spectator.html

This unique reception by gay men fractures normative masculinities. Farmer points out that the "dazzling images, sounds, and narratives" of movies not only expose desire but also teach desire that results in the formation of the fluid psychocultural discourses of sexuality which further compel audience to introspect about their own libidinal utterances. Inevitably it produces "a site of continuous interaction between the potential fantasmatic scenarios signalled by the text and the shifting psychosocial frames inhabited by the individual spectator" (http://www.glbtq.com/arts/film-spectator.html). Obviously the cinematic and photographic interpretations with regard to the specific gay spectators are bound to be ambivalent and the internal act of counter-constructions, on account of different diegetic spaces, allows and creates much necessary ruptures that prevent unilateral closure.

Significantly in Raj Rao's "Six Inches" (which has been discussed in Chapter 6, though in a different context), in the first photograph the protagonists cleverly manipulate the site of Chowpatty beach where many men have gathered sitting together and holding hands:

> Rashid and Ashok camouflage themselves in the crowd. Ashok has a camera hanging from his neck. He searches for an appropriate shot, then zeroes in on a pair who clasp each other so low on the waist that they virtually look like they're clasping arse. — Rai 1999b: 134-35

The boys think them to be foreign tourists trying to capture the various shades of exotic India and do not doubt their intentions. Similarly the second picture homosexualizes the busy Nariman Point and makes it look like a homosocial space and a hot hub for gay interaction. For another photograph a second-class compartment of the "train" comes into picture.

> The compartment is so over packed that the commuters, as they alight virtually look as if they are on the top of one another, especially as Ashok takes the picture from the floor level. — Ibid.: 136

For their last picture, they cunningly turn the religious space of *Dahihandi* festival into a homoerotic zone by manipulating the picture of wet male bodies falling on one another. All these photographs have been shot skilfully with such an angle that these straight spaces appear as queer sites and these non-sexual activities of straight men appear to be acts of homosexual mating. The site of *Dahihandi* festival specially follows the fourth principle of heterotopias as propounded by Foucault. According to Foucault, there are heterotopias of indefinitely accumulating time, for example, museums and libraries that will encompass in one place "all times, all epochs, all forms, all tastes, the idea of constituting a place of all times that is itself outside of time and inaccessible to its ravages, the project of organizing in this way a sort of perpetual and indefinite accumulation of time in an immobile place" (http://www.foucaullt.info/doc/documents/heterotopia/foucault.heterotopia.en.html). It is opposed to those heterotopias that in contrast represent time in its most transient, ephemeral and flowing nature. According to him, one example of such heterotopias is "festival". He further elaborates it by giving the example of fairgrounds. To quote his words:

> These heterotopias are not oriented towards the eternal, they are rather absolutely temporal [chroniques]. Such, for example, are the fairgrounds, these 'marvelous empty sites on the outskirts of the cities that teem once or twice a year with stands, displays heteroclite objects, wrestlers, snake-women, fortune-tellers, such as those Polynesian villages that offer a compact three weeks of primitive and eternal nudity to the inhabitants of the cities.
>
> — http://www.foucaullt.info/doc/documents/heterotopia/foucault.heterotopia.en.html

Significantly although the "*Dahihandi* festival" has been turned into a male orgy through homosexual gaze and humorously has been given a religious sanction too, but there are festivals like Aravani that take place every year at Villipuram in Tamil Nadu to celebrate the marriage of eunuchs (who come in a large number there from all over the country) to Aravan followed by temporary sexual romping in open spaces under full-moon sky. This is further followed by beauty contests and there is a certain kind of acceptance of all kinds of the so-called non-normative sexual behaviours which are not allowed after and before the festival time. In fact the state's acceptance of non-normative sexuality during a particular time period and space is evident from the fact that in 2008 an NGO named "Network of Positive People" distributed 3,000 condoms during Aravani festival ("Celebrating Their Uniqueness" in *The Hindustan Times*, 23 April 2008: 13). Interestingly the same newspaper clipping reports how the villagers affirm that after the euphoria in the morning they are left to clean the fields that look like a dump yard of used condoms. Further the newspaper reports that the local residents complain that their children bring back used condoms to home. This provides a very interesting intervention in terms of temporary sanction at a particular space for a certain time period (and thus emphasizing the temporality of non-normative sexual endeavours, though under religious sanction), which extends from open spaces (that assumes the form of festival heterotopias) to heteronormative home by the symbolic representation of children carrying used condoms to home. In this context it is important to note Mikhail Bakhtin's concept of "carnivalesque" that points out how the festival site recreates a symbolic "second life" where hegemonic structures are dismantled because the spirit of festivities provides an entry into the symbolic space of utopian freedom. Therefore some festivals or even at times marriage celebrations are by and large imbued with non-normative desires and work as a fertile location for transgressive desire, specially when perceived independently.

Thus there are homoerotic narratives like Ugra's story, "Chocolate" in which the accidental throwing of ink by one of the characters assumes symbolic meaning of Holi and the cultural codes of permissiveness associated with the festival of Holi come into the picture and lead to sexual intimacies:

> Seeing him pounce, Ramesh pretended to throw the ink-bottle at him, merely with the intention of frightening him. But look at this! The bottle remained in his hand but the cork came off. Dinkar Babu was soaked in ink! As if he had played Holi, he was drenched from head to foot . . . Ramesh stood stunned by this sudden turn of events. Dinkar caught hold of him and began to embrace and kiss him: Angry with me? With me? Darling, darling! — Ugra 2006: 42

Hence it gives impetus to the temporary entry of subaltern sexualities. Patiently festivals carry such power as to reinvest and radicalize the spaces immensely. No wonder in Raj Rao's *Hostel Room 131*, the imaginative recollection of Holi and the superimposing of it with alternative libidinal desires have been presented quite ingeniously. Likewise in the same novel, the

New-Year celebrations on 31 December at a public place provide an explicit exploration of the concept of "carnivalesque space" where at a particular time during festivities the heterosexist boundaries of a place become porous through which deviant longings can pour in. Siddharth and his paramour Sudhir were in crowd when the New-Year celebrations took place on the busy road of the town and amidst the celebration, the rampant sensuous intimacies, though for a short while, took place:

> It was an open-air pageant, free of cost and something he was not used to witnessing. But the highlight, surely, was that more than a couple of times someone in the crowd pinched his bottom and, once, even squeezed his dick. "Don't be a slut," Siddharth reprimanded him when he reported the matter, but Sudhir was flattered. That he, a small-towner, was desirable to Bombayites boosted his self-esteem . . . for this was one wanton night when they would be forgiven.
>
> — Patel 2010: 67

Thus the temporarily excluded liminal spaces or heterochronies (as Foucault calls them) create significant mutations not at the periphery only, but intrude the heterosexual spaces as well. Indeed these excluded or in-between places work potently to elicit the mechanism of power and use the structures and spaces of exclusion to reverse the power-paradigm and create a space of "emplacement".

At times the transgressive desires are deliberately placed inside the institutionalized heterosexual structure (for instance in temples and religious *ashrams*) and the technique of inversion is used to appropriate heteronorm. For instance in "Let Me Sin Then" by Dibyajyoti Sarma, the homosexual encounters have been depicted in Nalanda Vidyapeeth among monks and this deliberate placing of the same-sex desire in the religious space (in Gujarat there is a specific temple associated with sex-change, known as Bahuchara Mataji) is indeed a radical act of normalizing homoerotic desire and it negates the religious policing of homosexuality. Set in antiquity, the marriage scene inside a Shiva Temple between the two gay *bhikkhus* in Dibyajyoti's story radicalizes the religious place and ameliorates homophobia by superimposing the images of the two *bhikkhus* while they explore each other's body amid the rendering of *shlokas*. Then there is the use of the Banyan tree as a place for sensuous caressing rather than for *dhyan* (meditation). The gay marriage which is still struggling for acceptance both at social and legal level is being solemnized before a heterosexual deity Shiva:

> My eyes were moist and my mind went back to that lonely evening, when Varunmohan took me to the Shiva Temple on the top of the hill. He also carried some red *gulal* with him. Inside the temple, he smeared the red on my forehead, tied his sacred thread with mine, took my hand into his and recited that *sloka* which meant, *"today on, I accept you as my wife"*. Then he recited all those Vedic *slokas* that the *purohit* was now reciting. In front of that lonely God, I had become his wife, and he my husband. . . . — Sarma 2012: 104

However, the religious sanction through the temple-space creates an ambivalent disposition in terms of endorsement at one level and the regulation at the other. Almost in the similar manner the short story, "The Marriage of Somavat and Sumedha" by Devdutt Pattanaik, catalogues the subaltern sexual escapades of the two young men living in a temple as orphans with a holy cow that is a sole witness to their homoerotic liaison. Suroopa Mukherjee's *Across the Mystic Shore* is specially pertinent in this respect. The lesbian relationships originate and flower in the temple and *ashram* at the holy city of Banaras. Throughout the text the religious spaces have been invested with the same-sex longings and follow the politics of inversion. In the text, the very first meeting between the two lovers takes place in a Shiva Mandir before a Shivalinga, a significant heterosexual marker of divinity. During the worship of the Shivalinga, the proliferation of lesbian desire, by ceaseless accidental sensuous touching and spilling of the same milk on the body of one of the lovers which is meant to be offered to Shivalinga, is indeed a radical move of filling up the heterosexual puritan religious spaces with lesbian longings:

> The precinct of the temple was so narrow that it filled me with surprise. People jostled in that narrow space and I could feel my body lurching forward and touching hers. The delicacy of her skin and the contours of her breast covered by the blue edge of her *sari* carried for me a pattern of perfection. She was like the hallowed body of some goddess who dwelt in those streets, pure, without blemish, and yet obscene in her erotic appeal. Hands were pushing me from behind. Some of the milk from my clay pot splashed on the back of her neck. She cringed, the skin curling slightly. I noticed that a river of milk descended over her shoulder and plunged deep into the crevice between her breasts. I felt shock waves spiral through my loins. The clashing of cymbals and the sounds of chanting was deafening. We were moving deeper and deeper into the inner fold of the temple. The *linga* stood in the middle: dark. Bulbous and gorging the milk poured on its head with religious frenzy.
>
> — Mukherjee 2006: 163

Acorss the Mystic Shore is also remarkable for its delineation of lesbian motherhood (a very unique identity that helps in forming an alternative family structure) in the *ashram* space which is a classic example of an overlap of the fifth and sixth principles of "heterotopias". Since heterotopias prescribe a system of opening and closing that makes them pervious and impervious at the same time, they are not easily penetrable like a public space. According to Foucault, either the entry is compulsory as in the case of barracks and prisons or the individual has to go through the purification rights and in the Indian context the classic example can be cited from the fact that the inclusion of *hijra*s as *chela*s in *hijra* clan is only possible after various purification rituals. In fact, the *hijra*s are called real *hijra* only after going through *nirvanam* ceremony (emasculation). Contrary to these heterotopias, Foucault asserts that

> there are others . . . that seem to be pure and simple openings, but that generally hide curious exclusions. Everyone can enter into the new heterotopic sites, but in fact that is only an illusion — we think we enter where we are, by the very fact that we enter, excluded.
>
> — http://www.foucaullt.info/doc/documents/heterotopia/foucault.heterotopia.en.html

Ashram definitely is one of such sites where by the simple act of entry the law of displacement is enforced because it follows the sixth principle of Foucault's heterotopia according to which here are some heterotopic spaces that are as perfect, disciplined and meticulous as ours in contrast are messy, undisciplined and jumbled. He calls them not the heterotopias of illusion but of "compensation". He gives examples of puritan societies and Jesuit colonies. The puritanical *ashram* at Varanasi is indeed one such heterotopic site, for at one level with its strict regime, rules, regulations and discipline, it is more perfect than the spaces we encounter in usual day-to-day life, but on the other since it is autonomous and excluded in more than many ways, the usual societal rules do not operate there. This provides slippages and openings that help in the flourishing of the subaltern identities. *Sannyasis*, widows and people expelled from the society take refuge in *ashram* and make it both penetrable and impenetrable at the same time. Little wonder it becomes a unique site for exposing the eclectic dynamics of lesbian motherhood in Suroopa Mukherjee's *Across the Mystic Shore*. In this novel other than the two lovers and the midwife, no one in the *ashram* knows as who has actually given birth to the child. The advantage of procreation through heterosexual liaison, which is considered the greatest argument in favour of heterosexual mating and one of the strongest backlash at homoerotic passion, is negated by not only depicting lesbian desire but also by showcasing the formation of the alternative family structure with two mothers and a son. To quote from the text:

> Did Romola actually mean that she and Uma were trying to have a baby? That in fact they intended to use a real womb. But how? Then I saw the *ashram* for what it really was: a closed world, governed by its own rules. But how? How many delusions could flourish there? The prayer times, the communal eating, sleeping, waking and doing of household chores. Relationships that were undefined. How do you know your brother, father, mother, sister? The ascetic and the erotic co-existed. These ashramites were married to God and served his lust. I had seen pregnant women and suckling mothers inside the *ashram*. — Mukherjee 2006: 171

In quite a suggestive fashion, the story of the so-called forbidden room has been told to Romola by Uma. She talks about the secret rooms or spaces within household which are locked and how children get hold of the keys and open them, and just by being in those spaces they are able to unravel the forbidden things to themselves and to fellow-children. Uma told her that the children talked about the things that would have shocked elders. These secluded places have been compared to grandmothers' prayer rooms which are "heterotopias of contrast" as has been mentioned in this chapter. In this manner, the juxtaposing of space and identity has been made explicit by the author. Romola states:

> But forbidden spaces teach you the important lesson of learning to break rules in order to enter. You learn that you are alone in this world. The anger and joy you feel, they belong to you alone. Every door opens and closes for you in different ways. — Ibid.: 287-88

Romola also taught Uma that a very easy mode to bend rule

is to follow a small penance such as a missed meal or small prayer. Hence this autonomous mode of rules and regulations provides enough flexibility for the flourishing of descendant sexualities. It is in stark contrast to the outside world where these small punishments are not available to counter bolstering of homophobia. Naturally in this fashion the secluded world of four walls of *ashram* provides a unique space for lesbian motherhood which further negates all supremacist chauvinistic heterosexual propaganda of patriarchal family as the only available choice. In the words of the midwife:

> Believe me, I have never witnessed a birth that is so joyous, so completely devoid of the fear of pain. There were two women in the room, and they shared the experience like twins, joined body and soul. I felt my presence was redundant . . . the two women sang at high pitch. I was shocked, but mesmerized by the power they exuded. I began to sing with them, especially when they satirized and sanitized culture that views motherhood and childbirth as a woman's greatest birth right. — Mukherjee 2006: 216-17

In fact the midwife is so overwhelmed by this unique motherhood that she refuses to take her payment. Now in a way the religious sanction has been provided by placing the notion of lesbian motherhood in the *ashram* in the holy city of Banaras as has been done by Ruth Vanita — by the narration of the birth of Bhagirathi (from whose hair the holy Ganges emanates) by the two women (King Dilipa's wives after the death of the king) or the birth of *agni* by multiple mothers and Parvati's creation of androgynous God Ganesha as a form of parthenogenesis out of her own fluid to guard the homosocial space of her bathing — in the critical sphere of queer academia. It is further strengthened by the fact that the heterotopic space of *ashram* works as a suitable ground to counter the societal pressures regarding dissident sexualities because in one way even an ascetic flouts the rules of domesticated society. Little wonder the *ashrams* are placed at the outer fringe of the city.

Indeed Varanasi's unique character of being a place filled with mysticism and transcendentalism further adds a specific dimension to this whole issue of "emplacement" of city. To quote from the text:

> Is it something about this place, he wondered, that despite its strict religiosity Varanasi filled you with a sense of *masti*, and breaking all barriers? Like the *ghat*s, where veneration and commerce co-existed without flinching, and able-bodied men lay prone in states of indolence, while the place vibrated with the sights and sounds of devotion.
>
> — Ibid.: 252

In an interesting intervention, the novel showcases the placing of heterotopia within heterotopias (margins within margins). This creates spatial anxiety that results in the opening of a third space which further metamorphoses the erotic geography in such a fashion as the negotiation of fluid sexuality becomes a norm. When David wants to give Romola the security of a domestic space through marriage and wants to kiss her, she suggestively states that even within the *ashram* it is possible:

> "I know of a place where it is possible," she said mysteriously. He was taken aback by the simplicity of her proposition. If such a place existed in the *ashram* it had to be secret, yet at the same time widely known. . . . She led him to a large banyan tree, and sitting under its ancient roots she said to him, "You can touch me now. You remember I told you about this place where people meet and touch and kiss each other. This is it." He was astounded. "This is the place? But how? There is no privacy here. The whole world can see us." . . . "nobody can see us. These roots act as curtains. Haven't you noticed something? This tree faces the back of the building and there are no overlooking windows. This space is totally blocked out from anybody's vision, unless you are standing on a terrace. But at night it is too dark and no light can penetrate these roots". — Ibid.: 257-58

The synergistic relationship of the tree (a liminal space within heterotopic space of *ashram*) with Romola is explored in terms of their unique amalgam as seen by David. He envisages how the tree merges into Romola and Romola turns into a tree and this peculiar melting cannot be seen by anyone other than someone who is standing on the roof which as a site of intersection of public and private discourse, has been interpreted in the earlier section of this chapter. Thus the coexistence and mutual merging of three heterotopic sites, that is, tree, roof and *ashram*, create a space that can be easily termed as heterotopia within heterotopia which redlines the normative spaces and constructs a free-flowing pansexual spatiality. Unlike displacing the original heterosexual spaces and then reconstructing homoerotic zone, here Romola narrates her lesbian rendezvous with Uma under the tree and how the banyan tree is away from any sort of social scrutiny and policing. She then initiates David to take a plunge with her. Thus rather than displacing heterosexuality to make a place for same-sex union, here the narrator emphasizes that the particular space originally belongs to homosexual encounters, and by such fluid negotiation of sexuality the space has been sanitized for the so-called other forbidden liaison including heterosexual encounters outside a marriage. Importantly the process of inversion inscribes that heterotopias within heterotopias can make an accommodation for both homo and hetero encounters without any contradiction. To illustrate it, let us cite from the text:

> He saw her then, her body rooted to the tree, her eyes roving through the branches as though she wanted to pluck and eat the fruit that was furthest away from her. "Don't you like this place?" She asked, her voice hushed and full of wonder. "Uma and I often come here in the dark. At night the soft, shivering sound of leaves caught by a gentle breeze is like the music of the spheres. We watch the moon, looking like the belly button of the night witch, so naked and

> shameless. The brambles scratch our backs and the rotting moss on the bark fills us with its heady smell. We are drunk with the magic of being alive. I wonder why they never teach us this lesson in the *ashram*? Inhale, exhale are two exercises that we are taught, but under this tree we feel the pulse of the universe, beating without pause".
>
> — Ibid.: 258-59

Another interesting aspect of this matter is that schools or educational institutes are seen as spaces of somewhat relative autonomy as compared to the sphere of family, where patriarchal roles are stringently followed. Apparently the liberal discussion in Dawesar's *Babyji* on the same-sex desire in Anamika's school by a doctor and the various queries posed unabashedly by the students clearly evince the symbiotic relationship between space and sexuality, and how at times locating homoerotic desire outside domesticity in a somewhat gender neutral space is also a strategic move. There have been detailed questions and subsequent answers about homosexuality, transvestites, *hijra*s, lesbian and gay copulation in *Babyji*, as these kinds of queries and discussions are generally not permitted in domestic spaces. One very pertinent question is asked in the sex-counselling session in the school:

> "Ma'am if two men can have sex, does that mean two women can have sex?" She asked. . . . "Yes they can. . . . May be not sex as you know it. Maybe not penetrative heterosexual intercourse," . . . "To answer your question," the doctor continued, shifting her attention back to Sheela, her voice smooth once more , "women are capable of giving each other sexual pleasure, but once again this will not lead to procreation".
>
> — Dawesar 2005: 108

Thus the curriculum, whether in the form of biology class or sex education sessions, plays a pivotal role in reinvesting school and college environment with a certain openness that is a fertile ground for any sort of discussion on alternative sexualities.

Even if the formal curriculum is only about the heterosexuality, the informal curriculum which is called "hidden curriculum" by Nairan is a significant key to break the stereotypes as has been described in *Babyji*. In this novel, the formal sexual education is saturated with heteronormative assumptions but the informal counselling-session breaks the barriers and non-normativity becomes the focal point of the discussion. In this regard, quoting Valentine, Jon Binnie in "Sexuality, the Erotic and Geography: Epistemology, Methodology and Pedagogy" affirms:

> Visibility across the curriculum is important for dissident sexualities because it normalizes them. Otherwise the danger is that lesbian, gay and bisexualities are missed altogether or become relegated to the one-off "exotic other" lecture, which only serves to reinforce stereotypes and perpetuate the taken-for-granted heterosexuality of the university environment. — Binnie 2007: 37

Undoubtedly the correspondence between the formal and informal curriculum plays a key role in reorienting the taken-for-granted heteronormativity of the university space. Owing to this particular aspect of curriculum, university and school become unique sites for queer articulations. In fact, the first kiss between Sheela and Anamika in *Babyji* takes place in the school classroom, and in this manner there is a visibility of female transgressive desire in public domain, though not as explicit as in *The Boyfriend*. Ismat's *The Crooked Line*, Raj Rao's *Hostel Room 131* and Keval Sood's *Murgikhana* paint hostels as spaces which are imbued with Sapphic and homoerotic desires. Likewise in the short story, "Conference Sex", the educational space which is exclusively meant for cerebral stimulation is radicalized by portraying two lesbians engaged in unadulterated phallic longings bereft of any intellectual or emotional bonding. The temporality of conference space provides momentary opening and closing which is imperative for the negotiations of pansexualities. In *Vivek and I* by Mayur Patel, a particular problem regarding "coming out" of a teacher before his student in an educational space has been delineated ingeniously. There are some professional spaces like fashion industry and cinema where queer existence is relatively more acceptable, but the "coming out" of a teacher, being a role model, before his student is somewhat more difficult as has been described in *Vivek and I*. Kaushik, who is a school teacher, finds it quite difficult to "come out" before his student, Vivek, who happens to be his love interest. Similarly Miss Charan, who is a school teacher in Ismat's *The Crooked Line*, has to leave her job when her Sapphic longings have been discovered. In this connection, quoting Valentine, Jon Binnie in "Sexuality, the Erotic and Geography: Epistemology, Methodology and Pedagogy" argues that

> because of the assumption that mundane environments are coded as straight, lesbian, gay and bisexual staff are faced with the issue of whether to be out with their students . . . in the small and incestuous world of academia, once you are "out" there are few possibilities to retreat into the closet if the going gets tough. — Binnie 2007: 36

Indubitably if there is a considerable amount of freedom at educational spaces due to the relative autonomy, there is also a greater apprehension of "coming out" specially in teachers on account of their being seen as role models. None the less in countering this problem, the curriculum plays a vital role as has been documented in Dawesar's *Babyji*. The discussion surrounding sexuality opens many knots. As Valentine accepts that because of the mainstreaming of work on the geography of sexualities and the mass introduction of courses in which sexuality is discussed, there is a significant decrease in the antagonism against queer identities. Obviously the curriculum plays an important role in making an educational institute a queer-friendly domain. In this respect despite teacher being a role model of a certain kind, the autonomy and wisely designed curriculum can play an important part in transforming schools and universities into sites which work in favour of subaltern sexualities, and that is why there is a large number of queer texts that have schools, universities and hostels as background such as *The Crooked Line, Hostel Room 131, Babyji,* "Let Me Sin Then", *Murgikhana* and *Vivek and I.*

The bisexual spaces add another twist to the tale, for they tend to blur the distinction between the straight and the gay spaces in a way. But the question is whether they are able to create the much needed pansexual domains which should ideally mitigate the stringent binary opposition between the straight and the gay spaces or not. Quoting Hemmings Brown, Gavin Kath and Jason Lim argue that "bisexuals may think of either gay or straight spaces (or both) as 'home', but a bisexual identity is never predominant in either set of spaces, and although the presence of bisexuals may be acknowledged, it is seldom fully included" (p. 9). As in the story "Steps Taken Back" by Iqbal Deep, the protagonist lives with her partner in an apparently perfect lesbian household with a servant. The partner of the protagonist develops a relationship with the servant and the space turns from queer to straight. And the pain of the narrator is depicted quite poignantly but nowhere the inherent bisexuality of her partner is accepted, for either one is expected to be straight or queer and bisexuality is always hidden beneath these two identities. So the presentation of the exclusive bisexual space is still a myth specially in Indian literary texts. Further complicating the situation, Gavin Kath and Jason Lim, quoting Hubbard, state that

> . . . bisexual space is neither gay nor straight space, and the presence of bisexual identities in space is always partial.
>
> — 2007: 10

Her solution to this problem is to focus on witnessing the

spatial enactment of embodied acts and desires, although she has accepted that these seldom easily correlate to a self-identified bisexual identity. She has examined the production of bisexuality and the negotiation of bisexual desires in relation to other queer bodies in particular queer spaces. By taking this approach, it is Hemmings' intention to re-emphasize that desire is "'enacted through our bodies'and is site specific" (p. 10). In this connection, the story, "Valecha" by Bhupen Khakkar is specially significant because it beautifully creates that specific "third space" where a subtle interaction, rather than an antagonism, between hetero and homosexual desires takes place between them. Khakkar explains this in these words:

> I reluctantly went and sat. He caressed my legs and kept discussing legal matters with the woman. I figured out that the woman needed some help and Valecha was only too willing to do so. Then all of a sudden, their topic changed. They started winking lecherously, fooling around and cracking jokes. He rubbed my legs harder as they went along rambunctiously. I felt an undercurrent lust rising like fragrance in all three of us. — 2012: 54

Hence the negation of the strict binary opposition between the queer and the straight spaces is possible, but it is somewhat located in the metaphorical understanding of the space.

The use of the concept of space in shaping, altering and familiarizing of the sexual dissident identity is indeed a potent strategy, widely used in contemporary Indian creative homoerotic writings. However, the hierarchy within oppressed group is conspicuous from the fact that the visibility of public cruising places (public toilets and parks) and gay bars is rampant in the writings of Raj Rao and Mahesh Dattani, but such exclusive privatization of public spaces is missing in Indian lesbian literature by and large. By critiquing a number of literary texts, the present chapter aimed at highlighting the fact that there has been a deliberate heterosexualization after colonization and to contest it, among many other queer literary tools, the use of "space" as strategy to create homosocial spaces is of singular importance. An intricate analysis of certain texts brings out another aspect of this issue, and that is, the partial treatment accorded to lesbians and transgenders with respect to homosexualization of spaces in the Indian literary texts. Moreover the invasion of the deviant sexualities on heterosexualized spaces in one way negates the notion propounded by Duggan and illustrated by David Bell and Jon Binnie who assert that the new homonormativity and "gay villages" are ingenious tools to provide a separate identity to certain spaces but this exclusivity has pushed subaltern sexual identities towards a certain kind of periphery which creates place only for non-threatening lesbians and gay men. From another point of view they become instruments for spreading "pink economy" and produce sites which "are now complicit in reducing the 'gay public sphere' to sites of consumption and gentrified neighbourhood" (Casey 2007: 127).

The forgoing discussion gives rise to the question whether the intervention of homosexual identities into heterosexual sites is an act of redrawing of boundaries or a means to formulate spaces which accept gays and lesbians as long as they portray only non-threatening heteronormalized version of gay and lesbian identities. Then the question arises: is new homonormativity only for a particular kind of queer? And does this homosexualization of straight spatial formation have a backhand sinister plan of inclusion at the cost of endorsing mainstream capitalist social relations? Thus it is highly contestable whether the idea of separate gendered spaces — viz. Castro District in new Francisco, stylized or heavily marketed "gay district" or the "gay as now" adoption of Manchester, Newcastle and Melbourne for economic purposes or global rebranding — is an affirmative move, as it definitely gives impetus to "citizenship rights movement" or it is a backhand propagation of the non-threatening "new homonormativity". Hence the Indian literary texts, which primarily showcase not only the exclusive separate and accepted homosocial spaces — viz. kitchen, *Dahihandi* festival or gym — but also highlight the invasion of largely heterosexual spaces by queers in the form of homosexual mating on the conjugal bed or even at religious spaces, *ashrams* and universities (these places exclude any kind of libidinal longings let alone deviant desires), indubitably radicalize Indian spaces in quite an ingenious fashion.

Bibliography

Abbott, Justin E., 1985, *Bahina Bai: A Translation of Her Autobiographies and Verses*, New Delhi: Munshiram Manoharlal.

Adler, S. and J. Brenner, 1992, "Gender and Space: Lesbian and Gay Men in the City", *International Journal of Urban and Regional Research*, **16**(24): 34.

Advani, Rukun, 1994, *Beethoven Among the Cows*, New Delhi: Ravi Dayal.

Allman, K.M., 1996, "(Un)Natural Boundaries: Mixed Race, Gender and Sexuality", in *The Multiracial Experience: Racial Borders as the New Frontier*, ed. M.P.P. Root, Thousand Oaks, CA: Sage Publications.

Allport, Gordon Willard, 1979 (first published in 1954), *The Nature of Prejudice*, Basic Books: New York.

Alter, J., 1992, *The Wrestler's Body: Identity and Ideology in North India*, Berkeley and Los Angeles: University of California Press.

Ashley, Leonard R.N., 1982, "Dyke Diction: The Language of Lesbians", *Maledicta*, **VI**: 123-62. (Also in W. Dynes and S. Donaldsen (eds.) *Studies in Homosexuality*, 1994, Hamden, CT: Garland.)

Asian Age, 10 November 2003, p. 13; 28 October 2008, p. 10; 7 October, 2010, p. 3.

Bakhtin, Mikhail, 1941, *Rebelais and His World*, Bloomington: Indiana University Press.

———, 1929, *Problems of Dostoevsky's Poetics*, Minneapolis: University of Minnesota.

Barrett, Rusty, 1995, "Supermodels of the World, Unite! Political Economy and the Language of Performance Among African-American Drag Queens", in *Beyond the Lavender Lexicon*, ed. William L. Leap.

Bell, David and Jon Binnie, 2000, *The Sexual Citizen: Queer Politics and Beyond*, United Kingdom: Blackwell Publishers and Polity Press.

Bersani, Leo, 1995, *Homos*, Cambridge, MA: Harvard University Press.

Binnie, Jon, 1995, "Trading Places: Consumption, Sexuality and the Production of Queer Spaces", in *Mapping Desire: Geographies of Sexualities*, ed. D. Bell and G. Valentine, London: Routledge.

———, 2007, "Sexuality, the Erotic and Geography: Epistemology, Methodology and Pedagogy", in *Geographies of Sexualities: Theory, Practices and Politics*, ed. Kath Browne, Lim Jason and Gavin Brown, England: Ashgate Publishing.

Bose, Brinda and Subhabrata Bhattacharyya (eds.), 2007, *The Phobic and the Erotic: The Politics of Sexualities in Contemporary India*, United Kingdom: Seagull Books.

Bourdieu, P., 1984, *Distinction: A Social Critique of the Judgement of Taste*, London: Routledge and Kegan Paul.

Bristow, Joseph, 2007, *Sexuality*, New York: Routledge.

Brown, Michael, 1997, *RePlacing Citizenship: AIDS Activism and Radical Democracy*, New York: Guilford.

———, 2000, *Closet Space: Geographies of Metaphor from the Body to the Globe*, London: Routledge.

Butler, Judith, 1990, *Excitable Speech: A Politics of the Performance*, New York: Routledge.

Carter, Paul, 1987, *The Road to Botany Bay: An Essay in Spatial History*, London and Boston: Faber and Faber.

Casey, E. Mark, 2007, "The Queer Unwanted and Their Undesirable 'Otherness'", in *Geographies of Sexualities: Theory, Practices and Politics.*

Castells, M., 1983, *The City and the Grassroots*, London: Lawrence and Wishart.

Castle, Terry, 1993, *The Apparitional Lesbian: Female Homosexuality and Modern Culture*, New York: Columbia University Press.

Catvarah Karmagranthah (Prakrit and Sanskrit text), 1975, Pindavada: Bharatiya Pracyatattva Prakasana Samiti.

Chakravorty, Bhaswati, 2007, "Rights for the Third Gender: Problems of Identity and Recognition", in *The Phobic and the Erotic: The Politics of Sexualities in Contemporary India*, eds. Brinda Bose and Subhabrata Bhattacharyya, Calcutta: Seagull Books.

Chanana, Kuhu, 2012, "Interview with R. Raj Rao", in *An Evening Rainbow: Queer Writings in Bhasha Literatures*, New Delhi: Sanbun Publishers.

Chaudhary, Rajkamal, 1966, *Machali Mari Hui*, New Delhi: Rajkamal Prakashan.

Childers, J. and G. Hentiz, 1995, *The Columbia Dictionary of Modern Literary and Cultural Criticism*, New York.

Clarke, Cheryl, 1966, "Lesbianism: An Act of Resistance", in *Feminism and Sexuality: A Reader*, eds. Stevi Jackson and Sue Scott, New York: Columbia University Press.

Colette, Chiland, 2003, *Transsexualism: Illusion and Reality*, London: Sage Publications.

Connolly, W.E., 2002, *Neuropolitics: Thinking, Culture, Speed*, Minneapolis: University of Minnesota Press.

Daly, Mary, 1978, *Gyn/Ecology: The Metaethics of Radical Feminism*, Boston: Boston Press.

Dasavaikalika Sutra with Bhadrabahu's *Niryukti* and Agastyasimha's *Curni*, 1973, ed. Munipunyavijaya, Varanasi: Prakrit Text Society.

Dattani, Mahesh, 1999, "Night Queen", in *Yaraana*, ed. Hoshang Merchant, New Delhi: Penguin Books India.

———, 2000, "Do the Needful", in *Collected Plays*, New Delhi: Penguin Books India.

———, 2000, "On a Muggy Night in Mumbai", in *Collected Plays*, New Delhi: Penguin Books India.

———, 2000, "Seven Steps around the Fire", in *Collected Plays*, New Delhi: Penguin Books.

Dawesar, Abha, 2005, *Babyji*, New Delhi: Penguin Books India.

D'Emilio, John, 1992, "Capitalism and Gay Identity", in *Making Trouble: Essays on Gay History, Politics and the University*, New York: Routledge.

De, Shobha, 1992, *Strange Obsession*, New Delhi: Penguin.

Deccan Herald, 2 April 2010, p. 9; 8 January 2010, p. 5.

Deleuze, G., 1990, *The Logic of Sense*, London and New York: Continuum.

Dhasal, Namdeo, 1999, "Gandu Bagicha", in *Yaraana: The Gay Writing from India*, ed. Hoshang Merchant, New Delhi: Penguin Books India.

Duggan, Lisa, 1994, "Queering the State", *Social Text*, **39** (Summer 1994): 1-14.

Duncan, Nancy, 1996, *Body Space: Destablizing Geographies of Gender and Sexuality*, London and New York: Routledge.

Dykstra, Annie, 2012, "Pity that Blush", in *Close, Too Close: The Tranquebar Book of Queer Erotica*, eds. Meenu and Shruti, Chennai: Tranquebar Press.

Ellen, L. R., 2012, "Conference Sex", in *Close, Too Close: The Tranquebar Book of Queer Erotica*, eds. Meenu and Shruti, Chennai: Tranquebar Press.

Farmer, Brett, 2000, *Spectacular Passions: Cinema, Fantasy, Gay Male Spectatorships*, Duke: Durham University Press.

Foucault, Michel, 1967, "Of Other Spaces, Heterotopias", in http://www.foucault.info/doc/documents/heterotopia/foucault.heterotopia.en html.

Gahlot, Deepa, 1992, "Gay Is a Sad Word", in *Femina*, 8 September.

Ganguli, Kisari Mohan, tr., 1970, *The Mahabharata of Krishna Dvaipayana Vyasa*, New Delhi: Munshiram Manoharlal.

Gawankar, Madhav G., 1999, "The Jungle", in *Yaraana*, ed. Hoshang Merchant.

Ghosh, Shohini, 2007, "False Appearances and Mistaken Identities: The Phobic and the Erotic in Bombay Cinema's Queer Vision", in *The Phobic and the Erotic*, ed. Brinda Bose and Subhabrata Bhattacharyya.

Gopinath, Gayatri, 2007, *Impossible Desires: Queer Diaspora and South Asian Public Cultures*, Calcutta: Seagull Books.

Govindan, Padma and Aniruuddhan Vasudevan, 2011, "The Razor's Edge of Oppositionality: Exploring the Politics of Rights-based Activism by Transgender Women in Tamil Nadu", in *Law Like Love: Queer Perspectives on Law*, eds. Arvind Narrain and Alok Gupta, New Delhi: Yoda Press.

Hemmings, C., 2002, *Bisexual Spaces: A Geography of Sexuality and Gender*, London: Routledge.

Hindle, P., 1994, "Gay Communities and Gay Spaces in the City", in *The Margins of the City: Gay Men's Urban Lives*, ed. S. Whittle, Manchester: Arena.

Hooks, Bell, 1992, *Black Looks: Race and Representation*, London: Turnaround.

Ilyasova, K. Alex (November 2006), "Dykes on Bikes and the Regulation of Vulgarity", *International Journal of Motorcycle Studies*, retrieved on 21 August 2007.

Jackson, Stevi, 1996, "The Social Construction of Female Sexuality", in *Feminism and Sexuality: A Reader*, eds. Stevi Jackson and Sue Scott.

Kaplan, Morris, 1997, "Intimacy and Equality: The Question of Lesbian and Gay Marriage", in *Playing with Fire: Queer Politics, Queer Theories*, ed. Shane Phelan, New York: Routledge.

Kapur, Manju, 2002, *A Married Woman*, New Delhi: IndiaInk.

Kath, Gavin and Jason Lim, 2007, "Introduction, or Why Have a Book on Geographies of Sexualities", in *Geographies of Sexualities: Theory, Practices and Politics*, England: Ashgate Publishing Company.

Kawale, Rani, 2003, "A Kiss Is Just a Kiss . . . Or Is It? South Asian Lesbian and Bisexual Women and the Construction of Space", in *South Asian Women in the Diaspora*, ed. Nirmal Puwar, and Parvati Raghuram, Oxford, NY: Berg.

Keay, John, 2010, *India: A History*, UK: Harper Press.

Khakhar, Bhupen, 2012, "Valecha", in *An Evening Rainbow: Queer Writings in Bhasha Literatures*, ed. Kuhu Sharma Chanana, New Delhi: Sanbun Publishers.

Khandelwal, M., 2001, "Sexual Fluids, Emotions, Morality: Notes on the Gendering of Brahmacharya", in *Celibacy, Culture, and Society: The Anthropology of Sexual Abstinence*, ed. E. Sobo and S. Bell, Madison: University of Wisconsin Press.

Khare, R., 1984, *The Untouchable as Himself: Ideology, Identity and Pragmatism among the Lucknow Chamars*, New York: Cambridge University Press.

Klein, F., 1978, *The Bisexual Option: A Concept of One Hundred Percent Intimacy*, New York: Arbor House.

Knopp, Larry, 2007, "From Lesbian and Gay to Queer Geographies: Pasts, Prospects and Possibilities", in *Geographies of Sexualities: Theory, Practices and Politics*, eds. Kath Browne, Lim Jason and Gavin Brown, England: Ashgate Publishing Company.

Koertge, Noretta, 1984, *Valley of the Amazons*, New York: St. Martin's Press.

Koshy, Mridula, 2007, "A Large Girl", in *Katha: Short Stories by Indian Women*, New Delhi: Stanza.

Lamming, George, 1984, *The Pleasures of Exile*, London: Allison & Busby.

Leap, William L., 1995, *Beyond the Lavender Lexicon: Authenticity, Imagination and Appropriation in Lesbian and Gay Languages*, Newark: Gordon & Breach.

Lim, Jason, 2007, "Queer Critique and the Politics of Affect", in *Geographies of Sexualities: Theory, Practices and Politics*.

Malik, Michael G., 2012, "Dreams and Desire in Srinagar", in *Close, Too Close: The Tranquebar Book of Queer Erotica*.

Mangai, A., 2011, "Translator's Note: Revathi's Unarvum Unarvum", in

Our Lives, Our Words: Telling Aravani Lifestories, New Delhi: Yoda Stories.

Mansuri, Nazir, 2012, "The Sea Hawk", in *An Evening Rainbow: Queer Writings in Bhasha Literatures*, ed. Kuhu Chanana, New Delhi: Sanbun Publishers.

Matejskova, Tatiana, 2007, "Straights in Gay Bar: Negotiating Boundaries through Time-Spaces", in *Geographies of Sexualities: Theory, Practices and Politics*.

McDowell, L., 1997, *Capital Culture: Gender at Work in the City*, Oxford: Blackwell.

Mehta, Harshad, 2012, "Leech", in *An Evening Rainbow: Queer Writings in Bhasha Literatures*, ed. Kuhu Sharma Chanana, New Delhi: Sanbun Publishers.

Menon, Indu, 2012, "A Lesbian Cow", in *An Evening Rainbow: Queer Writings in Bhasha Literatures*, ed. Kuhu Sharma Chanana, New Delhi: Sanbun Publishers.

Merchant, Hoshang, 1999, "The Slaves", in *Yaarana*, ed. Hoshang Merchant, New Delhi: Penguin Books.

———, 2009, *Forbidden Sex/Texts: New India's Gay Poets*, New Delhi: Routledge.

———, 2011, *The Man Who Would Be Queen: Autobiographical Fictions*, New Delhi: Penguin Books.

Mishra, Hiranmayee, 2007, "A Tale of a Rainy Night", in *The Voyage Out: Contemporary Oriya Short Stories by Women*, ed. Sumanyu Satpathy, Bhubaneswar: Rupantar.

Mukherjee, Suroopa, 2006, *Across the Mystic Shore*, New Delhi: Pan Macmillian.

Muraleedharan, T., 2005, "Crisis in Desire: A Queer Reading of Cinema and Desire in Kerala", in *Because I Have a Voice: Queer Politics in India*, eds. Arvind Narrain and Gautam Bhan, New Delhi: Yoda Press.

Nair, Anita, 2001, *Ladies Coupé: A Novel in Parts*, New Delhi: Penguin Books India.

Nair, Sridevi K., *Writing the Lesbian: Literary Culture in India*, http://deepblue.lib.umich.edu/bitsream/202742/64620/1/nair-1.pdf.

Namjoshi, Suniti, 1981, *Feminist Fables*, London: Sheba Feminist Publishers.

———, 1985, *The Conversations of Cow*, London: The Women's Press.

———, 2000, *Goja: An Autobiographical Myth*, Melbourne: Spinifex Press.

Nanda, Serena, 1999, *Neither Man Nor Woman: The Hijras of India*, London: International Thomson Publishing Europe.

"Naz Foundation vs. Government of New Capital Territory of Delhi and Others", *Delhi Law Times*, **160**(2009): 277 at para 50.

Namjoshi, Suniti, 1980, *The Jackass and the Lady*, Calcutta: Writers Workshop.

———, 1982, *The Authentic Lie*, Frederiction, Canada: Fiddlehead.

———, 1984, *From the Bedside Books of Nightmares*, Canada: Fiddlehead.

———, 1986, *Flesh and Paper* with Gillian Hanscombe, UK: Jezebel Tapes and Books.

———, 1989, *Because of India: Selected Poems*, London: Onlywomen Press.

———, 1989, *The Mothers of Maya Diip*, London: The Women's Press.

———, 2006, *Sycorax: New Fables and Poems*, New Delhi: Penguin Books India.

Narrain, Arvind, 2007, "Queer Struggles Around the Law: The Contemporary Context", in *Sexualities*, ed. Nivedita Menon, New Delhi: Women Unlimited.

Nayar, Pramod K., 2007, "Queering Cultural Studies: Notes Towards a Framework", in *The Phobic and the Erotic: The Politics of Sexualities in Contemporary India*, ed. Brinda Bose and Subhabrata Bhattacharyya, Calcutta: Seagull Books.

Ochs, Robyn, 1996, "Biphobia: It Goes More Than Two Ways", in *Bisexuality: The Psychology and Politics of an Invisible Minority*, ed. A. Beth Firestein, California: Sage Publications.

Panja, Shormishtha, 2006, "The Ghost Who Talks: Terry Castle's *The Apparitional Lesbian* and Gender Discourse", in *Lesbian Voices, Canada & the World Theory, Literature, Cinema*, ed. Subash Chandra, New Delhi: Allied Publisher.

Patel, Mayur, 2010, *Vivek and I*, New Delhi: Penguin Books.

Pollak, Michael, 1985, "Male Homosexuality — Or Happiness in the Ghetto", in *Western Sexuality: Practice and Precept in Past and Present Times*, eds. Ariès Philippe and Andrè Bèjin, tr. Anthony Forster, Oxford: B. Blackwell.

Puri, Jyoti, 2003, "Outing the Global Gay" (circulated as a draft), presented at a conference on "Postcolonialism, Sexuality and the Law" organized by the Centre for Feminist Legal Research, New Delhi.

Radicalesbians, 1973, "The Woman Identified Woman", in *Radical Feminism*, eds. A. Koedt, E. Levine and A Rapone, New York: Times Books.

Rajendran, Aneeta, 2007, "(Un)Familiar Spaces: The Erotic Geographies of Contemporary Lesbian Indian Novel", in http:// www.interdisplinary.net/critical-issues/transformations/persons-and sexuality/project-archives/ 4th/session-1-representations/.

Rao, R. Raj, 1999, "Moonlight Tandoori", in *Yaraana*, ed. Hoshang Merchant.

———, 1999, "Six Inches", in *Yaraana*, ed. Hoshang Merchant.

———, 2003, *The Boyfriend*, New Delhi: Penguin Books India.

———, 2009, "Introduction", in *Whistling in the Dark: Twenty-one Queer Interviews*, eds. R. Raj Rao and Dibyajyoti Sarma, New Delhi: Sage Publication.

———, 2010, *Hostel Room 131*, New Delhi: Penguin Books India.

Rao, R. Raj and Dibyajyoti Sarma, 2009, *Whistling in the Dark: Twenty-One Queer Interviews*, New Delhi: Sage Publication.

Rashid, Abdul Khalid, 2012, "Incomplete Human", in *An Evening Rainbow: Queer Writings in Bhasha Literatures*, ed. Kuhu Sharma Chanana, New Delhi: Sanbun Publishers.

Reddy, Gayatri, 2006, *With Respect to Sex*, New Delhi: Yoda Press.

Revathi, A., 2010, *The Truth About Me*, New Delhi: Penguin India.

———, 2011, *Our Lives, Our Words: Telling Aravani Lifestories*, New Delhi: Yoda Press.

Rich, Adrienne, 1975, "When We Dead Awaken: Writing as Revision", *Adrienne Rich's Poetry*, ed. Barabara Gelpi, Charlesworth and Albert Gelpi, New York: W.W. Norton & Company.

Richardson, Diane, 1996, "Constructing Lesbian Sexualities", in *Feminism and Sexuality: A Reader*, eds. Stevi Jackson and Sue Scott, Edinburgh: Edinburgh University.

Roshanabadi, Qamar, 1999, "Vande Mataram!", *Facing the Mirror: Lesbians Writings from India*, ed. Ashwini Sukthankar, New Delhi: Penguin Books India.

Rothenberg, T., 1995, "And She Told Two Friends: Lesbian Creating Urban Social Space", in *Mapping Desire: Geographies of Sexualities*, ed. D. Bell and G. Valentine.

Sahoo, Sarojini, 2007, "Behind the Scene", in *The Voyage Out: Contemporary Oriya Short Stories by Women*, ed. Sumanyu Satpathy, Bhubaneswar: Rupantar.

Sami, Praveen, "Furor over a Film", in *Frontline* 15, 26, 19 December 1998 – 1 January 1999, 10 January 2008 <http:// www.hinduonnet.com/ fline/fl1526/15260430.htm>.

Sarma, Dibyajyoti, 2012, "Let Me Sin Then", in *An Evening Rainbow: Queer Writings in Bhasha Literatures*.

Satya, 2012, "I Hate Wet Tissues", in *Close, Too Close: The Tranquebar Book of Queer Erotica*, eds. Meenu and Shruti, Chennai: Tranquebar Press.

Seidman, Steven, 1998, "Are We All in the Closet?: Notes Towards a Sociological and Cultural Turn in Queer Theory", in *European Journal of Cultural Studies*, **1**: 177-92.

Sharma, Maya, 2006, *Loving Women: Being Lesbian in Unprivileged India*, New Delhi: Yoda Press.

Shivani, 2007, "Manik", in *Kaustri Mrig*, New Delhi: Penguin Books India.

Shree, Geetanjali, 2001, *Tirohit*, New Delhi: Rajkamal Prakashan.

Singh, Dayanita, 2001, "Myself Mona Ahmed", in http://en, wikipedia.org/ wiki/third-gender.

Singh, Khushwant, 1990, *Delhi: A Novel*, New Delhi: Penguin Books.

Sitapati, Vinay, 2009, "Sex Change for Free", in http.// www.samesame. com.au/forum/showthread.php?t==7865.

Smith, Patricia Juliana, 1995, "'And I Wondered if She Might Kiss Me': Lesbian Panic as Narrative Strategy in British Women's Fiction", in *Modern Fiction Studies*, **41**: 3-4 (Fall–Winter).

Soja, Edward W., 1996, *Thirdspace: Journeys to Los Angeles and Other Real-and-Imagined Places*, Oxford: Basil Blackwell.

Sood, Keval, 2013, *Murgikhana*, New Delhi: Shilalekh.

Sukirath, 2012, "The Home", in *An Evening Rainbow: Queer Writings in Bhasha Literatures*, ed. Kuhu Sharma Chanana, New Delhi: Sanbun Publishers.

Sukthankar, Ashwini, 1999, *Facing the Mirror: Lesbian Writings from India*, New Delhi: Penguin Books India.

———, 2011, "Complicating Genders", in *Because I Have a Voice: Queer Politics in India*, eds. Arvind Narrain and Gautam Bhan, New Delhi: Yoda Press.

Thadani, Giti, 1996, *Sakhiyani: Lesbian Desire in Ancient and Modern India*, London: Cassell.

The Hindustan Times, 23 April 2008.

Times of India, 14 June 2008, p. 19; 23 July 2010, p. 11; 6 February 2011, p. 4.

Trawick, M., 1990, *Notes on Love in a Tamil Family*, Berkeley and Los Angeles: University of California Press.

Ugra, Pandey Bechan Sharma, 2006, "Chocolate", in *Chocolate, and Other Writings on Male–Male Desire*, tr. Ruth Vanita, New Delhi: Oxford University Press.

Valentine, G., 1989, "(Hetero)sexing Space: Lesbian Perceptions and Experiences of Everyday Spaces", *Enviornment and Planning D: Society and Space*, **11**: 395-13.

———, 1993, "Negotiating and Managing Multiple Sexual Identities: Lesbian Time–Space Strategies", in *Transactions of the Institute of British Geographers NS*, **18**(2): 237-38.

Vanita, Ruth, 1996, *Sappho and the Virgin Mary: Same-Sex Love and the English Literary Tradition*, New York: Columbia University Press.

Vanita, Ruth and Saleem Kidwai, 2000, *Same-Sex Love in India: Readings from Literature and History*, New Delhi: Macmillan India.

———, 2005, *Gandhi's Tiger and Sita's Smile: Essays on Gender, Sexuality and Culture*, New Delhi: Yoda Press.

———, 2005, *Love's Rite: Same-Sex Marriage in India and the West*, New Delhi: Penguin Books.

———, 2012, *Gender, Sex and the City: Urdu Rekhti Poetry, 1780-1870*, New Delhi: Orient Blackswan.

Vatsyayana, 2011, *Kamasutra: A Guide to the Art of Pleasure*, tr. A.N.D. Haskar, New Delhi: Penguin Books.

Veyne, Paul, 1985, " Homosexuality in Ancient Rome", in *Western Sexuality: Practice and Percept in Past and Present Times*, eds. Aries Philippe and Andre Bejin, tr. Anthony Forster, Oxford: B. Blackwell.

Vijayasree, C., 2001, *Suniti Namjoshi: The Artful Transgressor*, Jaipur and New Delhi: Rawat Publishers.

Wald, J., 1997, "Outlaw Mothers", in *Hastings Women's Law Journal*, **8**: 1.

Wolf, Naomi, 1991, *The Beauty Myth: How Images of Beauty Are Used Against Women*, New York: Harper Collins Publications.

Wolfson, Evan, 1996, "Why We Should Fight for the Freedom to Marry: The Challenges and Opportunities that Will Follow a Win in Hawaii", in *Journal of Gay, Lesbian and Bisexual Identity*, **1**: 79-89.

Zwilling, Leonard and Michael J. Sweet, 1993, "The First Medicalization: The Taxonomy and Etiology of Queers in Classical Indian Medicine", in *Journal of the History of Sexuality*, **6**(3).

———, 2000, "The Evolution of Third-Sex Construction in Ancient India: A Study in Ambiguity", in *Invented Identities: The Interplay of Gender, Religion and Politics in India*, eds. Julia Leslie and Mary McGee, New York: Oxford University Press.

Index

acceptance of
homosexuality, 211
unique transgender body, 54
act(s) of
normalizing homoerotic desire, 245
subjugation, 185
gay copulation, 220
Adam, bondage of, 116
Adler, S., 210
Advani, Rukun, 12, 121
A.K. Modelling Agency, 141-42
Allen, Dennis, 94
Allman, K.M., 209
all-pervasive nature of
gay desire, 221
lesbian longing, 215
Allport, Gordon Willard, 62
all-women space, 104-05
alternate sexuality, 143
alternative
family structure, 93, 106
lesbian family structure, 181
sexual
choices, 78
styles of living, 129
American Psychiatric Association, 144
androgynous anatomy, 96
anthropomorphic lesbian identity, 112
anti-retroviral therapy, 149
apparitional lesbianism, 166, 198
Aravani festival, 51, 231, 242
Arthashastra, 200
Ashley, Leonard R.N., 10
Ashvamedha, myth of, 174

Bachchan, Amitabh, 225
badai hijras, 69
Bagemihl, Bruce, 78
Bahuchara Mataji, 244
Bahucharji, goddess of, 51
Bai, Bahina, 12
Bakhtin, Mikhail, 22, 243
Baksh, Maulvi Mukarram, 170
Balzac, Honoré de, 189
Barrett, Rusty, 8-9
Barthes, Roland, 85
Baudelaire, Charles, 166
beauty myth, false notion of, 193
Bedharaj Mata, 90
Behra, Sanju, 65
Bell, David, 6, 34, 94, 96, 107, 109, 257
Bersani, Leo, 157
Bhagiratha, 172-73
Bhagirathi, 4, 249
bhangi(s), 130-31

Bhasha writings, 2
Bhattacharyya, Subhabrata, 33
Bhishma, 188
bikes on dykes, 9
Binnie, Jon, 6, 34, 94, 107, 109, 210, 214, 253-54, 257
biphobia, 98
- internalized, 75
- sources of, 89
- specific problem of, 25

bisexual
- bonds, 78
- desires, 256
- identity, 256

Bose, Brinda, 33
Bourdieu, P., 209
brahmacarya, articulations of, 88
Brenner, J., 210
Bristow, Joseph, 128
British
- atrocities, living symbol of, 81
- hyper-masculinity, 87

British Retention League, 81
Brown, Hemmings, 214, 255
Brown, Michael, 6, 221-22
burlesque feminine behaviour among *hijras*, 83
butch and femme, 101, 193
- identities, 42, 183
- stereotypes, 183
- stereotypical degenerative model, 203

Butler, Judith, 120, 183, 206

Caleri Report, 196, 231
carnivalesque spaces, 21
Carter, Paul, 232
Carter's concept, 232
Casey, E. Mark, 257
Castell, Manuel, 209
Castle, Terry, 3, 166, 198, 213
Chakravorty, Bhaswati, 63, 98
Chanana, Kuhu, 76, 123
Chandra, Subash, 184
Chaudhary, Rajkamal, 3-4, 46-47, 161-62, 185, 187-89, 192, 205, 213
Chiland, Colette, 71
Childers, J., 206
Chughtai, Ismat, 178, 253-54
citizenship rights movement, 258
Clarke, Cheryl, 26, 161, 180
class
- and homosexuality, complex matrix of, 129
- dissolved hierarchy of, 132

classless and casteless same-sex union, utopia of, 138
coded and secretive language, 151
coding of lesbians, absence of, 161
coercive heterosexuality, 30, 145
- victims of, 179

coming out, 229, 254
compulsive
- heteronormativity, 154
- heterosexuality, 115, 176-77, 180

concept of
- affective bond, 209
- carnivalesque, 22
    - space, 244

privacy, 221
self-ghosting, 3
sexual citizenship, 33
swardspeak, 9
topophilia, 209
true *sannyasi*, 87
virtual memory, 229
Connolly, William, 229-30
contemporary Indian queer writings, 4
conventional heterosexual spaces, 211
Coplan, Cora, 157
sex counselling-session in school, 253
counter-culture, 25
Creet, Julia, 110
Criminal Tribes Act (1871), 17-18, 50, 52-56
crude emasculation, 69

D'Emilio, John, 15, 93-94, 129
Dahihandi festival, 21, 140, 241-42, 258
dalit literature, 125
Daly, Mary, 114
Damayanti, 172
Dannecker, Martin, 142
Dattani, Mahesh, 1, 17-18, 22, 53, 55, 62-63, 68, 79, 84-85, 90, 97, 131, 143-44, 146, 156, 158-59, 221, 256
Dawesar, Abha, 3, 7, 10, 20, 24, 27-28, 30, 33, 39-41, 125, 213, 219, 252, 254
De, Shobha, 12, 47
Deep, Iqbal, 255
deep-rooted
internalized biphobia, 68
transphobia, 76
Deleuze's theory of "affect", 228
delineation of lesbian motherhood, 246
Detha, Vijaydan, 26-27
Dharmendra, 225
Dhasal, Namdeo, 221
Diagnostic and Statistical Manual of Mental Disorders, 144
Dickinson, Emily, 185
disabled entity, symbol of, 90
dissident androgyny, tool of, 86
Dnyaneshwar, 149
doganas, 101
Dollimore, Jonathan , 15, 131
Dollimore's notion of need of elusive "other", 123
Douglas, Michael, 229
Duggan, Lisa, 33, 257
dykes on bikes, 9
dykes with tykes, 9
Dykstra, Annie, 222

eagalitarian lesbian rendezvous, 193
eclectic mapping of queer spaces, 109
eclectic nature of
homoerotic experience, 181
passive/active dichotomy, 136
sexuality, 106
effeminate picture of Indian man, 32

egalitarian
- ethics of self-control, 89
- same-sex love, 216
- structure of same-sex love, 28
- structured relationship, 183

ego-dystonic
- homosexual, 145
- homosexuality, 144, 146
- sexuality, 144

Ellen, L.R., 23-24, 234
emasculated corporeal self, 89
emotional satisfaction and happiness, 129
even same-sex relationship, exploitive nature of, 42
exclusive gay household, 215
exploration of
- feminine sexuality, 39, 164, 200
- plurality and multiplicity of lesbian experience, 29

Faderman, Lillian, 165, 187, 204
fallacious concept of all consuming motherly love, 36
falsified notion of
- masculinity, 133
- their hyperlibidinousness, 62

familial citizenship, 93
fantasmic spectatorship, psychoanalytic concept of, 240
Farmer, Brett, 225, 240
female
- desire, re-sexualization of, 102
- homoerotic
  - desire, 195
  - passion, 202
- transgressive longings, 34

female-colonial subject, 108
feminine sexuality,
- exploration of, 39, 164, 200
- repressed module of, 84
- regressive module of, 197

femininity, symbol of, 70
- holistic realization of, 28
- potent tool of, 173

first *hijra* anthology, 52fluid
- continuum, 60
- homosexuality, 184
- identity, 65
- negotiation of sexuality, 213

forbidden desires, 238
Ford, Harrison, 229
Foucauldian
- heterotopias, 234
- term(s), 128, 218, 223

Foucault, Michel, 20-21, 209, 218, 235, 241, 247
Foucault's heterotopia, sixth principle of, 247
free-flowing pansexual spatiality, 251
Freud, Singmund, 74, 145

Gahlot, Deepa, 202
Gandhi, M.K., 86-87
Gandhi, Leela, 54
Gautier, Theophile, 166
Gawankar, Madhav G., 140
gay
- and lesbian anthologies, 52
- copulation, 79, 252
  - acts of, 220
- culture, 159

desire, all-pervasive nature of, 221
district, 257
gaze, 227
identity, 127-28, 150, 152, 159, 220
lingo, 127, 151
marriage, 93, 95, 245
mating, 62
prostitution, logistics of, 133
queens, 150
sex, 122
subculture(s), 118, 127, 150, 155, 160, 196
visibility, 148
lesbian and *hijra* anthologies, 1
gender identities, 169
gendered structure, 41
Gere, Richard, 229
Ghosh, Shohini, 14, 122, 225
ghosting of
lesbianism, 167
lesbians, 3, 166, 198, 199, 213
Gibson, Mel, 229
glorified motherhood, myth of 27
God's eunuch, 87
Goddess Mata, 69
Gokhale, Namita, 154
Goodall, Jane, 78
Gopinath, Gayatri, 42, 132, 219
Gordon, Stephen, 189, 194
Govindan, Padma, 77
gynecomastia, 75

Hall, Radcliff, 189
Hardy, Thomas, 189
Harley, Vincent, 77
Heidegger, Martin, 208
Hemmings, C., 209, 256
Hentiz, G., 206
hetero and homosexual passion, overlapping of, 213
heteronormative
society, 128, 170
structure, 190
world, hostility of, 152
heteronormativity, 103
heteropatriarchal
family pattern, critique of, 97
ideology, 171
paradigm, 95
subjugation, 86
world, 104
heterosexual
city space, 215
coercion, 194
ill effects of, 185
domesticity, 181
familial structure, 213
framework, hegemonic structures of, 158
marriage, non-egalitarian nature of, 155
mating, marker of, 24
matrix, 212, 215
monogamous mother, woman as a, 107
ordering of desire, 185
relationship, procreative nature of, 200
subjugation, 233
superiority, 45
heterosexuality, coercive nature of, 164, 193

heterotopia(s), 223, 242
  Foucault's concept of, 19
  of contrast, 248
  of crisis, 20, 218, 223, 235
  of deviation, 223
  principles of, 246
  within heterotopias, 250-51
hidden curriculum, 24, 253
hijra(s)
  anthology, 69
  as a tribe, acceptance of, 56
  community(ies), 51, 55, 66, 68, 75
  family
    structure, 98
    value of alternative, 97
  gory death rituals of, 53
  identification of, 63
  identity, 2, 17, 25, 49, 52-53, 55, 85, 90, 96
  namelessness of, 57
  oppression of, 18
  structural violence against, 67
  terminology, 61
  uplift of, 19, 52
Hindle, P., 210
Hindu/Muslim religious riots, 92
homo/hetero dichotomy, 223
homoerotic
  behaviour, 77
  desire,
    act of normalizing, 245
    assertion of, 231
    domestication of, 102
  experience, eclectic nature of, 181
  liaison, 245
  longings, 226
  negotiation, 186
  passion, 47, 157, 176, 191, 248
    resexualization of, 47
  presence, 226
  tales, 225
  writings in Bhasha literatures, 1
  zone, 241, 251
homoeroticism, 115, 204
  familiarization of, 211
homophobia, 190, 193, 219
  and biphobia, overlap between, 18, 59
  exhibition of, 197
  internalized, 130, 134, 140-41, 204
  of heterosexuals, 59
homophobic
  anxiety, 159
  blackmailer, 150
  myth, 118
homosexual
  gaze, 239, 242
  identity(ies), 210, 257
  leanings, 103
  literary productions, 2
  lovers, 225
  mating, 140, 200, 258
  slang, dictionary of, 151
homosexuality
  acceptance of, 211
  decriminalization of, 49
  fluidity of, 182
  impact of class on, 16
  intersection of class and, 140
  native perception of, 113
  of convenience, 178
    advocates of, 179
  religious policing of, 245
  subversive patterns of, 117

homosexualization of
  heteropatriarchal, amalgam of, 220
  spaces, 2, 208, 220, 257
homosocial space(s), 233, 235, 241, 258
Hubbard, Janae, 255
Hyderabadi *hijras*,
  death rituals of, 76
  ethnography of, 90

ICD-10, WHO's classification of mental and behavioural disorders 144
idea of normalcy, 125
ideal
  notion of love, 177
  sphere for pansexuality, 220
identity crisis, dilemma of, 162
in-between
  entity, 228
  liminal space, 223
  sexuality, 83
Indian
  lesbian
    literature, history of, 5
    motherhood, 4
  literary lesbian history, 207
  middle-class dilemma of identity crisis, 174
  nationalist struggle, 32
  queer
    academia, 25
    literary production, 2
    literary texts, 14
    literature, 207
  sexual minorities, 210
Indianizing the queer culture, 117
Insha, Ibne, 101
instinctive bisexuality, 177
intention of evincing
  homoerotic liaison, 38
intentional ambiguity, 99
internalized
  biphobia, 75
  hierarchy of class superiority, 137
  homophobia, 130, 134, 140-41, 204
  lesbophobia, 197
  transphobia, 72-73
International Bill of Gender Rights, 77
International Conference on Transgender Law and Employment Policy 1995, 77
inter-sex bodies, 72
intersexed identity, 65
invisibility of *hijras*, issue of, 53
Irving, John, 69
issue of
  invisibility of *hijras*, 53
  sexual citizenship, 52

Jaan, Kamla, 64
Jackson, Stevi, 176
James, Henry, 166
Jan Sahib, 101
janana, 101
Jogmaya Temple, 91
Johnston, Lynda, 221
Judeo–Christian–Islamic Tradition, 188
juxtaposing of motherhood and lesbianism, 108

Kafur, Malik, 135
Kakar, Sudhir, 86
KALI, 118, 231
Kamasutra, 168
Kameny, Franklin, 94
Kamla Bua, 50
kandra hijras, 69
Kant, Immanuel, 208
Kaplan, Morris, 94-95
Kapoor, Rishi, 225
Kapoor, Shashi, 225
Kapur, Manju, 3, 46, 161-62, 174, 179, 183-84, 212, 224, 230-31
kapurusatva, 87
Karnad, Girish, 219
Kath, Gavin, 255
Kawale, Rani, 10, 110-11, 119, 210, 219-20, 224-25
Keay, John, 135
Kessler, Udis, 60
Ketu, Katrak H., 107
Khakkar, Bhupen, 256
Khalji, Ala-ud-din, 135
Khandelwal, Meena, 88
khangis,
  language of, 11, 120
  speech of, 121
Khanna, Rajesh, 225
Khanna, Vinod, 225
Khare, Ravinder, 88
Khwaja Sahib, 91
Kidwai, Saleem, 1, 4, 27, 188, 212
King Dilipa, 3, 172, 249
Kinnar Sammelan, 231
KISS, 118-19, 220, 231
Klein, F., 61
Knopp, Larry, 22, 233, 239
Koedt, A., 44, 177, 187, 205
Koertge, Noretta, 115
Koshy, Mridula, 20, 214, 217-18
Krishna, image of, 171
Krishna's son Samba, 51
Krittivasa Ramayana, 172
Kureishi, Hanif, 132

Lamming, George, 111
language of
  khangis, 11, 120
  lesbians, 118
lavender lexicon, 11
Lawrence, D.H., 201
Leap, William, 8
Lefebvre, Henri, 208
lesbian(s)
  and transgender intimacies, public acceptance of, 233
  anthology, 124
  appropriation of heteropatriarchal space, 104
  as authentic citizens, 114
  continuum, reflection of, 112
  desire, unthinkability of, 213
  diasporic identity, 109
  eroticism, 122
  experience, plurality of, 161
  experiences of Indian upper middle-class married women, 3
  exploration, 175
  fabulation, 6, 125
  feminism, 42

ghosting of, 3, 166, 198-99, 213
ghosting, 193
contradictory aspects of, 168
dichotomy of, 169
identity, 12, 110-11, 113, 121, 173, 232
crisis in, 192
language of, 118-19
liaison, 190
life story, 45
literature, history of, 197
longing, all-pervasive nature of, 215
love, 103, 174
is holistic, 37
supremacy of, 47
lovemaking, 223, 236
marginalization, 210
mating, 222
motherhood, 171, 249
myth-making, 115
panic, 3, 43, 184, 193, 197, 206, 218
relationships, invisibility of, 166
rights, 112
sexuality, specificity of, 206
site, emergence of, 23
tales from Bhasha literature, 5
visibility, 4
lesbian's sex-encounters, plausibility of, 122
lesbian-ecriture, 120
lesbianism
and ghosting, connection between, 167
as a political tool of emancipation, 47
definition of, 165
de-sexualization of, 187
ghosting of, 167
in the feminist context, 27
of convenience, 178
overarching phenomenon of, 29
re-sexualization of, 187
re-sexualizing, 165, 206
with heterosexism, co-existence of, 174
lesbophobia, 189
internalized, 197
lesbophobic, 102
anxiety(ies), 101, 195-97
regional tales, 25
society, 169, 194
Levine, E., 44, 187, 205
LGBTQ
cause, 207
circles, 196
identity in Indian literary spaces, 210
movement, 2
LGBTQIA, 118
Lim, Jason, 228-30, 255
liminal
identity, 126
sexuality, 71
love, ideal notion of, 177
Lucknow, *nawab*s of, 102

Mahabharata, 188
Mahabhashya, 63
Mahila Aghadi, 31
male
and female twin identity, 60
body, feminization of, 160
fantasies, voyeuristic

pleasures of, 205
female binary, stringent conceptualization of, 57
heterosexual lesbophobia, 163
prostitution, 136
supremacist imperialism, 190
Malik, Michael, 20-21, 238
Mangai, A., 58
Mansuri, Nazir, 11, 13
Manu-Smriti, 12
marginal people, 62
marginalized
identity, 158
of sexual and racial minority, 5
marital rape and domestic violence, victims of, 38
masculinity,
falsified notion of, 133
terrible appropriation of, 41
Matejskova, Tatiana, 221
matrimony, usual pleasures of, 199
McDowell, L., 209
Meenu, 72
Mehta, Deepa, 31, 225
Mehta, Harshad, 12
Menon, Indu, 11, 13, 26
Merchant, Hoshang, 1, 15-16, 113, 127-28, 136, 196
Mirza, Heidi, 110
Mishra, Hiranmayee, 5, 197, 201
Mishra, Nalini, 199
mock marriage, 134
Mother India, 31-32, 114
Mukherjee, Suroopa, 7, 20, 26, 172, 245-49
multidimensional plurality, 127
Mulvey, Laura, 46, 205
Muraleedharan, T., 227
Murugam, Perumal, 58
myth of
Ashvamedha, 174
glorified motherhood, 27

Nair, Anita, 3, 20, 27-28, 30, 35-36, 40, 42-44, 213, 219, 236
Nair, Sridevi K., 31-32, 41, 114
Namjoshi, Suniti, 1, 5, 7, 11, 13, 103-05, 107-09, 110, 112-14, 116-21, 124-26
Nanda, Serena, 83
Nandy, Ashish, 86
narcissistic streak, 202
extension of, 192
Narrain, Arvind, 150
National Federation of Indian Women, 196
natural order, laws of, 86
Nayar, Pramod K., 206
Naz judgement, 55
new homonormativity, 258
Newton, Isaac, 208
NGO Forum at Fourth World Conference on Women, 231
nirvanam ceremony, 247
non-normative
desires, 243
relationships, normalizing of, 212
sexual endeavours, temporality of, 243

O'Murray, Stephen, 183
Ochs, Robyn, 17-18, 59-60, 62
Onir, 196
oppression of
 hijras, 18
 complex network of, 52
 women in gay subculture, 153
oppressive
 coercive heterosexuality, 29
 heterosexual structure, 206
 idea of middle-class stability, 25
 sexual slavery, 138
"other", stoic symbol of, 111
outcast gay culture, 128
over-glorification of beauty, notion of, 181

Panja, Shormishtha, 166
pansexuality(ies), 61, 71, 193
 is a part of natural order, 77
 classic symbol of, 63
 ideal sphere for, 220
 negotiations of, 254
passive/active dichotomy, 133
Patanjali, 63
Patel, Jabbar, 219, 244
Patel, Mayur, 20-21, 24, 228, 230, 254
Patil, Amruta, 1
patriarchal
 mindset, 106
 notion of masculinity, 133
 structure, annihilation of, 174
 subjugation, 106, 157, 161
Pattanaik, Devdutt, 245
Pendleton, Eva, 93
phallocentricism, tales of, 114
physical abuse, tool of, 70
plurality and multiplicity of lesbian experience, exploration of, 29
Pollak, Michael, 141, 151-52, 159
Polybius, 208
Posidonius, 208
Pran, 225
privacy of gay bars, notion of, 222
procreative-sex and motherhood, valorization of, 180
psychiatric abuse, victim of, 146
Purana Kila, 80
Puri, Jyoti, 27
Puwar, Nirmal, 119

queer
 activism, 95
 larger framework of, 211
 aesthetics, 8, 47, 123, 125-26
 citizenship, 113
 family pattern, 108
 gaze, 222, 226
 geographies, boundaries of, 228
 identity, 129, 208
 language, 120
 reinventing of, 10
 literary tradition, 2
 movement, 147
 or transgressive aesthetics, 45
 relationships, transitoriness of, 25
 spaces, 228
 theory, 118

visibility, 225
queer-erotica, 1
queer-friendly environment, 239
queerness by heteronormativity, appropriation of, 147

racism on homosexuality, effect of, 153
Radha–Krishna tradition, 187
radical anti-gay marriage stand, 96
Rado, Sandor, 74, 145
Rajendran, Aneeta, 211
Rangin, Sa'adat Yar Khan, 101, 121, 191
Rao, Raj, 8, 10, 15, 17, 21-22, 24, 26, 39, 45, 74, 95, 123, 125, 127-28, 131, 134, 137-38, 146-47, 151-52, 155, 159, 169, 196, 220, 225-26, 230, 233, 235, 239-40, 253, 256
Rashid, Abdul Khalid, 17, 235
Rauhofer, Judith, 93
Redcliff, Ann, 194
Reddy, Gayatri, 19, 70, 76, 83, 85-86, 88-90, 92, 99
Reich, Wilhelm, 142
rekhti
an offshoot of *ghazal*, 101
male-poets, 103
poetry, 4, 10, 100, 104, 120, 216-18
poets, 102-03
reparative therapies, 74, 145
re-sexualization of
female desire, 102
homoerotic passion, 47
lesbianism, 187
re-sexualizing lesbianism, 165, 206
respectability, middle-class issues of, 84
Revathi, A., 1, 52, 61, 64, 69, 82
Rich, Adrienne, 115, 177, 187, 204
Richardson, Diane, 44, 165, 187, 205
Rose, Ippadikku, 50
Roshanabadi, Qamar, 32, 114

Sade, Marquis D, 189
Sahoo, Sarojini, 20-21, 235-36
sakhi space, safe zone of, 204
same-sex
activities, 139
couple, 95, 170
desire, 37, 102, 125, 199, 219, 244
non-procreative nature of, 200
normalization of, 211
framework, 37
leaning, 157
liaison, 141, 201
longings, 189, 245
love, 48, 128, 162, 169, 190
classless and casteless paradigm of, 43
non-exploitative nature of, 29
secondary aspect of, 187
lovers, 171-72, 237
marriage, 94, 96
mating, 166, 217
partners, 60
passion, 157

relation(ship), 103, 169
union, 48, 138, 251
dynamics of, 127
Sapphic
and homoerotic desires, 253
desire, 47, 233
longings, 254
relationships, 5
Sarma, Dibyajyoti, 39, 152, 155, 244-45
Satpathy, Sumanyu, 197
Satya, 17, 72-73
security, false sense of, 25
Sedgwick, E. Kosofsky, 206
Seidman, Steven, 82
self-ghosting, 166
self-hatred, 94
Selvadurai, Shyam, 153
semen anxiety, 87
sex-change
clinic, 74
operation, 76
surgeries, 71-72, 76
sex-counselling session, 252
sex-reassignment
psychological and physical effects of, 53
saga, 77
surgery, 73-75, 99
crippling effects of, 18
sexual
and gender roles, fixities of, 116
binaries, colonial logic of, 87
citizenship
concept of, 33
issue of, 52
rights, 97
dissident identity, 256
gratification, portrayal of, 166
identity, 221
and space, overlapping of, 209
realization of, 175
stereotypical concept of, 211
minority(ies), 130, 150, 223
oppression, 161
orientation, modern concept of, 174
renunciation, 87
starvation, demonizing effects of, 190
studies, dichotomous model of, 99
subcultures, 34
urge, extermination of, 72
sexuality,
eclectic nature of, 106
fluid negotiation of, 213
sexually repressed Indian women, 83
Shabnum Mausi, 50
Shakuntala, 172
Sharma, Maya, 1, 5, 124, 161, 195-96, 231
Sharma, Parvati, 1
Shi, 68
Shikandi/Amba story, 51
Shitole, Manohar, 134
Shivani, 3, 197, 201, 203
Shree, Geetanjali, 3, 7, 26, 40, 46, 161-64, 167-69, 172-73, 212, 215, 217
Shroff, Jaya, 65
Shruti, 72
Siddharth, 225
silence, strategy of, 184

silencing
- sexual minorities, techniques of erasure for, 19
- technique, 149
- techniques of, 99

Singh, Dayanita, 63, 76, 80
Singh, Khushwant, 8, 17-18, 53, 56, 64, 78-79, 90
Singh, Sonia, 235
Sinha, Shatrughan, 225
Sitapati, Vinay, 70
Smith, Patricia Juliana, 3, 184, 197
Soja, Edward, 209
somatic authentic lesbian norm, 111
Sood, Keval, 12, 253
Soundarajan, Santhi, 65
South Asian
- dykes, 210
- queer activism, 224

space and sexual identity, 210
- double bind of, 110
- interdisciplinary prominence of, 209
- overlapping of, 19
- relationship between, 211
- symbiotic relationship between, 2

space(s)
- and sexual leanings, interconnections between, 219
- and sexuality, symbiotic relationship between, 252
- in Indian literary texts, (re)appropriation of, 210
- theorization of, 208

space–time compression, 211
spatial identity, 221
Spivak, Gayatri, 27, 93, 95
stoic symbol of "other", 111
Stone, Sharon, 229
Stonewall Movement, 232
Strabo, 208
stringent hyper-masculinity, 87
subaltern
- identities, 247
- sexual
  - escapades, 245
- sexual identities, 1
- sexuality(ies), 2, 24, 243, 255

Subarna, 199
Subramaniyam, Kalki, 50
subversive
- heterosexual domesticity, 181
- heterosexual pattern, 47

Sukirath, 215
Sukthankar, Ashwini, 1, 26, 29, 32, 44-45, 77, 149, 179, 195, 203-04, 212, 235
Sukumarika, tale of, 51
Sweet, Michael J., 63
Swenson, May, 100
symbiotic relationship between
- space and identity, 209
- space and sexual identity, 2
- space and sexuality, 252

symbol of
- disabled entity, 90
- femininity, 70

Thadani, Giti, 26, 37, 44, 46, 162, 173-74, 187, 200, 204, 212, 235
thayamma nirvanam, 69

Tolkappiyam, 58
transgender
 beauty contests, 51
 identity, gross appropriation of, 80
transgression, moment of, 96
transgressive
 desire, visibilizing of, 206
 desires, 234
 relationships, projection of, 224
transphobia, 53, 66, 68, 73
 internalized, 72-73
transphobic anxiety, 64
Tripathy, Laxmi, 50
two-gender mould identity, 65

Ugra, Pandey Bechan Sharma, 32, 47, 239, 243
unadulterated sexual mating, 165
uncertainity principle, 46
unique transgender body, acceptance of, 54
upward social mobility, 40
utopian
 freedom, symbolic space of, 243
 notion of all women-space, 29
 world of classless and casteless gay world, 133

Valentine, G., 209, 214, 221, 253-54
Vanita, Ruth, 1, 4, 10-12, 14, 26-27, 37, 95, 102, 116, 120-23, 158, 162, 169-70, 172, 188-89, 191, 212, 216, 249
Vasudevan, Aniruuddhan, 77
Vasudevan, Ravi, 227
Vatsyayana, 168
Veyne, Paul, 135
victims of
 coerced heterosexuality, 179
 marital rape and domestic violence, 38
 patriarchal subjugation, victims of, 106
Vijayasree, C., 115-18, 121, 126
Vinaya tradition, development of, 59

Wald, J., 171
Warn, Sara, 4, 171
Warner, Michael, 94
Weeks, Jeffrey, 97
Western
 framework of popular visual culture, 4
 heteropatriarchal division, 62
 queer literary theory framework, 118
 theoretical apparatus, 27
Wittig, Monique, 123
Wittman, Carl, 93
Wolf, Naomi, 191, 202
Wolfson, Evan, 94
women in
 gay subculture, oppression of, 153
 heterosexual family, subjugation of, 105
Woolf, Virginia, 122, 167

Yi fu Tuan, 209

Zwilling, Leonard, 63